D0375015

Bear Flag Rising

FORGE BOOKS BY DALE L. WALKER

Legends and Lies: Great Mysteries of the American West
The Boys of '98: Theodore Roosevelt and the Rough Riders
Bear Flag Rising: The Conquest of California, 1846

Bear Flag Rising

❋

THE CONQUEST
of CALIFORNIA, 1846

DALE L. WALKER

A TOM DOHERTY ASSOCIATES BOOK
NEW YORK

BEAR FLAG RISING: THE CONQUEST OF CALIFORNIA, 1846

Copyright © 1999 by Dale L. Walker

The photograph on page 70 of John Charles Frémont by Mathew Brady, albumen silver
print, 1861, NPG.80.308, is used by permission of the National Portrait Gallery,
Smithsonian Institution. Gift of Dr. Mary W. Juday.

The photograph on page 146 of Robert Field Stockton [photographer unknown],
daguerreotype, ICHi-12579, ca. 1845-1850, is used by permission of the
Chicago Historical Society.

The portrait on page 164 of Stephen Watts Kearny [artist unknown], #907328, is
reproduced from the Collections of the Library of Congress and is used by permission.

This book is printed on acid-free paper.

A Forge Book
Published by Tom Doherty Associates, LLC
175 Fifth Avenue
New York, NY 10010

Forge® is a registered trademark of Tom Doherty Associates, LLC

Book design by Leah Carlson-Stanisic

Map © 1999 by Miguel Roces

Library of Congress Cataloging-in-Publication Data
Walker, Dale L.
Bear Flag rising: the conquest of California, 1846 / Dale L.
Walker. — 1st ed.
p.   cm.
"A Tom Doherty Associates book."
Includes bibliographical references (p.   ).
ISBN 0-312-86685-2 (acid-free paper)
1. California—History—1846–1850.   2. Bear Flag Revolt, 1846.
3. Mexican War, 1846–1848—Campaigns—California.   4. California—
History —To 1846.   I. Title.
F864.W26   1999
979.4 03—dc21   99-21742
                                              CIP

First Edition: July 1999

Printed in the United States of America

0 9 8 7 6 5 4 3 2 1

TO WESTERN WRITERS OF AMERICA, INC.

Mexico can never exert any real governmental authority over such a country. . . . The Anglo-Saxon foot is already on its borders. Already the advance guard of the irresistible army of the Anglo-Saxon emigration has begun to pour down upon it, armed with the plough and the rifle. . . .

—John Louis O'Sullivan, *The United States Magazine and Democratic Review,* July–August, 1845

If I were a Mexican, I would tell you, "Have you not enough room in your own country to bury your dead men? If you come into mine, we will greet you with bloody hands and welcome you to hospitable graves.

—Sen. Thomas Corwin of Ohio, February 11, 1846

We go to war with Mexico solely for the purpose of conquering an honorable and permanent space. Whilst we intend to prosecute the war with vigor, both by land and by sea, we shall bear the olive branch in one hand and the sword in the other; and whenever she will accept the former, we shall sheathe the latter.

—James Buchanan, Secretary of State, 1846

Poor Mexico, so far from God, so near the United States.

—Mexican proverb

CONTENTS

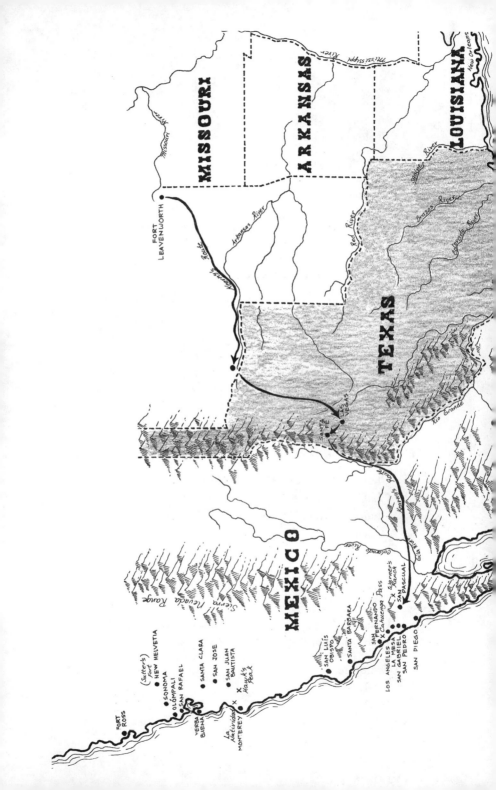

INTRODUCTION

❀

The conquest of California is representative of a concept as old and arrogant as humankind. A New York lawyer-editor named John Louis O'Sullivan called this idea "Manifest Destiny," the useful phrase printed in a summer, 1845, magazine editorial arguing in favor of the annexation of Texas by the United States. He wrote of Texas' "absorption" into the Union as "the inevitable fulfillment of the general law which is rolling our population westward," and California, he predicted, would also fall away from an "imbecile and distracted Mexico." In the minatory tones of an awakened giant, O'Sullivan said, "The Anglo-Saxon foot is already on its borders. Already the advance guard of the irresistible army of Anglo-Saxon emigration has begun to pour down upon it. . . ."

Manifest Destiny was a new phrase for an ancient abstraction that has steered and muddled every nation, primitive and civilized, since national attitudes of superiority arose.

(Substituting "Spaniard" for "Anglo-Saxon" in O'Sullivan's editorial results in a pronunciamento that might have guided Cortéz and his conquistadores when they conquered Mexico in 1520 and when his successors claimed California for Spain in 1769. At the time of the events of *Bear Flag Rising*, the British, who wrote the text on spreading Anglo-Saxon "civilization" around the globe, were warring against the Maoris in New Zealand and the Sikhs in India.)

The spirit of Manifest Destiny, the belief that it was the fate, perhaps divinely written, of the United States to rule the North American continent, was anything but an idle notion. It was a virulent force from our national beginnings, and in 1846, it swept like a rush of air into a vacuum from the Continental Divide to the Pacific, guided by what Bernard DeVoto called "the logic of geography."

❖

Bear Flag Rising is the story of three agents of Manifest Destiny in collision with one another while on a common mission: the annexation by military force of the Mexican province of Alta California by the United States.

The event signaling the opening of the takeover occurred on June 14, 1846, when a band of backwoods malcontents raised the berry-juice-painted petticoat known as the Bear Flag over the plaza of the northern California village of Sonoma. The *process* of conquest, however, had begun six months earlier, upon the arrival in the Far West of John Charles Frémont, the first of the three linked but unbonded conquerors.

The Bear Flag is the perfect symbol of the conquest; Frémont, the highly imperfect human manifestation of it. Firmly wedged between the other two men and abraded by them, he inspired and abetted the Sonoma rising and stood at the epicenter of the thirteen-month storm that followed it. He is the looming presence of the California campaign.

He is also one of our history's enduring enigmas, a thoroughgoing man of action, easy to admire but difficult to like. A pathmarker if not a pathfinder, he is at various times an *agent provocateur*, Byronic hero, brilliant leader of men, and pathetic egoist. One of his signal characteristics is that, like the ostrich, his eye is bigger than his brain. He sees panoramas, but details, many of them urgent, confound him. What remains fixed in his character and life are his unbounded hubris and ambition, and the devotion to him of his wife, Jessie.

The second of the triad of conquerors is Robert Field Stockton, a commodore of the navy and confidant of presidents. He is wealthy, imperious, elegant, grandiloquent, and ruthless—a born satrap. He dreams of military glory, a spectacular sea fight, a great overland march to battle, some chance to prove himself, to ensure himself an eminent niche in history. He is smallish in stature and as excitable as Lord Nelson, whom he admires.

And the third figure in the story is Stephen Watts Kearny, a general of dragoons, a briary old-school martinet blooded in Indian wars. He is a master of tasks, but like his contemporary, Zachary Taylor, a primitive tactician. He is courageous in battle and, in appropriate company, courtly in manner, but he is foolish and vindictive in many critical matters, and like generals before and after his time, he surrounds himself with the like-minded and hears little in opposition to his thinking except from his enemies.

These contentious men, around whom the spectacle of the conquest tumbles and swirls like a Mojave dust devil, and the color and drama of the California conquest, preoccupy this book.

While *Bear Flag Rising* is about the California campaign from an American perspective, I have tried, at some length, to provide a picture of pre-conquest California and to do justice to the Californian "side" in the 1845—47 era, especially in recounting how leaders such as José Castro, Pío Pico, and Andrés Pico rose to oppose, as best they could with no assistance from Mexico, an event each knew was inevitable: the loss of their beloved land, and their way of life, to the interlopers.

—*Dale L. Walker*
June 14, 1998

The Californios called them "Bostons."

These were the Americans who came around Cape Horn from Eastern seaports, the principal ones on the Massachusetts coast, to the Pacific Rim in the half-century before the conquest.

The first American ship to visit California was the *Otter*, out of Boston, which dropped its hook in Monterey Bay in October, 1796, en route to the Sandwich Islands and China with a cargo of sea-otter pelts. The captain of this small vessel, one Ebenezer Dorr, had several convicts aboard, escapees from the Australian penal colony at Botany Bay who had paid him to take them to the United States. Dorr asked permission of Monterey's commandante to land these "English sailors" but was politely refused. In the dark, and in the first recorded instance of the Americans wearing out their welcome, he landed them anyway.

❀

In the dozen languorous years before the conquest, many other Bostons ventured unbidden to California. Some of them stayed, tolerated as foreign residents. One who came and returned home and wrote an influential book about his adventures was an uncommon sailor out of Cambridge, Massachusetts, named Richard Henry Dana.

His grandfather, a jurist, had been a delegate to the Continental Congress and United States minister to Russia; his father was a poet and essayist and founder of the influential literary journal, *The North American Review,* and his favorite teacher in private school was a certain serene transcendentalist and aspiring Unitarian minister, Ralph Waldo Emerson.

In 1831, at age sixteen, Dana entered Harvard but a bout with measles left his eyesight impaired and, feeling "useless, pitied, and dissatisfied," he left the college after two years to cast about for some answer to his failing health. He found it, to his family's alarm, in the port of Boston.

"There is a witchery in the sea," he later wrote, and the tall-masted ships he saw, and the carefree sailors at work on their decks, romanced him. He might have embarked as a passenger or, through his family's influence, as a merchant officer, but on August 14, 1834, he traded his frock coat, silk topper, and kid gloves for the rough duds of the ship's slop chest—a pair of baggy duck trousers, a checked pullover shirt, and a black-varnished tarpaulin hat "with half a fathom of black ribbon hanging over the left eye"—when he signed on as a common seaman on the brig *Pilgrim,* outward-bound for Cape Horn and Mexican California.

"There is not so hopeless and pitiable an object in the world as a landsman beginning a sailor's life," he said of the beginning of his two-year adventure. In fact, he had no notion of just how wretched life before the mast could be. He had swapped more than clothes: he had traded silk sheets in a warm and spacious home for a hammock slung in the crew's quarters below the *Pilgrim's* forecastle, amidst coils of rope, rigging, spare sails, stores, and the eternal stink of the bilges; he had traded sumptuous meals served at a damask-covered table for cold salt beef scummed with grease, and "scouse" (biscuits pounded into crumbs and mixed and boiled with beef), potatoes, and pepper; he had traded brainwork for picking oakum—old rope pieces untwisted and picked into shreds, then tarred for use in caulking—and for flensing the skin off his knees in endless days spent holystoning decks; he had traded intellectual talk with poets and pedants for the stupefying chatter of his deckmates and the fearsome pronouncements of the *Pilgrim's* tyrannical captain, a self-described "regular down-east johnny-cake" who promised his crew, "If you ain't careful, I'll make a hell of heaven."

Most of the voyage to California was hellish, but not all of it. Dana learned to love the capstan songs the sailors sang, to delight in their effusions over the grog ration that was passed around in bad weather; and he was filled with awe to witness such seagoing phenomena as the weirdly beautiful corposant—Saint Elmo's Fire—that crawled along the masts and yards in stormy weather.

By the time the *Pilgrim* had slugged its way south in high seas to the Falkland Islands and the coast of Patagonia, he had learned much of sailing-ship nomenclature, writing in his journal of the "fine breeze from the northward, topmast and topgallant studding-sails set, and every prospect of a speedy and pleasant passage round." He also studied Bowditch on the voyage south and learned to identify such navigational phenomena as the Magellen Clouds—three small nebulae, two bright, one dim—seen just above the horizon soon after crossing the southern tropic, and, directly overhead at Cape Horn, the four stars of the Southern Cross, one of the brightest constellations in the heavens.

Three and a half months out, the *Pilgrim* anchored off Juan Fernández—Robinson Crusoe's island—four hundred miles west of Valparaiso, to fill water casks, and on January 13, 1835, sighted the California coast. It took the eighty-six-foot Boston brig five days to beat its way one hundred miles upcoast to its trade destination, fighting head winds and smashing seas so unrelenting that the ship sprung its foretopmast and was driven hundreds of miles off course. But on January 18, the *Pilgrim* sailed past Point Pinos, the headland entrance of the twenty-four-mile-wide Bay of Monterey, and Dana saw the town. Before him lay a pretty collection of whitewashed adobe buildings with red-tiled roofs, a customshouse, and a square presidio, Mexican flag fluttering above it, all huddled neatly on the edge of a large, pine-wooded cove "green as nature could make it."

The bay and the town teemed with commerce. Since Monterey had the only customshouse on the coast, all trading vessels were required to drop anchor there, enter their cargoes in the registry, undergo a haphazard inspection by harbor authorities, and receive permission to traffic in the other ports north and south. Ships from New England threaded through the anchorages of ships from Mexico, Central and South America, England, France, Genoa, the Sandwich Islands, China, and Japan; on the beach and in town, trader captains and sailors, hide droghers, shag-bearded trappers in greasy buckskins, Kanakas, Indians, freighters, and laborers jostled with presidio soldiers and monied gentlemen in stovepipe hats.

Since Dana spoke Spanish, the *Pilgrim*'s captain appointed him interpreter, and in the year the brig wandered up and down the coast with its cargo of spirits, tea, coffee, sugar, spices, raisins, molasses, hardware, tinware, crockery, cutlery, calicoes and cottons from Lowell, boots and shoes from Lynn, crepes, silks, shawls, scarves, jewelry, combs, furniture—"everything that can be imagined, from Chinese fireworks to English cartwheels"—the husky, curly-headed New Englander kept a meticulous journal, subsequently published as *Two Years Before the Mast.*

He loved the majesty of the Spanish language and the beauty of its intonations among the citizenry. "Every common ruffian-looking fellow, with a slouched hat, blanket cloak, dirty underdress, and soiled leather leggings, appeared to me to be speaking elegant Spanish," he wrote. "A common bullock-driver, on horseback, delivering a message, seemed to speak like an ambassador at a royal audience."

He admired the dress of the Californios (the Mexican natives of California). The men, at least those of some substance, wore dark, flat-topped, broad-brimmed, silk-lined sombreros with gilt or figured bands; short, vest-like silk jackets; shirts made of broadcloth or velveteen, laced with gilt and open at the neck; pantaloons open at the sides below the knee; white stockings and Indian-made, gold-embroidered deerskin shoes; broad sashes, often blood-red, cinching the waist; dark blue or black cloaks of broadcloth with velvet trimmings; and colorful serapes slung over their shoulders.

"Every rich man looks like a grandee and every poor scamp like a broken-down gentleman," he wrote.

He saw ladies in silks, crepes, crinolines, and calicoes, all made in the European style but with short sleeves, leaving the arm bare, and loose around the waist—"corsets not being in use." They wore shoes of kid or satin, bright sashes or belts, necklaces and silver-filigreed pendant earrings, and since they wore no bonnets, their hair, loose or in long braids, was decorated and held in place by tall combs.

People of pure Spanish blood, he said, had clear "brunette" complexions. The Indians, who ran about naked except for "a small piece of cloth, kept up by a wide leather strap round his waist," were darker.

The Californios were caste-conscious, Dana recorded: "The least drop of Spanish blood, if it be only of quadroon or octoroon, is sufficient to raise one from the position of a serf, and entitle him to wear a suit of clothes—boots, hat, cloak, spurs, long knife, all complete, though coarse and dirty as it may be—and to call himself Español, and to hold property, if he can get any."

Horses—smallish, wiry animals—were prevalent in their daily lives, and it was so commonplace to see men and women on horseback that he thought of the Californios as centaurs, but he was disgusted by the neglect and downright cruelty shown to the beasts. The men may have been *caballeros,* but only insofar as the word meant "horsemen." They were not gentlemen. He wrote,

They can hardly go from one house to another without getting on a horse, there being generally several standing tied to the doorposts of the little cottages. When they wish to show their activity, they make no use of their stirrups in mounting, but striking the horse, spring into the saddle as he starts, and sticking their longs spurs into him, go off on the full run. Their spurs are cruel things, having four or five rowels, each an inch in length, dull and rusty. The flanks of the horses are often sore from them, and I have seen men come in from chasing bullocks with their horses' hind legs and quarters covered with blood.

He said that when the people embarked on long journeys, "they rode one horse down, and catch another, throw the saddle and bridle upon him, and after riding him down, take a third, and so on to the end of the journey."

The Californios, even the "Dons," Dana wrote disdainfully, were an "idle, thriftless people" who could "make nothing for themselves." Here, he said, was a land abounding in grapes, "yet they buy, at a great price, bad wine made in Boston and brought round by us, and retail it among themselves at a *real* (twelve and a half cents) by the small wine glass." He said that cowhides, "which they value at two dollars in money, they barter for something which costs seventy-five cents in Boston; and buy shoes (as like as not made from their own hides, which have been carried twice around Cape Horn) at three and four dollars. . . ."

He told of a country where none but "Papists" could own property or even remain more than a few weeks ashore unless assigned to a trade vessel; a place with no system of credit, no banks, no investments except in cattle, no schools, and no discernible governance.

He told of a vast, bizarre, lazy and decadent land, immensely rich (if more in the potential than the tangible), whose people, other then a handful of "grandees," had no education and no initiative and seemed to be in a geographical and cultural limbo, as if apathetically awaiting conquest.

"In the hands of an enterprising people, what a country this might be!" he wrote.

❉

Three hundred years before Dana's advent, the Spaniards, an enterprising people, had thought the same thing.

PART I

❖

The *Coast* *of*
Cathay

✣

CHAPTER ONE

The Spaniards

1

Juan Rodríguez Cabrillo had commanded a company of cross-bowmen in the march by Hernán Cortés to the Aztec capital of Tenochitlán in 1519, and for these and other military labors, he had earned the confidence of the viceroyalty of Mexico. After two decades of service to Spain in the New World, the Portuguese-born officer was given his first command—an odd assignment for a soldier, but an important one. In June, 1542, he sailed north from the port of La Natividad, on the Pacific coast of Mexico, his flagship the caravel *San Salvador* accompanied by a smaller vessel, the *Victoria.*

Cabrillo's mission, assigned him by the viceroy, was to explore the uncharted "coast of Cathay," believed to be a large island somewhere in the north, and perhaps discover any number of fabled places: the Strait of Anián, a northwest passage between the two great oceans; or the seaport of Quivira, a land said to contain Seven Cities of Gold ruled by El Dorado, a king whose subjects dusted him with gold every morning and washed it off every night.

He might even find the island mentioned in a popular work by the Spaniard Ordóñez de Montalvo titled *Las sergas de Esplandián* ("The Deeds of Esplandián"), published in Madrid in 1510. This tale told how the Christians in Constantinople had fought a force of black Amazons led by Queen Califía of the island of California. The island was said to be located "at the right hand of the Indies" and close to the Terrestrial Paradise, a place bounteous in gold and guarded by griffins that carried unwary intruders high into the sky and dropped them to their deaths.

Whatever he was searching for, the record of Cabrillo's voyage, written about thirteen years later, states that on "Sunday, July 2 [1542], they sighted California."

He sailed up the unknown coast, charting islands, bays, inlets, reefs and rocks, among the latter a dangerous group he named the Habre Ojos—"Watch Out." In September, he visited a "good harbor" that he named San Miguel (soon called San Diego), found ways to talk with coastal Indians, and sailed on, often far to seaward to avoid fierce winds and the terrifying crash of the ocean on the cliffs and rock-girded beaches. He sighted but did not visit a wide-mouthed harbor 450 miles north of San Miguel and named it Baía de los Pinos (probably Monterey Bay), and in mid-November, after sailing past a great fog-shrouded place that would become known in three hundred years as the Golden Gate, the *San Salvador* and *Victoria* anchored in a large bay about six hundred miles north of San Miguel. This anchorage was visited thirty-five years later by the English freebooter, Sir Francis Drake, and given his name.

On the return voyage, somewhere in the islands off Santa Barbara Channel on January 3, 1543, Cabrillo died of an infection caused by having broken his arm and shoulder in a shipboard fall, but he had made his mark: this Portuguese-Spaniard soldier-mariner found the land that had been named before it had been seen.

❀

After Cabrillo's expedition, 227 years passed before the Spaniards made their first settlement there, but in the waiting, California was rediscovered many times.

Galleons from the Philippine Islands, a Spanish possession from 1564 and governed by a viceroyalty of New Spain, built a profitable trade between Manila and Mexico and skirted the California coast laden with cargoes of silks, damasks, spices, chinaware, wax, and other exotic goods of the Far East. The rules of the trade called for the galleons, outward-bound from Manila, to follow the Great Circle. This route took them northeast toward Japan, then due east along the forty-first parallel to the vicinity of Cape Mendocino, westernmost point of the California coast, then south past Baja California to Acapulco. There were at least two hundred Manila galleon voyages to Mexico and many of them, perhaps most, touched on the California shore to fill water casks, cut wood, and search for game.

2

Then Drake came. He and his corsairs sailed from Plymouth in November, 1577, with a fleet of six vessels led by the hundred-ton *Golden Hind*. They ran south to the Cape Verdes and into the Strait of Magellan, took seventeen days to thread the hellish Horn, and, as they entered the Pacific, endured a storm that lasted fifty-two days, destroyed some of their ships and sent others scurrying back to England. Now alone, a speck on the measureless ocean, Drake worried the battered *Hind* north along the gale-swept western coast of South America, his cutthroat crew sacking Spanish towns from Chile north to Mexico and filling the hold of the flagship with gold and silver bullion and plate, pearls and emeralds, and all manner of plunder. The *Hind* captured and looted many Spanish ships as well. One of them, bound for Panama, had the memorable name *Cacafuego* ("Shitfire") and was grappled to the *Hind* off Lima. It was found to contain so much booty—twenty-six tons of silver bullion, eighty pounds of gold, plus weapons, gunpowder, clothing, and religious artifacts—that it took three days for Drake's pinnaces to transfer the cargo to his flagship.

The master mariner sailed on and spent a month in the summer of 1579 on the California coast, careening, refitting and provisioning the *Golden Hind,* and claiming the land, which he named Nova Albion, for his patron, Elizabeth I. Drake may have entered the Golden Gate, though he made no mention of the spectacular bay that lay inside the headlands. He did trade with the Miwok Indians of the northern coast and may have journeyed as far north as the future Bodega Bay before sailing west for Mindanao, Java, the Indian Ocean, the Cape of Good Hope, and home to Plymouth in September, 1580, completing his circumnavigation of the globe in two years and nine months.

✦

The Englishman's claim of New Albion does not seem to have greatly disturbed the Spanish crown or its viceregal authorities in the New World, but since a port was needed for the Manila galleon trade, Spain did send several expeditions to the California coast in the years following Drake's foray.

The most significant of these explorations was that of the *adelantado* (merchant-adventurer) Sebastián Vizcaíno, who set out from Acapulco with two ships in the spring of 1602. In December, he arrived off Cabrillo's Bay of San Miguel, which he renamed for his flagship *San Diego,* then moved north, bestowing names, most of them holy names, on the islands, points, and inlets he spied— Santa Catalina, Santa Barbara, Punta Concepción. At Santa Catalina, he saw many Indian canoes made of cedar and pine, their seams caulked with brea from seepages along the coast, some of them carrying fifteen men who rowed like galley slaves.

The prize discovery of Vizcaíno's expedition was the sighting of a magnificent harbor. It was, he said, "the best port that could be desired, for besides being sheltered from all the winds, it has many pines for masts and yards, and live oaks, and white oaks, and water in great quantity, all near the shore." He spoke of the bay being "excellent for shipping," sheltered from the winds, ideal to provide security and protection for ships from Manila, and a climate resembling that of Castile.

He named it for the viceroy of Mexico, the Conde de Monterey.

3

By the time the Spaniards made their first mission foothold there in 1769, the immense and still unmapped land they called California was inhabited by native peoples, perhaps 150,000 in all, in at least a hundred tribes and clans. In the north were people such as the Shasta, Modoc, Northern Paiute, the coastal Pomo, Miwok, Costanoan, and others; in the midlands were the Washo, Paiute, Shoshone, Salinan, and Yukot; in the south, the Chumash, Serrano, Diegueño, Gabrielino, Mojave, and Yuma.

They knew little of the vastness and diversity of their land for they were not nomadic and for twelve thousand years had subsisted on whatever their small domains provided.

Among many tribes, acorns provided the staple food. These were pounded and ground by mortar and pestle into a fatty, nutritious flour, winnowed by tossing in a basket, washed free of their bitter tannic acid, and rolled into a mush or unleavened cakes, seasoned with wood ashes, bits of meat or fish, and baked in earthen ovens. In the deserts, mesquite beans were a staple; in forested areas, piñon nuts. Hunters, using snares, pit traps, and arrows with obsidian points, killed deer and other small game; coastal tribes fished with nets and hooks and harpoon-like spears, gathered shellfish, and caught small fish by using buckeyes to poison pools and eddies. Mojaves and Yumas and the people of the Colorado River region grew corn, beans, and pumpkins; the more primitive tribes ate insects and grubbed for roots.

Many of the mid- and southern-California Indians lived in conical or domed huts made of poles and brush and banked with dirt; in the north, there were solid frame dwellings of redwood planks.

There were basket-makers among some of these people, clever

weavers using sedge, bulrush, willow, bracken, or tule reeds, who often decorated their works with stained bird feathers. The baskets were used for gathering and winnowing, and those of finest weave were filled with water and hot stones, for cooking.

Along the coast, boats were made of tule balsa, and rafts of rushes; in the far northwest, dugout canoes were fashioned from redwood trunks.

Artisans made arrow points of obsidian, stones, and shells; made awls and pots, charms, pendants, dentalium or clamshell beads (used for money); others made music from clap-sticks, deer hooves, turtle shells, gourds, bone whistles, and animal-skin drums.

In some places, the natives were naked; in others, they wore skirts of plant fibers or animal skins, and slept on furs and deer-hides.

Most of these disparate people were exogamous, mixing and marrying among one another; the men were polygamous, the marriages made by agreement or purchase.

Religion and medicine were guided by a shaman; sometimes drugs were a part of the religion, as in the northern San Joaquin Valley and among certain southern tribes that developed a *toloache,* or jimsonweed cult.

The Spaniards, including the missionaries, who invaded their lands were contemptuous of the Indians, describing them as lazy, filthy, immoral savages.

4

In May, 1769, a Spanish officer named Gaspar de Portolá led an expedition of fifty soldiers, servants, Christianized Indians (called "neophytes"), and missionaries from northern Baja California to the bay founded by Juan Rodríguez Cabrillo 227 years earlier.

At the head of the brown-robed Franciscan fathers in Portolá's party was a Spanish farmer's son, born on Majorca in 1713, Fray (Friar) Junípero Serra, father-president of the missions in Baja.

Portolá took possession of San Diego on July 1, established it as a presidio, and on July 16, Serra proclaimed the first mission of Alta California and named it San Diego de Alcalá.

San Diego was the earliest of twenty-one missions founded in California, each a day's journey apart and connected by a rude wagon trail called El Camino Real (the Royal Road). The northernmost of the missions, San Francisco Solano de Sonoma (Sonoma a Miwok word meaning "earth village"), was founded by Franciscans in 1823, two years after Mexico won its independence from Spain. For all its isolation from the governance of California, Sonoma became among the most prosperous of the missions. It had rich pasturage around it for herds of cattle, horses, and sheep; the grainfields were irrigated by water piped from springs; there were grapes for wine-making, and orchards of pears and apples, pomegranates, figs, and olives.

During California's "pastoral" era (1769–1833), eighty-two thousand Indians lived, worked, and died in a feudal peonage in the missions. These neophytes were the church's slaves, given instruction in Christianity, working throughout their lives as menials in the mission fields as planters and harvesters, adobe brick-makers, and butchers of cattle for the growing hide-and-tallow industry.

In the sixty-four years that followed the founding of the San Diego mission, two-thirds of the native peoples died, most of them from the diseases brought by their conquerors: cholera, dysentery, smallpox, tuberculosis, syphilis, diphtheria, typhoid, and scarlet fever.

❖

CHAPTER TWO

The Mexicans

1

As the colony of Alta California grew, the Spanish rulers in Mexico found it increasingly difficult to garrison their remote Pacific province, or even to supply it with needed goods. Ships from Mexican ports and especially from Spain, faced long, costly, and hazardous voyages to this isolated outpost, and when the wars of independence from Spain began in 1810, these supply-ship voyages ceased entirely.

In 1821, Mexico gained its independence from Spain, and in September, 1822, California became a Mexican territory. For a time, the new mother country made an effort to exert control over its stepchild, which it promoted to a "department" in 1836. Governors were appointed from Mexico City, and a *disputación,* a sort of provincial legislature, was established. This body met only when the governor ordered, and as a result, the business of state devolved into a petty despotism, with little or no guidance from home. Mexico, preoccupied with its own perpetual inner turmoil, adopted a laissez-faire policy toward the department of California, as it did toward its New Mexico colony, allowing both to drift and find ways of maintaining themselves.

Just as California's goods, guidance, and governance were ignored by Mexico, so did matters of security languish. Many of the soldiers who were sent to the province were ex-convicts and the meanest scrapings from the streets of Mexico, unqualified for the job and as little interested in service outside their home country as were the pressed or shanghaied seamen from England and America. The Californios detested these *cholos* (half-breeds) and *borrachos* (drunks), as they called them, and Governor Juan Bautista Alvarado said of them, "The majority of these soldiers were corrupt and lustful, and so audacious that not even their officers dared to impede their mutinies and other demonstrations. . . ."

Another conflict between the central government in Mexico and the Californios had to do with the secularization of the province's missions in the period 1834—1840, converting them to parish churches and selling off their great landholdings to private individuals. This enabled the wealthy to establish large private ranchos— an estate usually at least four square miles in size, some as large as thirty square miles—and haciendas, most of them over five square leagues, or twenty thousand acres, in size.

2

In the absence of shipments of goods from Mexico, trade opened in Alta California to the outside world, especially in the ports of San Diego, Monterey, and San Francisco Bay. In 1822, the first foreign trading ship, a British vessel, arrived, soon followed by a Boston trader; within months, both British and American agents were ashore and thriving.

Although the Californios had some wheat, timber, beaver and otter skins, wine, and *aguardiente* to sell, the mainstay trade in early California lay in cattle hides and tallow and, to a lesser extent, in other cattle by-products such as suet, lard, and pickled beef.

Cowhides (called "California banknotes" by the Americans), scraped, salted, and dried, fetched up to two American dollars each, and by 1846, California was producing up to eighty thousand hides annually. Tallow, packed in rawhide *botas* (bags), was valued at two dollars per *arroba* (twenty-five pounds), and twenty-five thousand *arrobas* were traded annually at peak production.

The hide-and-tallow market had its main depot at San Diego, where the hides were dumped from carts onto the beach and "droghers" cleaned and salted them, staked them in the sun to dry, folded them lengthwise, hair side in, and made great, ungainly bundles of them. These were taken by pack mules or oxcarts for transfer to small boats, then stacked into the trade ships' holds, the hides for boot and shoemaking in New England, the tallow for soap and candles.

Other anchorages for this specialized commerce were established off San Luís Rey, San Juan Capistrano, San Pedro (serving Los Angeles), Santa Barbara, San Luís Obispo, Monterey, Santa Clara, and Yerba Buena, the village that came to be San Francisco.

Trading vessels from many nations visited the California ports, paying duties that provided a $75,000-a-year income for the province. American ships were the most frequent and active traders and brought every conceivable commodity from the United States, from brooms to cookstoves, pianos to kegs of nails. The Californios manufactured nothing and were therefore needful of everything. As Dana recorded in his journal, even the soap and candles made from their own tallow were traded to them, as were boots and shoes and saddles made from their cowhides.

A typical cargo of trade goods out of Boston and a return shipload of hides brought a three-hundred-percent profit to the trading company.

3

In 1786, the first non-Spanish visitor since Drake made a call at the Pacific coast of North America. This was the French explorer Compte de Lapérouse, who spent ten days in Monterey Bay before sailing on to Kamchatka, the Philippines, and Australia, and to being swallowed up by the Pacific and never seen again. Neither Drake, nor Lapérouse, nor the American adventurer John Ledyard—who, in the service of the illustrious English explorer Captain James Cook, came to the north California coast in 1778—made a significant impression on the Spanish throne or its viceroys in the New World.

They continued to come, increasingly bothersome intruders: by the 1790s, Russian and British ships were in the North Pacific killing sea otters, seals, and whales—sperms, graybacks, humpbacks, rights, and blues. By 1801, some eighteen thousand sea otters had been slaughtered in California waters, their pelts worth three hundred dollars each in Canton. By 1820, this animal, which had flourished from the Aleutians to Baja California, had been virtually extinguished.

In 1818, Monterey and San Juan Capistrano were plundered and burned by pirate patriots from two privateers sailing under the Argentine flag and commanded by a Frenchman, Hippolyte de Bouchard, a freebooter fighting against Spain in South America. So distant was the Pacific outpost from the main theaters of action in South America and Mexico that Bouchard's foray was California's only brush with the wars of independence from Spain.

Russians came to San Francisco Bay from Sitka in 1806, sent in the brigantine *Juno* by Aleksandr Baranov, head of the Russian American Fur Company, to buy supplies for his scurvy-plagued and starving colonists in Alaska and to trade cloth, agricultural implements, tools, and furniture. The Russians, dreaming of a trans-Pacific empire, gained from Spanish authorities a temporary trading concession, and fifty miles north of San Francisco Bay they built a timber palisade and blockhouses slotted with rifle loopholes—sixty buildings in all—and armed the place, which they called Rossiya, or Fort Ross, with cannon. Soon afterward, the Russian fur traders built another post at Bodega Point, eighteen miles south of Fort Ross, and stationed eighty trapper-traders and fifty Aleut Indians there.

Even though the Spanish, and later the Mexican, authorities in California were confident that the Russians would make no advances closer to San Francisco Bay, as a precaution, the mission town of Sonoma was garrisoned and armed with nine brass cannons.

4

The original American resident of California, a genuine Boston man and merchant seaman named Thomas W. Doak, came to Monterey in 1816 on the trader *Albatross*. He may have been sent ashore to recover from some illness, or may simply have deserted his ship. Not much is known about him except that he married into a Spanish family, worked as a carpenter, and died in about 1848.

A few other Americans ventured to California in the dying years of Spanish hegemony, but most of them arrived after Mexican independence.

Jedediah Strong Smith, born in the Susquehanna Valley of southern New York, became the first American to cross into California by a land route. So respected in the mountaineer fraternity that he was called "Captain Smith" and "Mr. Smith" by men who rarely deferred to anyone, he carried a butcher's knife in his belt and a bible in his bedroll and was described as "half grizzly and half preacher" by his comrades.

In November, 1826, Smith led a party of beaver trappers across the Mojave Desert and into the San Bernardino Valley of California, completing the first overland crossing of the southwestern route to the Pacific. At the San Gabriel Mission near Pueblo de Los Angeles, he and his men were at first welcomed and treated cordially by the village *alcalde* (magistrate) but soon fell under suspicion. Fur traders were unknown in the province at the time and Smith had difficulty in explaining his purpose and profession. The Mexican authorities ended up calling him a *pescador* (fisherman) and considered imprisoning him in San Diego until they could figure out what he and his ruffian-like crew were up to. Only the intervention of the master of an American trading ship anchored in San Diego Harbor kept this from happening, but in the spring of 1827, Smith and his men were ordered to leave California.

The Yankee-trader captain took Smith north to San Pedro Bay. There he was reunited with his trapper party, equipped with new provisions and horses, and seemed to obey orders to quit the country when he retraced his route over the San Bernardino Mountains. But instead of returning east, he led his party north to the San Joaquin River Valley, which proved to be rich beaver grounds, and wintered there.

In May, 1827, after trapping along the Stanislaus River and amassing a haul of fifteen hundred pounds of furs, the captain and his men tried to cross the mountain barrier east of their trapping camp but were turned back, losing five horses along the way, by the heavy snow and ferocious winds in the passes. His main party left behind, Smith and two others made a second push and succeeded in getting through, thus becoming the first white men to cross the Sierra Nevada range.

The foray into California by Jedediah Smith and his trapper band set an ominous pattern.

In 1830, working with a seasoned mountain man named Ewing Young and a party of forty fur men, a nineteen-year-old Kentuckian named Christopher Houston Carson made his first expedition to California, entering the San Gabriel Mission by Jed Smith's Mojave route. The Ewing Young party, without sanction, trapped north as far as the Sacramento River, burned several Indian villages after a number of their horses were stolen, then ran into trouble upon returning to Los Angeles. There, pueblo officials demanded to know what authorization Young had to travel, trap, and kill Indians in California. When he could provide no papers, threats were made to jail him and his party. Kit Carson claimed that the Mexicans tried to ply Young and his men with liquor to make it easier to arrest them. In any event, Young wanted to get home before his furs were confiscated and so led his brigade out of the territory to the Colorado River.

All this was precedent. Twenty years after Jed Smith and fifteen years after Ewing Young left their tracks in California, the process was repeated: an American, with a band of freebooters, Kit Carson among them, entered California uninvited, was ordered to leave, and refused.

❀

CHAPTER THREE

The Californios

1

John Bidwell, a New Yorker from Chautauqua County and former schoolteacher who came to the Pacific coast in 1841, told of how a friend or stranger paid a visit to the home of a Californio and stayed overnight. All that was necessary, Bidwell said, was to bring your own blankets and a knife with which to cut meat from a common haunch. When you finished eating, you delivered your plate to your hostess and said *"Muchas grácias, Señora,"* and she would answer *"Buen provecho."*

This example of the gregariousness, generosity, and hospitality of the *gente de razón* (people of means) was echoed by many others in the dying days of Old California. Visitors wrote of being invited to picnics, lavish weddings, birthday celebrations, religious festivals, fandangos, rodeos, and amusements such as horseback grizzly-bear hunts, wild-horse roundups, and bull-and-bear baitings.

Many of the American visitors bit the hand extended to them.

In 1841, a United States Navy explorer named Charles Wilkes led a six-ship expedition to chart the Pacific coast, with particular attention given to San Francisco Bay. He had serious things to report to his superiors in Washington: he was amazed by the expanse of the bay, big enough, he said, to shelter all the world's navies, with prevailing winds that put it on sea-lanes linking ports in India, China, Japan, and Manila to the Pacific coast of North America. San Francisco was the potential key to the Orient trade, he said in his voluminous report, especially since the next significant harbor north, at Juan de Fuca Strait, was eight hundred miles distant, and San Diego Bay lay over five hundred miles to the south.

Except for a cursory look at the village of Santa Clara, at the extreme southern tip of San Francisco Bay, Wilkes himself seems rarely to have gone ashore, but others in his expedition did and kept diaries and journals on what they saw and experienced.

A party of officers from one of his ships, the sloop-of-war *Vincennes,* examined the village of Yerba Buena, a woebegone settlement consisting of a few ruined adobes and a poop-deck cabin from a wrecked sailing ship serving as somebody's home. They also visited Sonoma, the northernmost presidio of California, and were greeted by the eminent military commander of the northern frontier, Mariano Guadalupe Vallejo, whom many believed to be the most powerful man in California. The commandante led the officers on a tour of Casa Grande, the Vallejo home adjoining the garrison's barracks, and one of the Americans jotted a note describing the furnishings of the home as gaudy—in particular, certain chairs that had come from the Sandwich Islands. Colonel Vallejo was ill during the visit, but this did not diminish his hospitality and the visitors were invited to dinner. Some of the officers found the food execrable—served cold and every bite, one said, "poisoned" with red peppers and garlic.

The colonel's brother, Salvador, and three soldiers from the presidio, took the Wilkes party on a tour of the Sonoma countryside, a sportsman's Eden with thousands of ducks and geese in the marshes and deer so plentiful they were killed for their tallow. In the presidio barracks, one of the American officers counted thirteen soldiers and described them as "mere boys with enormous swords and a pair of nascent moustaches, deerskin boots and that everlasting serape or blanket with a hole in the middle for the head."

The Americans also saw an Indian village of three hundred people and left with the image of naked savages living in hovels made of tree branches, eating bullock meat and acorns.

The *Vincennes* men suffered another meal of chile and tortillas with the Vallejos and were later invited to a *baile* where they were shocked to see the ladies smoking cigarillos.

2

Most of the callers who left a record of their experience among the Californios ignored the naked Indian and his stick-and-mud hovel and the poor farmworker crowded with ten or fifteen others in a small one-room adobe. Most visitors wrote of California as the land of the Don, who, dwelling on his rancho, presided over his picturesque and spacious lands.

The Don's domain typically lay across rolling hills and creek-crossed valleys; his home was a whitewashed adobe structure with a red-tiled roof, and verandas shaded by sycamores and oaks. He might have a melon patch, grow corn, grapes, and olives for his own use. He had so many horses that he hunted and killed hundreds of them to preserve his pasturage for his cows, and let hundreds of others run free, trailing a rope for easy capture when needed.

The ranchero's source of income and his life's passion lay in his cattle. They were wide-horned, long-legged, lean, and tough animals that roamed his unfenced estate at will and required little attention until the periodic *rodeos* (roundups), in which the ranch's *vaqueros* would brand and notch the ears of the calves and record their numbers on tally-sticks—one notch per ten head.

After the rodeo, the next and final time the animals were rounded up was for the *matanza*, the slaughtering. Since the cattle were valuable to the Californios principally for their hides and their fat by-products, only a few choice haunches were kept, together with some meat to be cut into long strips, soaked in brine and dried. This black *carne seca* (which American cowboys called jerky) was carried by the *vaqueros* in their saddlebags. The rest of the hide-

and-fat-stripped carcasses were left to the buzzards, wolves, and coyotes.

It never seems to have occurred to the rancheros to venture into the dairy business. "It was very common at many haciendas for the owners to say that while they had six or seven thousand head of cattle, they could not offer a traveler a glass of milk if he requested it," the Monterey customs official Antonio María Osio wrote in an 1851 memoir. "They gladly would offer him a calf, but they only used the meat they could eat at one sitting. They would dump the rest out in the same fields where they would sleep or nap while their animals grazed and rested."

That there was very little money in California seemed unimportant to the Don. He lived content in the assurance that everything he needed was available from the traders, most of them Yankees, whose ships carried foodstuffs, drygoods, hardware, guns and powder, liquors, furniture—even pianos and billiard tables—to trade for "California banknotes" and tallow.

Nor was education a matter of much consequence to him. Most of California's native-born were illiterate. No system of education, and therefore no schools, existed in the province in the 1840s or at any time before that. For one thing, the Franciscan fathers feared education, convinced that reading and writing would foment such dangerous things as rebellion and godlessness, and only a few of the many governors who came to the province attempted to change the system.

3

And so for three hundred years after Juan Rodríguez Cabrillo spied the sun-washed coast of Cathay from the quarterdeck of the *San Salvador,* Mexican California drifted, a remote, neglected satellite suspended in a governmental vacuum.

Mexico may have regarded its Pacific "department" as the inestimably precious jewel in its colonial crown and dreaded the prospect of losing it, but Californios could not remember a time

when the home country had made a demonstration of any such regard. Mexico City's laissez-faire policy toward its possessions north
of the Rio Grande, the product of its own incessant inner turmoil
and of the two thousand miles of desert and mountain that sepa-
rated it from the Pacific Rim, begat a similar policy in California.
The *gente de razón* simply ceased worrying about their putative
mother country. It had never seriously governed California to
begin with, and the last fragile ties, those held by the church, were
broken in 1834 when the missions, which had birthed such towns as
San Luís Obispo, San Juan Bautista, San Juan Capistrano, and
Sonoma, were secularized. Then, even the Indians were released
from patronage and governance.

After nearly a quarter-century of neglect, California had evolved
into a semi-autonomous colony that regarded its home country as
little more than an absentee landlord, a tax collector who contributed nothing to earn his revenue. Mexico supplied a string of
nominal "governors" to mind the political affairs of its cherished
department, but these affairs were elementary in nature and of little
interest to the average Californio.

Talk of a schism with Mexico was commonplace in the years between the 1834 secularization of the missions and 1845. Many Californios felt that a revolution would be easy, perhaps bloodless: the
home country had no serious military presence there beyond four
decrepit presidios along the coast, San Diego to Yerba Buena, each
with a handful of slothful soldiers and some rusty cannons. In fact,
in the period 1836–1845, there were four desultory revolts against
Mexican authority, although none of them resulted in significant
changes in the governance of California.

Some Californios remained loyal to Mexico, others favored an
independent state and opposed any foreign intervention; still others leaned toward annexation by England, France, or the most
prominent of the trader-nations, the United States.

By 1845, internecine rivalries and territorial jealousies characterized the politics of Mexican California. The province was un-
officially divided into two regions, with San Luís Obispo the

demarcation point at the approximate mid-coast. South of this tiny port town to the border with Baja California lived the southern populace, the *abajeños* (those below); north of San Luís Obispo to Bodega Bay and beyond lay the country of the northerners, the *arribeños* (those above). What political guidance the province could claim was centered in the south at Pueblo de Los Angeles, an adobe village with a population of fifteen hundred, where the governor, a man named Pío Pico, resided. He had little influence among the farflung *arribeños:* in Monterey, just four hundred miles north of Los Angeles, the senior military officer in California, General José Castro, served as quasi-governor; and in Yerba Buena and Sonoma, neither Pico nor Castro, who disliked each other and who were at odds over control of the departmental treasury and customs income, exerted any significant influence.

4

In 1845, Alta California had a population of about twenty-five thousand, of which perhaps fifteen thousand to seventeen thousand were Indians, a sad remnant, about a tenth of the number of native inhabitants there when Spain built its first mission on their lands in 1769. The eight thousand or so non-natives included as many as twelve hundred foreigners—Russians, British, Germans, Sandwich Islanders, and a smattering of other nationalities. Americans were by far the most numerous of the outlanders, numbering at least eight hundred of the twelve hundred, most of whom had settled in the northern Sacramento Valley.

What lured the Yankees there probably began with the tales told by the Bostons—the sea captains and tars such as Ebenezer Dorr and, especially, Richard Henry Dana—who came to San Diego and Monterey and San Francisco Bay and departed in wonderment at the sheer immensity of the place, its salubrious climate, its primeval beauty, hidden riches, limitless potential.

Since there is nothing like a financial disaster to create a migration, economic factors played a part in the luring. In the spring of

1837, just two months after the inauguration of Martin Van Buren as President, a panic erupted when New York banks suspended the conversion of paper money into gold and silver. The practice spread, nine hundred banks failed, there were marches by the unemployed, food riots erupted in many cities, and a six-year economic depression followed.

The Texas example also provided a precedent in propelling Americans to the Pacific.

When Mexico won its independence from Spain in 1821, several hundred Americans had been permitted—welcomed, in fact—to "colonize" the Mexican state of Texas y Coahuila, requiring only that the settlers convert to Catholicism and take Mexican citizenship. Then, with Mexico's attention diverted by internal revolutions, counterrevolutions, coups, and insurrections, the American Texans, employing the old lie of being deprived of religious and economic freedom, of being oppressed by a cruel and despotic regime, began talking of independence, of revolution. In 1836, after defeating a Mexican army sent to quell the revolt, the Texans proclaimed themselves a republic and began to work toward winning annexation by the United States.

On December 29, 1845, Texas became the twenty-eighth state of the Union.

The trails broken, the Oregon Trail in particular, were another factor in California emigration. These breakthroughs rose from the explorations of men such as Jedediah Smith, Ewing Young, Joseph Reddeford Walker, James Clyman, Tom Fitzpatrick, and army explorers such as John Charles Frémont.

The Oregon experience certainly heightened "California fever."

By 1845, the American population in Oregon territory was nearing ten thousand, an astonishing number considering that the first real overland covered-wagon migration to Oregon had taken place only four years previously when a pioneering party of seventy emigrants left Westport, Missouri, and joined up with a group of Catholic missionaries headed for the Columbia River. Within three years, these pioneers had built seventeen flour and sawmills, were raising twenty thousand head of cattle, and had harvested a hundred thousand bushels of wheat.

Congressman William Gilpin of Missouri told his congressional colleagues in 1846: "Half a dozen years ago, the Willamette was occupied by beaver and eagles; it now exhibits an American republic, with a government, agriculture, mills, and commerce."

Of that original 1841 Oregon-bound emigrant party of seventy people, thirty-two turned southward at Fort Hall on the Snake River in Idaho. This group made its way to the fertile, isolated Sacramento Valley, close to Sutter's Fort, the perfect place to be left alone.

✣

Nueva Helvetia

1

Those who journeyed for the first time down the western foothills of the Sierra Nevada and followed the American River into Mexican California must have stopped and rubbed their eyes as they reached the slight bend in the river near its joining with the Sacramento. Before them lay a wonder of the West: an immense, tawny fortress, its adobe walls fifteen feet high and three feet thick, its corner bastions protected by twelve brass cannons, all surrounded by tilled, plantation-like fields.

Sutter's Fort, as significant a wilderness sentinel as Bent's Fort on the Arkansas, lay at the center of a much larger and even more impressive enterprise. This was John Augustus Sutter's "Nueva Helvetia"—New Switzerland—a fifty-thousand-acre empire that in peak times employed five hundred workers: Indian field hands, who were paid in special coins redeemable only at Sutter's stores, and *vaqueros,* farmers, gardeners, blacksmiths, gunsmiths, carpenters, tanners, blanket-weavers, hunters, trappers, sawyers, shepherds, millwrights, and distillers. There were even hired hands to run a launch down the Sacramento to the bays of San Pablo and San Francisco carrying loads of hides, furs, wheat, and produce, returning with lumber from the coastal redwood groves and other supplies.

The visionary, and at times improvident, lord of this spectacular domain was an amiable and hospitable entrepreneur born in Baden, Germany, of Swiss ancestry. Sutter had had a fecund marriage but an unhappy one, perhaps because of his extravagances, meager earnings, and business failures in Switzerland. Whatever the cause, he deserted his wife and five children and emigrated to the United States in 1834. He settled in St. Louis and for a time entered the Santa Fé trade and trapped beaver in the Rocky Mountains. In 1838, he removed to Oregon territory, and in July of the next year, after a circuitous voyage to Sitka in Russian Alaska, Vancouver, and the Sandwich Islands, arrived in San Francisco Bay as a self-proclaimed former captain of the Swiss Guards.

A charming, ambitious dynamo who had learned the Spanish language in his Santa Fé days, Sutter quickly became acquainted with influential provincial authorities, and in 1840 he secured from Governor Juan Bautista Alvarado permission to establish a rancho in the unsettled Sacramento Valley. He began with trapping and wild-grape brandy making, employed Indians, Kanakas, Californians, and vagabond foreign settlers, and expanded into cattle raising and wheat farming. He cleared land, built an irrigation system and a mill. In 1841, when he swore fealty to Mexico, he was granted a parcel of land eleven square leagues in size. So rapidly did he rise in wealth and influence that he was able to purchase Fort Ross on thirty thousand dollars in credit from the Russian-American Fur Company, and gained in the sale the fort's horses, cattle, and forty cannons.

Soon after acquiring the fort, with Governor Alvarado's blessing and precisely three hundred years after Cabrillo first sighted the California coast, Sutter's workers constructed a 425-by-170-foot mud-brick fort at New Helvetia, ostensibly to protect the northern boundary of California from Indian depredations and unwanted intruders.

The Swiss had earned the trust of his absentee masters. He had become a citizen of Mexico, won a huge and spectacularly productive land grant, was called "General," and had the status of a provincial official. He was empowered to enforce the laws of Alta California, to dispense justice, and—a notable responsibility—to prevent Indian raids and "the robberies committed by adventurers from the United States."

His stature among some key Californios was diminished by his participation, on the wrong side, in the revolt against the last Mexican-appointed governor of the province.

Brigadier General Manuel Micheltorena, a native of Oaxaca, was sent to San Diego in 1841 and took with him an "army" of three hundred thugs liberated from Mexican prisons and jails. These *cholos,* unpaid and undisciplined, soon ran amok, terrorizing the *abajeños* by their drunkenness, threats, and pillaging of shops and homes.

Micheltorena, congenial but lazy, earned the loyalty of Sutter and the Americans in the north by permitting the Swiss to make land grants to foreign emigrants, but by the end of 1844, the *cholo* rampages had alienated the true Californios. The governor's predecessor, Juan Bautista Alvarado, the man who had given Sutter permission to build New Helvetia, now organized a revolt and enlisted his friend, General José Castro of Monterey, to lead his 220-man army of rebels.

The former governor had reason to trust Castro. In April, 1840, Alvarado had learned of a planned uprising by foreigners intent on taking control of the province. The foreigners, it was said, were led by one Isaac Graham, a Virginia-born trapper who had settled at Natividad, near Monterey. Castro captured Graham and his confederate, an Englishman named William R. Garner, and marched them in irons to Monterey, where they were charged with fomenting rebellion and taken by ship to Tepic, in Baja California. There, apparently through the influence and bribery of the British consul, they were released and permitted to return to Monterey.

Sutter and his handful of loyalists reached Los Angeles in February, 1845, to join forces with Micheltorena. Most of his original force had evaporated, returning to their farms and homesteads in the north when it appeared that Micheltorena was doomed to failure. All that remained in Sutter's miniature army were some Walla Walla and other Indians, and a few American settlers working land near New Helvetia: Moses Carson, Kit's half-brother, a rancher in the Russian River area; Ezekial Merritt, a coarse, often whiskey-raddled trapper and frontiersman; Peter Lassen, a Dane, a blacksmith, and a naturalized Mexican citizen who owned a sawmill at Santa Cruz and a 26,000-acre land-grant rancho in the Sacramento Valley; and John Bidwell, Sutter's trusted assistant at the fort and aide-de-camp in the field.

The rebellion ended bloodlessly on February 20, 1845, in the "battle" at Cahuenga Pass near Los Angeles. Micheltorena surrendered to Alvarado and Castro and subsequently returned to Mexico.

Sutter and his men, at first taken prisoner, were soon forgiven and pardoned by Alvarado.

Pío Pico, a Californio by birth and a cavalry commander under Alvarado, replaced Micheltorena, taking office in Los Angeles. He may have sensed that he would be the last governor before his homeland was wrested from Mexico, for he seemed to advocate an alliance of some kind with the French or British to stave off the Americans, who had already made serious inroads into his country. American settlers in California he viewed as "lawless adventurers" and "avaricious strangers." He wrote,

We are threatened by hordes of Yankee emigrants; already the wagons of these perfidious people have scaled the almost inaccessible summits of the Sierra Nevadas, crossed the entire continent and penetrated the fruitful valley of the Sacramento. They are cultivating farms, establishing vineyards, erecting mills, sawing up lumber, building workshops and a thousand and one other things which seem natural to them but which Californians neglect or despise—we cannot stand alone against them.

Despite such words, Sutter continued to encourage emigrants, including Americans, even urging the new government to grant to foreigners two-league parcels of wilderness lands along the San Joaquin River and tributaries of it such as the Stanislaus and Merced, and offering parcels of his own grant to newcomers.

The motive behind his largesse may have been his indebtedness—Sutter owed the Russians most of the thirty thousand dollars he had agreed to pay for Fort Ross—but he was nonetheless exceedingly charitable with his money and manpower. Many times he dispatched his men across the Sierra to assist stranded or desperate emigrant parties; he was a convivial and generous host and a benefactor to the down-and-out. John Bidwell, one of the thirty-two emigrants who had come to the Sacramento Valley in 1841, said of the lord of New Helvetia, "He employed men, not because always needed or could profitably employ them, but because in the kindness of his heart it simply became a habit to employ everybody who wanted employment."

Bidwell himself worked for Sutter, serving "the General" as majordomo and bookkeeper.

Not all the Americans making their way to Sutter's Fort were farmers or others seeking gainful employment. California historian Hubert H. Bancroft said that some of the arrivals were deserters from ships visiting coastal trade ports: "Reckless, daring, and unprincipled men, with nothing to lose." He said there were also a number of men—"mere filibusters"—looking not for work, but for glory, wealth, and power under what they felt was a soon-forthcoming American takeover of the province, men who looked upon the Californios as inferior humans who had to be taught the beauties of freedom and the ways of a civilized nation.

In this, Bancroft was practically defining the spirit of expansionism defined in the summer of 1845 by John Louis O'Sullivan as "Manifest Destiny."

Manuel Micheltorena, early in his troubled tenure as governor, had a notable run-in with American trespassers, an affair that served as an omen, bright as a signal rocket, that the United States would be arriving soon and intended to stay.

On October 18, 1842, an American naval officer of Welsh ancestry named Thomas ap Catesby Jones arrived off Monterey in his flag-ship, the frigate *United States*, accompanied by a sloop-of-war, the *Cyane*. Commodore Jones and a party of officers and sailors came ashore and to the astonishment of ex-governor Juan Alvarado, port officials, and townspeople, announced that he was taking possession of Monterey in the name of the government of the United States.

As it happened, Jones, commander of American naval forces in the Pacific, had been at anchor off Callao, Peru, when he received some newspaper articles and dispatches leading him to believe that the United States and Mexico were at war—apparently over the Texas dispute. Since there were no telegraphic stations in the West and all military instructions came to Pacific outposts by way of Cape Horn, the commodore concluded that in the absence of orders to the contrary, he needed to sail for California instantly and seize it. Otherwise, Mexico might do something drastic, such as ceding the province to England.

Alvarado, appalled at Catesby Jones' surrender demand, signed the proclamation dazedly. A Mexican customs official who witnessed the sudden capitulation wrote of the "true Californios, people who loved their country and were proud of their nationality," as having been forced to witness a painful ceremony in which the flag of Mexico was replaced with the Stars and Stripes: "This flag was alleged to be the symbol of liberty, but that was actually a lie. It belonged to an oppressor who displayed arrogance against the weak," the official wrote.

The comic conquest of Monterey lasted for a single day, the reversal effected by another American, Thomas O. Larkin, a Boston man who had come to California via the Sandwich Islands in 1832.

Serving as interpreter between Jones and Alvarado, Larkin showed the American some Mexican newspapers and commercial mail, all of more recent date than the material the commodore had read while off Callao, revealing that no state of war existed.

Thomas ap Catesby Jones apologized, restored the Mexican flag and province to Alvarado and his stunned subordinates, and sailed south to make his apologies to the governor.

Micheltorena meantime had issued a bombastic call to arms to repel the American invaders, and upon receiving the commodore and dining with him, presented the officer with a bill for the damages done to Monterey and its citizenry: he asked for fifteen thousand dollars in cash, sixteen hundred military uniforms, and some musical instruments.

Jones thought Micheltorena was joking but was ushered from the governor's office before he laughed out loud.

The preemptive conqueror of Monterey was recalled and temporarily relieved of his command. Washington disavowed responsibility for his actions.

Larkin took office as consul for the United States at Monterey in April, 1844.

By 1845, the American colony in northern California had become a source of grave concern to leaders such as Pío Pico and José Castro. The Graham and Jones affairs had left scars, reminders of the audacity and untrustworthiness of the American "adventurers," and with Mexico teetering on the brink of a war with the United States, the Californios decided that the flow of these intruders must be stopped.

Meantime, Sutter, ostensibly answerable to General Castro of Monterey, but with his loyalties split, said of the Americans: "Nothing can stop this migration. In case of opposition, they would fight like lions."

✳

PART II

Bear Flag
Rising

✸

CHAPTER FIVE

The Dark Horse

1

"He has no wit, no literature, no point of argument, no gracefulness of delivery, no elegance of language, no philosophy, no pathos, no felicitous impromptus; nothing that can constitute an orator, but confidence, fluency, and labor."

This mixed assessment of James Knox Polk was offered in 1834 by John Quincy Adams when he and Polk were opposite-aisle colleagues in Congress. The former President's remarks on the future President were perspicacious but not news to his party. Jacksonian Democrats knew more about Polk's limitations than his strengths, and when they brought him to the power of the presidency, they did so tentatively; they really did not know what to expect of him.

Born in North Carolina in 1795, he grew up in Tennessee, the son of a prosperous planter. A sickly boy from birth, at age seventeen, "Jimmy" Polk survived an operation for gallstones, a risky procedure performed with only liquor as anesthetic. He recovered slowly but never fully; fragile health shadowed his life.

He studied law at the University of North Carolina, served in the Tennessee House of Representatives, and was elected to Congress in 1825, the year after his marriage to Sarah Childress, daughter of a plantation owner in Murfreesboro. She was a homely, lively, charming, and well-educated helpmate, a devout Presbyterian who frowned on drinking and dancing and doted on her husband, believed him to be a man of destiny, and protected him. He confided in her as in no other while he served six terms in Congress, including two years as Speaker. He was an unwavering supporter of Andrew Jackson's presidency and opponent of John Quincy Adams'. Sarah was delighted when he retired from Congress to serve a term as governor of Tennessee. They had no children.

At the Democratic Party convention at the Odd Fellows' Hall in Baltimore, May 27–30, 1844, Martin Van Buren of Kinderhook, New York, appeared to be the favorite for the nomination. He had seemingly impeccable Jacksonian credentials: he had served as Old Hickory's secretary of state and vice president and had succeeded Jackson in the presidency. But as chief executive, Van Buren had fallen afoul of Southerners—the heart of Jackson's party—in opposing the annexation of Texas, which had declared its independence from Mexico in 1836. Northern politicians opposed the admission of Texas to the Union as another slave state, and Van Buren agreed with them. Democrats with long memories remembered the words of the most celebrated of the Alamo defenders, David Crockett, who, as a Tennessee congressman in 1835, said, "Van Buren is as opposite to General Jackson as dung is to a diamond."

Van Buren's support eroded after the first ballot in Baltimore, and the other candidates—Lewis Cass of Michigan, Richard M. Johnson of Kentucky, and James Buchanan of Pennsylvania—did not catch on. Polk, whom some believed might make a good vice president, was not in attendance at the convention when his name came up in the eighth ballot, and when he was nominated on the ninth, he became the original "dark horse." He accepted by letter, expressing appreciation for the endorsement of his mentor, Andrew Jackson, and the honor bestowed on him by the delegates in Baltimore. He pledged to a one-term presidency—a tenet that Polk firmly believed was implicit in Jacksonian ideology (although Jackson served two terms)—and began the effort to defeat his Whig opponent, Henry Clay of Kentucky.

The Texas issue defeated Clay. Like Van Buren, he courted Northern favor and the abolitionist vote by his anti-annexation stance while Polk, criticized as "Jackson's puppet" and praised as "Young Hickory," stood steadfast behind the movement to admit Texas to the Union. Jackson favored the measure, and the outgoing President, John Tyler, had signed the treaty of annexation just the month before the Polk-Clay campaign opened.

Polk won the election in true dark-horse fashion. The November, 1844, results showed him nudging Clay out by 37,000 votes out of 2,600,000 cast. In electoral votes, Polk had 275, representing twenty-six states, to Clay's 105 and eleven states.

"Young Hickory," age forty-nine years and 122 days, took office as the eleventh President of the United States on March 4, 1845, three months before Andrew Jackson died in Nashville at age seventy-eight. Polk's inauguration was the first reported by telegraph.

❋

His religion, it was said, was politics, and had been so since 1820 when he had been admitted to the bar in Tennessee. He had no discernible interests other than politics. He had no hobbies, sports, or pastimes, was neither a reader, a dreamer, a talker nor a laugher— "no wit, no literature," in John Quincy Adams' words. In a place and pursuit in which men mingled, drank and smoked and made promises, Polk did none of these things and had no intimates other than Sarah Polk.

He was lean, thin-lipped, morose, walked erectly, and dressed scrupulously. He had deep-set gray eyes and a high-browed head with graying hair brushed straight back behind his ears. To many, he gave the appearance of a formidable schoolmaster, cold, suspicious, pompous, narrow. It was believed that his distant and humorless nature was the product of his lifelong delicate health, worsened by his years in Washington. The miasmal swamps bordering the Potomac and their infestations of mosquitoes and flies gave rise to malarial and typhoid fevers, and dysentery, dangerous to a healthy man, murderous to one of such a delicate constitution as Polk's.

One attribute was granted to him by even his most vociferous opponents: James Knox Polk had *focus*, an utterly clear vision of what he intended to accomplish in his single term as President.

In his inaugural address, he spoke of the Republic of Texas and its impending annexation. "Our Union is a confederation of independent States," he said, "whose policy is peace with each other and all the world. To enlarge its limits is to extend the dominions of peace over additional territories and increasing millions." He seemed to hint that there were other lands that would benefit from annexation but said, somewhat abstrusely, that the rest of the world had nothing to fear from American military ambition and that the Texas example should be looked upon "not as the conquest of a nation seeking to extend her dominions by arms and violence, but as the peaceful acquisition . . ."

He also advocated free trade and was determined to lower taxes on imported goods, but few, other than trade-and-tariff authorities, cared about such dull matters. What Polk only hinted at in his inaugural speech was a breathtaking plan to nearly double the geographical size of the United States: he intended to preside over statehood for Texas (which included all the territory north from the Rio Grande to the Arkansas River and as far west as Santa Fé); he would push the British out of Oregon; and he would "acquire," preferably by purchase through diplomacy, Mexico's territory lying between the Continental Divide and the Pacific, with California the *ne-plus-ultra* objective.

In accomplishing all this, he hoped to avoid war, but he was willing to wage war if diplomacy failed.

In the expansionist 1840s, there were many "questions"—a word used in political and diplomatic circles to denote the conflict between one or more nations over some other nation's property. In Europe, the "Eastern question" had to do with England's concerns that Russia might swoop down Central Asia to Constantinople and threaten British India. This question eventually resulted in the Crimean War.

James Knox Polk, when he took office in March, 1845, had several questions to answer, the most important of them focused on Mexico. Even the "Oregon question" had a Mexican connection.

Oregon territory (including the present states of Oregon, Washington, Idaho, and parts of Montana and Wyoming west of the Continental Divide) had been under "joint occupancy" by the United States and England since Secretary of State John Quincy Adams had negotiated a treaty between the two countries in 1818. Oregon became a "question" when the first Americans, most of them Methodist missionaries, came to the Willamette Valley, south of the Columbia River, in the 1830s. This advent was followed by the "Oregon Fever" emigration a decade later, when reports of cheap land there arrived in the eastern United States. The British moved their Hudson's Bay Company headquarters to Vancouver Island, virtually conceding control to the Americans of the territory between Puget Sound south to the boundary with Mexican California.

But England still hovered over the territory, its presence an American expansionist's nightmare. British warships paid visits to the Oregon coast and were sighted as far south as Acapulco. Did the British covet California? Might they seize it from Mexico, or purchase it? And what were the Russians doing plying the sea-lanes of the northern coasts? And the French and the Prussians?

American claims on Oregon rested on the 54°—40' line of latitude, encompassing all of Vancouver Island, and one of the campaign slogans that helped Polk's election was "Fifty-four Forty or Fight!" The President, while willing to negotiate the latitude, said our "title" to Oregon was "clear and unquestionable," and one of his first moves as President was to ask Congress to give England one year's notice that the United States would assert its claim to Oregon.

A convention signed on June 15, 1846, ended the joint occupancy and Oregonians were notified that they were now American citizens.

This was the resolution of the first of Polk's objectives as President.

❀

The "Texas question" had been hanging in the air for a decade and it was on the Texas experience, and the precedent set by it, that Polk's designs on California pivoted.

In 1821, soon after winning its independence from Spain, Mexico had welcomed several hundred American settlers to its northern province of Texas y Coahuila. These emigrants, most of them Southerners from slave states, won important concessions from Mexico—they were allowed to keep slaves, were protected from debts they had incurred in the United States—and by 1830, some thirty thousand Americans had posted notice that they were "Gone to Texas." But Mexico's internal turbulence, its changes in leadership and policy, eventually led to harsher laws, trade restrictions, and attempts to control the flow of emigrants to its Rio Grande territory. Out of Mexico's anarchy grew the Texas independence movement that culminated in the American setback at the Alamo on March 6, 1836, and Sam Houston's annihilation of the Mexican army at San Jacinto six weeks later.

Mexico never relinquished its province to the Americans, nor did it recognize the existence of the Republic of Texas. Offers by the United States to purchase the province were rebuffed. It was a certainty that the American annexation of Texas would mean war, and it was this eventuality that faced President Polk when he took office. His predecessor, John Tyler, as the last act of his administration, sponsored a resolution to annex the Republic of Texas.

In the first summer of the Polk presidency, John Louis O'Sullivan's extraordinary "Manifest Destiny" call to arms appeared in the July—August issue of his paper, *The United States Magazine and Democratic Review,* arguing in favor of the annexation of Texas. The lawyer-editor articulated the doctrine with some prescience in writing that after Texas was absorbed into the Union, "California will, probably, next fall away from the loose affiliation which, in such a country like Mexico, holds a remote province in a slight equivocal kind of dependence on the metropolis."

He said that "the Anglo-Saxon foot" was already on California's borders, and what he called "the advance guard of the irresistible army of the Anglo-Saxon emigration" was already pouring down into the province "armed with the plough and the rifle" in the first stage of a process, not far distant, "when the Empires of the Atlantic and the Pacific would again flow together into one."

3

While the phrase "Manifest Destiny" did not appear in the President's speeches, journal, or correspondence, the essence of the concept to James Knox Polk was political scripture. Oregon's boundary was in negotiation, and joint sovereignty of the territory with England would soon end; the annexation of Texas had all but been accomplished in the month he took office. But he knew that Mexico was unlikely to yield to diplomacy or a cash offering for its territory north of the Rio Grande and west to the Pacific—New Mexico and, the Koh-i-noor in the crown, California.

Seventeen days after Polk took office, he had a special meeting with his secretary of the navy, George Bancroft. This urbane Massachusetts Democrat, a distinguished historian and author* who would soon see his dream of a naval academy at Annapolis come true, had among other distinctions that of being as close to a confidant as the President allowed. On March 21, 1845, as a result of their meeting, Bancroft sent a secret message by warship around Cape Horn to the Peruvian coastal port of Callao ordering Commodore John D. Sloat, commander of the navy's Pacific Squadron, to proceed to the west coast of Mexico.

Sloat, age sixty-five, a New Yorker and forty-five-year veteran of the navy who had fought pirates in the West Indies and the British in the War of 1812, moved cautiously. His squadron consisted of the fifty-four-gun flagship *Savannah,* the *Congress,* of sixty guns, the sloops-of-war *Warren, Portsmouth,* and *Levant,* each carrying twenty-four guns, the armed schooner *Shark,* and a transport, *Erie.* One additional ship later joined Sloat's flotilla as a reinforcement, the sloop *Cyane,* which sailed from Norfolk, Virginia, that summer, taking fifty-six days to reach Rio de Janeiro and another fifty-three battling the Horn to Valparaiso.

The *Cyane* joined Sloat's squadron in November, and by then the commodore had received additional orders from his government: Bancroft's new messages said that if Sloat learned "beyond a doubt" that the United States and Mexico were at war, he was to sail north immediately, seize San Francisco Bay, and blockade or occupy other California ports as he deemed necessary. In so doing, he would "preserve, if possible, the most friendly relations with the inhabitants" of the province and be "assiduously careful to avoid any act which could be construed as an act of aggression."

Since no transcontinental telegraph system existed in 1845, nor a canal across Central America to the Pacific, Bancroft's secret orders to Commodore Sloat were carried by courier on a sailing ship

---

Not to be confused with the California historian, Hubert H. Bancroft.

and were many months in transit. Even more months passed before Sloat could provision his Pacific Squadron and make his voyage north from Callao to Mazatlán, the principal seaport on the west coast of Mexico.

In mid-June, before Bancroft's orders reached Sloat, other orders, these to the army, were carried from Washington to Fort Jesup, in the Red River Valley of Louisiana. The dispatches, from Polk's secretary of war, William Marcy, to the Fort Jesup commanding officer, Brigadier General Zachary Taylor, represented an even more overt acknowledgment of impending war than Bancroft's directive to Sloat. Taylor was instructed to move his force of about two thousand men to a camp below New Orleans, where they would embark on steamers down the Mississippi to the Gulf of Mexico, thence to another camp on Corpus Christi Bay in Texas. Taylor had commanded Fort Jesup and its euphemistically named "Army of Observation" for over a year, since, during the Tyler administration, Texas annexation had seemed imminent and with it, anticipated troubles with Mexico on the Rio Grande. The potential for such difficulties was exacerbated by the appearance in the Gulf in May, 1845, of a particularly warlike naval officer commanding the flagship *Princeton* and a small flotilla. Commodore Robert Field Stockton of New Jersey seemed to be an emissary for President Polk as he visited Galveston and spent his time assessing local attitudes toward annexation and sending urgent but unnecessary messages to Washington warning of Mexican threats if the United States interfered in Texas.

By the end of July, Stockton had returned home, the government of the Republic of Texas had approved the annexation treaty, and General Zachary Taylor had disembarked his force—now renamed the "Army of Occupation"—at Corpus Christi, just below the mouth of the Nueces River. By October, this army of over thirty-five hundred men had been divided into four infantry regiments, one of which was comprised of dragoons (cavalrymen who fought dismounted as infantry), and four of artillery. At the time, the entire standing army of the United States numbered only eight thousand, most of whom were Indian fighters scattered around frontier posts from the Florida swamps to the Kansas plains.

Taylor had no detailed orders or plan, no idea of the size or whereabouts of the Mexican army; he was camped in country where firewood was scarce, the water brackish. An enormous train of camp followers trailed the army and sold liquor to the troops, nearly half of which were Irish and German immigrants, tough fighters but owing no particular allegiance to the United States. Desertions were commonplace.

The general and his restless army stayed put for six months.

4

By the end of his first nine months in office, President Polk had a squadron of warships cruising off Mazatlán and an army camped in Texas. His War and State Departments had generated other significant missions as well, several adding to the country's war footing, one a forlorn attempt to avert war.

In October, 1845, when reinforcements were reaching Zachary Taylor's Army of Occupation in the Texas sand dunes, Polk's secretary of state, James Buchanan, sent secret instructions to Thomas O. Larkin, consul for the United States at Monterey and the most influential American in Mexican California. Now age forty-three, Larkin had ventured to Monterey in 1832 and with a capital of five hundred dollars, opened a small store and flour mill. From this modest beginning grew a prosperous trade in horses, furs, lumber, and flour with Mexico and the Sandwich Islands. Remarkably, he never took Mexican citizenship and managed to stay aloof from provincial politics. Described as "prudent and praiseworthy," he was tactful, practical, and honorable, a pleasant man of sound, conservative judgment. As consul since 1842, he had from the beginning assiduously reported his somewhat alarmist views on the activities of his British and French counterparts.

The Buchanan dispatch, dated October 17, 1845, and carried on the frigate *Congress* around Cape Horn to the Sandwich Islands, reached Larkin via a merchant vessel. It appointed him a confidential agent of the State Department at a salary of six dollars a day, and instructed him to take advantage of any signs of unrest among the Californios, to "conciliate" them and urge their support of annexation by the United States. In these efforts he would be aided by the American vice consul, William Leidesdorff at Yerba Buena, the settlement in San Francisco Bay. Larkin was to make clear to his influential contacts that the United States could not interfere in matters between California and Mexico City, but that in the event of hostilities between Mexico and the United States, if California asserted its independence, Washington would "render her all the kind offices in our power as a Sister Republic." Larkin was also to spread the word that if Californians wished to unite "their destiny with ours, they would be received as brethren."

Larkin leaked this information to a number of American influentials and worked to win the support of Don Mariano Vallejo. This powerful and independent *jefe político* of Sonoma, north of San Francisco Bay, Larkin described as "very studious for a Californian . . . formal, stiff, pompous and exacting . . . pleasant and condescending, anxious for popularity and the good will of others." The consul felt that he would be a valuable ally and would support annexation. Colonel Vallejo, whose two sisters were married to Americans and who had many American friends, was a wealthy man. He owned 175,000 acres of land stretching from San Francisco Bay north to the Valley of the Moon. He had encouraged emigration to California since, he said, he was powerless to prevent it. He was a Californio patriot, not a Mexican patriot, who felt that the future of California lay with friendly relations with the United States.

❖

In the executive mansion in May, 1845, Polk's guest list included the Senate's most impassioned expansionist, Thomas Hart Benton of Missouri, and Benton's son-in-law, the celebrated explorer Captain John Charles Frémont, recently returned from an army Topographical Corps expedition to Oregon and California.

Frémont gave the President a detailed account of his journey west, spoke of the limitless potential of Oregon and California, and of the importance of continuing the exploration of the region toward preparing accurate data and maps. He told Polk that existing maps were not dependable and gave as an example a map he had examined in the Library of Congress that depicted the Great Salt Lake as being linked to the Pacific by three large rivers. None of these rivers existed, Frémont said. He had been there.

The President listened, asked questions, and in his journal noted only that Frémont was "young" and "impulsive." But since Mexico and its provinces of New Mexico and, especially, California preoccupied him that summer, he must have closely questioned the explorer, who was preparing to embark on a new westward expedition. There had been disturbing reports circulating in Washington that the British, whose presence in Oregon was problem enough, had designs on California and perhaps were even being welcomed there by Mexico. Polk may have viewed the impulsive captain of topographers as an instrument to upset those plans. Frémont might be able to determine, in the event of war with Mexico, the degree of resistance the United States could face in California and how much assistance could be expected from the American settlers there.

Frémont himself later noticeably omitted mention of the President when he wrote of the meeting: "California stood out as the chief subject in the impending war; and with Mr. Benton and other governing men at Washington, it became a firm resolve to hold it for the United States. . . ."

On the evening of October 30, 1845, while Zachary Taylor and his army were waiting on the Nueces River, and as Thomas Larkin in Monterey was assimilating his secret instructions from the State

Department, and Captain Frémont's new exploring party had reached the Great Salt Lake, the President made note in his diary of what became a momentous meeting with a minor military officer: "I had a confidential conversation with Lieut. Gillespie of the Marine Corps, at eight o'clock P.M., on the subject of his secret mission on which he was about to go to California. His secret instructions and the letter to Thomas O. Larkin, United States consul at Monterey, in the Department of State, will explain the object of his mission."

The marine had been selected for the assignment by Navy Secretary George Bancroft and while the details and purpose of his mission were never adequately explained, Lieutenant Archibald Hamilton Gillespie, who would soon leave Washington loaded with mysterious papers, was destined for a role in the unfolding events that was far more significant than that of courier.

A tall, red-haired career officer with a stylish, pointed beard and an air of self-importance, Gillespie was thirty-three at the time he met with the President. A native of Pennsylvania who had been orphaned at a young age, he enlisted in the marines at age twenty, rose to the rank of sergeant, then received a commission upon reenlisting. His superiors regarded him as a dependable, intelligent officer and a natural leader. He had had seagoing experience in the Pacific and, key to his new assignment, he spoke fluent Spanish.

Before departing Washington, the ambitious lieutenant wrote Secretary Bancroft: "I cannot say what I would wish at a moment like this, setting forth on an adventurous enterprize, but I can assure you, you will not regret having named me for this service."

When Gillespie boarded a commercial steamer bound for Vera Cruz on November 16, he carried with him instructions for Consul Larkin (which he subsequently memorized and destroyed); orders for Commodore John Sloat of the United States Pacific Squadron at Mazatlán; a letter to Captain Frémont of the Topographical Engineers, who had departed five months earlier on a "surveying expedition" to California; and a packet of letters to Frémont from his wife Jessie, daughter of Senator Thomas Hart Benton, and from the senator as well.

He traveled in mufti, posing as an invalid Scotch-whiskey sales-man with interests in California. He planned to cross Mexico in a *diligencia* (stagecoach) to Mazatlán, rendezvous there with Com-modore Sloat, then proceed to Monterey to meet with Larkin and to find Frémont.

❀

The President's final duty of 1845 involved yet another mission—a peace feeler to Mexico. To carry out this difficult if not impossible task, he appointed a former Louisiana congressman named John Slidell to travel to Vera Cruz. As Minister Extraordinary and Plenipotentiary, Slidell was to attempt to negotiate a boundary be-tween the two countries, specifically the Rio Grande, with Mexico ceding all the territory east and north of the river for a sum of money yet to be determined. If Mexico demonstrated a willingness to sell New Mexico and California, the United States would offer up to forty million dollars for them.

Slidell's timing was unfortunate. He arrived on the Mexican coast at the end of the year, just as one government fell and another rose. In January, 1846, the new regime, headed by the anti-Yankee army general Mariano Paredes y Arrillaga, not only refused Slidell an audience, but rejected all points of the proposed negotiation. There would be no recognition of the annexation of Texas by the United States, no boundary agreement, no sale of Mexican terri-tory. Indeed, Paredes announced that he intended to march to the Rio Grande and defend Texas.

Eighteen forty-five thus ended. Texas was admitted to the Union on December 28, Mexico was preparing to send an army north to the Rio Grande, Zachary Taylor's army was poised to meet that army, and John Charles Frémont and his rough crew were marching into California.

John Charles Frémont.

❈

CHAPTER SIX

Frémont

1

When John Charles Frémont led his buccaneer's band of buck-skinned mountain men, French-Canadians, and Delaware Indians down the western slope of the Sierra Nevada and into Sutter's Fort in the winter of 1845, he had been six months on trail out of St. Louis. He loved the trail and camp, loved riding with a stalwart company of frontiersmen whose loyalty he prized above all things. In the prairies, deserts, and mountain passes, he had a singleness of purpose; in remote places, he found serenity in work, none of it too routine. Finding good game, graze, wood and water for making camp became a small daily triumph. He relished such chores as ordering cook fires started and tents pitched, and assigning pickets in two-hour shifts to watch the hobbled horses and pack animals, and to listen for unfamiliar sounds. He delighted in working into the night on his papers under the flickering light of a bull's-eye lantern, and rousting the men at daybreak to cook meat and boil coffee for breakfast and to break camp. He found satisfaction in supervising the packing of mules and rolling stock for resuming the march at no later than six-thirty; he found solace in jotting, sketching, mapping, and making astronomical observations.

He was never happier than in journeying—the going there

rather than the getting there. The trail brought out all his gifts. He had a cool daring in times of peril. He was decisive—pointing the way, saying yes or no. He innovated, added to his assignment, and returned to his superiors with more than they had bargained for.

Above all, he had a singular facility in commanding diverse and difficult men. He had experienced classrooms and drawing rooms, danced at balls and galas, sat in the sanctums of men of wealth and power, spoken confidently to the President of the United States. Yet he easily inspired the loyalty of men who knew nothing of social graces, were suspicious of education, wealth, and power, who could not name the President of the United States.

The men who rode with him into Sutter's Fort knew no rules or laws except the natural ones that governed the wilderness and their ability to survive in it. To all else, they were utterly independent and insubordinate, yet Frémont, time and again, led them.

The trail's end revealed another John Charles Frémont. On the journey, he could keep his balance while teetering between mountaintop and desert. But when he arrived at his destination, he resembled a sailor suddenly cast ashore, confounded by surer footing. In places shared by a citizenry and the trappings of civilization, the master of all the exigencies of the journey became a moody, directionless figure. Those he led and who enjoyed his company at the campfire and in the command tent now found him uncompanionable—peremptory, worried, humorless, quick to perceive a slight.

He was an essential adventurer and man of action, and inaction confused and braked his racing mind and turned it toward ruinous matters, such as politics and ambition.

He was an impatient man who believed that his destiny for greatness had been preordained and writ large in the celestial record. He had known for many years that his fate lay in the trackless lands west of the Mississippi and now, riding into the Sacramento Valley in December, 1845, a month from his thirty-third birthday, Frémont saw his destiny in finer focus. He had sensed it eighteen months ago when he first laid eyes on Sutter's Fort.

2

Frémont's father, John Charles, Senior, whose history is sketchy, was a royalist who fled from Napoleonic France, took ship to Santo Domingo, was captured by the British and spent some months in a West Indies prison before being permitted to emigrate to the United States. In 1808, he appeared in Richmond, Virginia, and there, while teaching at a private academy, met Anne Whiting Pryor, wife of an elderly horse-breeder and former military man. Anne and Charles ran away together and settled in Savannah, Georgia. On January 21, 1813, their first child, John Charles, was born and not long afterward, upon the death of Pryor, the couple married.

After Charles Frémont died of pneumonia in 1818, Anne took her son and her two other children to Charleston, where she subsisted on a small inheritance and by taking in boarders. In his early teens, John attended Charleston College, excelling in math and sciences, and although expelled at least once for habitual absences from his classes, he earned enough credits to land a teaching job in the city. Soon afterward, through the intervention of a family friend, Frémont, not yet twenty, was given a post as math instructor on the USS *Natchez*, embarking on a two-year cruise to South America.

Frémont's patron was Joel Roberts Poinsett, a Jacksonian politician who became the first American minister to Mexico (and the man who introduced to the United States the red tropical flower bearing his name). In 1837, as secretary of war in President Martin Van Buren's cabinet, Poinsett again used his influence on Frémont's behalf and was able to obtain for his protégé a commission as a lieutenant in the newly formed U.S. Topographical Corps. This appointment, and the subsequent posting to two surveys of the territory between the Mississippi and Missouri rivers, sealed Frémont's future. In the Minnesota and Dakota Territory, he worked alongside the eminent French topographer Joseph Nicollet, a man he loved as the father he had never known and whom he characterized as his "Yale College and Harvard," and he saw his life's work lying before him like one of Nicollet's magnificent maps.

Poinsett, stirred by the young man's brilliance, manners, and natural charm, bestowed one other favor on his friend. This, the most significant gift in Frémont's life, occurred in Washington when his patron introduced the lieutenant to the man who, more than Poinsett, or even more than Nicollet, would touch and transform his life. Senator Thomas Hart Benton of Missouri was the supreme expansionist leader in Congress and the principal supporter of government-sponsored surveys and explorations of the West. Frémont began dining often at the Benton home. He was held in thrall by Benton's table talk—the huge, craggy-faced senator was a polished orator no matter the size of his audience—and by Benton's lively and beautiful teenage daughter, Jessie. She in turn fell instantly in love with the handsome, articulate, Gallic-mannered Southerner.

When Benton learned of their romance, Frémont felt the full fury of the senator's notoriously volcanic temper and saw the map of his future turn to ashes. Benton forbade any contact between his beloved daughter and the penniless upstart who had betrayed his hospitality and trust. Soon after their confrontation, Poinsett, probably at Benton's instruction, sent the lieutenant off in the summer of 1841 on an expedition to survey Iowa Territory.

His three-month exile from Washington did nothing to cool the young couple's ardor, however, and Frémont and Jessie Benton eloped and married that October. Benton's wrath subsided after Jessie threatened to abandon him completely, and thereafter, with one future parting, the senator and his son-in-law became partners in their shared ambition to "open the West" and make it American.

3

In 1842, Benton and his expansionist political brethren muscled a thirty-thousand-dollar appropriation from Congress to survey the Oregon Trail, the growing route for emigration to the Pacific. The plan called for Joseph Nicollet to lead the expedition, but the Frenchman fell ill and Frémont, who had been assigned to serve as second in command, led the party. They journeyed to the fabled South Pass on the Continental Divide in Wyoming Territory—a saddle in the central Rocky Mountains, the great overland gateway to the Pacific—and the four-month venture inspired a detailed map and survey, and a splendid report. It also produced the first meeting between Frémont and a small, freckled, stoop-shouldered mountain man named Christopher Houston "Kit" Carson. This unprepossessing figure would eagerly share his deep and hard-won knowledge of the Western wilderness with the man he called "the Colonel" and follow Frémont—guide him, yet follow him—unstintingly in the years of adventure and conquest ahead.

Of the great inspirations in Frémont's life—his mother, Joel Poinsett, Joseph Nicollet, Thomas Hart Benton and Jessie Benton—Carson occupied a special niche. Frémont loved the little gray-eyed Kentuckian and came to regard him, and write of him, as the very apotheosis of the Western frontier, one whose name ought to be linked to those of Ulysses, Jason, Hector, Nimrod, the Norse heroes, and the knights of the Round Table.

Carson had been orphaned at a young age and had run away from home at sixteen to work as a wrangler on the Santa Fé Trail. Over the next decade, with the town of Taos, the fur-trade center eighty miles northeast of Santa Fé in Mexican New Mexico, as his *pied-à-terre*, Kit found work as a teamster. In 1828, working with Ewing Young and his fur brigade of forty men, he made his first expedition to California. In this venture, he was involved in a fight with Klamath Indians as the trappers made their way north along the Sacramento River.

Over the years before he met Frémont, Carson trapped with such fabled frontiersmen as Jim Bridger, Joe Meek, and Tom "Broken Hand" Fitzpatrick, fought Crow, Blackfeet, and Comanche war parties, and traveled the rivers and mountains from Missouri to the Pacific, from the Canadian border to the Rio Grande. He fought a duel with a French trapper at the Green River trappers' rendezvous in the summer of 1835 in which he "got his hair parted" and wounded his adversary. He married an Arapaho girl and after she died, "took up" with a Cheyenne woman. He trapped and hunted for the Hudson's Bay Company on the Mary's River in Nevada and on the Madison in Wyoming, traded among the Navajo, and worked as a hunter out of Bent's Fort on the Arkansas.

In May, 1842, on a steamer headed up the Missouri, he met Frémont and they struck up an enduring friendship. On the deck of the riverboat, Carson, then thirty-three, volunteered to join the explorer on the Oregon Trail journey and, as he later remembered the moment, said, "I told him that I had been some time in the mountains and thought I could guide him to any point he wished to go."

Frémont made some inquiries and hired Carson as scout and guide at a hundred dollars a month.

The Oregon Trail expedition ended in the late summer of 1842. Carson left Frémont at Fort Laramie, Wyoming, and in January, 1843, traveled on to Bent's Fort, then to Taos. In February, he converted to Catholicism and married María Josefa Jaramillo, age fifteen. She was the daughter of a prominent citizen of Taos and sister-in-law of Charles Bent, who had opened Bent's Fort in 1833. Seventeen years earlier, Charles Bent had hired a then-sixteen-year-old runaway named Kit Carson as a horse wrangler on a trading expedition to Santa Fé.

❀

Frémont returned to Washington in October and worked furiously with Jessie, dictating to her in numbing detail the facts of the journey. Jessie took her husband's data and observations and transformed them into a work of literature—lustrously written, as exciting as an adventure novel, filled with descriptive passages, lore, colorful anecdotes, and advice to overland travelers. The report, something entirely new among the normally labored prose of government documents, was printed in an edition of ten thousand copies and made available to the public. The book appeared in the spring of 1843, and despite its ponderous title, *A Report of an Exploration of the Country Lying Between the Missouri River and the Rocky Mountains on the Line of the Kansas and Great Platte Rivers*, it won instant acclaim in the press.

Thomas Hart Benton, the chief Oregon Trail and westward emigration boomer in Congress, was thrilled with the work of his son-in-law, and vindicated in having pushed him to succeed Joseph Nicollet to lead the expedition. The senator jumped on the success of the Oregon Trail report and engineered a follow-up mission for Frémont. This time, the exploration would continue on over the South Pass and to the mouth of the Columbia River, in Oregon territory.

In May, 1843, Frémont organized his party in St. Louis. Among the thirty who signed on were men who had followed or guided him to South Pass the year before, and others who would be notable Frémont men in years to come. Kit Carson joined the party at Bent's Fort, and Kit's friend Tom "Broken Hand" Fitzpatrick also came aboard. This big Irishman had trapped and traded among Blackfeet, Crows, Arikaras, Pawnees, Cheyennes, Shoshones, Arapahos, and Sioux since 1816, and had guided a wagon train from Missouri to Oregon in 1841. His hair had turned snow-white after a run-in with a Gros Ventre war party in 1832, and his left hand had been maimed in the dim past when a firearm exploded.

Other expedition members, trusted trailsmen, included the voyageurs Basil Lajeunesse and his brother François; Theodore Talbot, a Kentucky senator's son who became Frémont's loyal lieutenant and second in command; and an eighteen-year-old free black man, Jacob Dodson, one of the Benton family's servants.

In St. Louis, Frémont obtained permission to draw some breech-loading, smoothbore Hall muskets, carbines, and gunpowder from the city's army arsenal. The request was approved by an officer who would reenter Frémont's life in years to come. This was Colonel Stephen Watts Kearny, commander of the Third Military Department. A longtime friend of Senator Benton's, he had known Jessie since her childhood.

When Frémont first met him at Jefferson Barracks in St. Louis, Kearny, not yet fifty years old, was a thirty-year army veteran whose first battle had been at Queenston Heights, above the Niagara River in Canada, in the War of 1812. Since 1836, he had commanded one of the army's elite units, the First Dragoon Regiment, headquartered at Fort Leavenworth, Kansas, and in 1843, in St. Louis.

He was a stiff, humorless, ploddingly unimaginative professional soldier with a reputation as a martinet. He was also courageous and dependable, an officer whose life had followed a single path, that which connected the orders of his superiors to his prompt and exact execution of them.

Kearny greeted Frémont cordially at Jefferson Barracks and no doubt asked about Senator Benton, Jessie, and the Frémonts' newly born daughter. Then he signed the application for arms and powder and does not seem to have questioned the request for a brass howitzer, which Frémont thought would be useful in the event of Indian attack. The gun, its thirty-three-inch brass barrel mounted on a large-wheeled carriage, had been patterned after the French cannons used by mountain troops in Algeria and the Pyrenees. With its range of a thousand yards, the twelve-pounder (from the weight of the iron ball it fired) was the lightest piece of army artillery. For a peaceful, exploratory expedition, it was an odd and cumbersome weapon to choose, but Frémont was oblivious to the possibility that a cannon might look warlike to the Mexicans, some of whose territory he would need to cross, or to the British, who held Oregon territory in a fragile joint sovereignty with the United States. These fears did occur to those in command of the Topographical Corps and the Ordnance Department in Washington, but no orders to return the howitzer to the armory were received by the explorer before he and his party departed St. Louis on May 13. The cannon, and its powder and ball, was dragged over some three thousand miles of wilderness until abandoned many months later in a Sierra snowdrift.

❁

Early in September, the expedition reached the Great Salt Lake, and in November, Fort Vancouver, in Oregon territory. There its assignment ostensibly expired, but instead of turning toward home, Frémont led his men south to explore the Great Basin country between the Rockies and Sierra Nevada. Then, in a move that delighted Benton and his California-covetous colleagues, he took his party across the Sierras in January, 1844, and into Mexican California. They reached Sutter's Fort in the first week of March, purchased forage, supplies, and pack animals, and rested for nearly three weeks. Frémont and John A. Sutter met frequently over food and wine and exchanged information and philosophical ideas. The convivial empresario of New Helvetia made certain that the explorer understood his dream of empire and how strongly he encouraged emigrants to his lands, particularly Americans. Sutter saw the future of California as an American province, and Frémont agreed.

The expedition resumed its journey late in the month, this time heading south down the San Joaquin Valley and into the Mojave Desert, then northeast again, through Nevada, Utah, and back to Bent's Fort on July 1.

In August, Frémont returned to St. Louis, where he was reunited with Jessie and her parents. Soon after that, the family embarked by stagecoach for Washington, where the explorer and his beloved amanuensis set to work on his new report.

4

In his absence, Frémont learned, his father-in-law had been present—and nearly killed—in an awful explosion aboard the steam frigate *Princeton* while on a Potomac cruise. The calamity had occurred on the last day of February past, at the time the explorer and his men were making their way toward Sutter's Fort.

The *Princeton* was the navy's finest steamship, the first to be driven by screw propellers instead of sidewheels, a man-of-war equipped with the most powerful gun battery afloat: twelve forty-two-pound carronades—blunt-barreled, short-range cannons—plus two monster guns, the biggest in existence, capable of firing a 225-pound iron round shot. Each of these cannons measured fifteen feet from butt to two-foot-wide muzzle, and each weighed fourteen tons.

The commanding officer of the *Princeton*, Captain Robert Field Stockton, had supervised the ship's construction in Philadelphia the year before, and in February, 1844, had taken four hundred Washington dignitaries on a Potomac cruise. Among his special guests were President John Tyler, Tyler's son, daughter and son-in-law, cabinet members, the secretary of the navy, certain powerful members of Congress, including Senator Benton, and seventy-six-year-old Dolley Madison, widow of the fourth President of the United States.

As the frigate steamed toward Fort Washington and Mount Vernon, the ship's band playing "Hail, Columbia," Captain Stockton proudly demonstrated his guns, firing twenty-one-gun salutes with the carronades and twice ordering the firing of the Peacemaker, one of the mammoth cannons, after which the guests went below to the officers' mess for a lavish banquet and champagne toasts. When Navy Secretary Thomas W. Gilmer asked Stockton for one final demonstration of the Peacemaker, the captain went on deck to supervise it, followed by many of the *Princeton*'s visitors.

Senator Benton with Senator S. S. Phelps of Vermont and other guests gathered at the starboard rail; Tyler's secretary of state, Abel Upshur, and Secretary Gilmer among others watched from the port side. As the gun crew loaded the Peacemaker with a twenty-five-pound blank powder charge, the President and his family remained below, listening to the band.

When Stockton shouted "Fire!" the great gun blew to pieces at a point about two feet from the breech, hurtling a one-ton chunk of steel backward, its shrapnel spraying the port rail and instantly killing Secretaries Upshur and Gilmer and four others.

Stockton, standing at the gun, miraculously survived, though the blast singed the hair from his head and the beard from his face.

Benton had escaped, shaken and in shock, but uninjured.

A court of inquiry later cleared the captain of any responsibility for the tragic accident and determined that the source of the gun explosion lay in a metallurgical problem.

Stockton, three months later, commanded the *Princeton* in the Gulf of Mexico and within a year and a half was promoted to the rank of commodore. His new assignment called for him to take command of the navy's Pacific Squadron and to proceed on his new flagship *Congress* around Cape Horn to Mexican California.

With publication of his second book-length report, three times longer than the first and ten thousand copies printed and distributed, Frémont seemed to have reached the apogee of his career. Winfield Scott, commanding general of the army, had recommended him for promotion to a brevet captaincy (approved by President John Tyler just before he left office); the explorer had become a national hero, called "the Pathfinder," his name a symbol of American fortitude, adventure, and spirit. He was dashing and handsome, exuding a Gallic charm and a Childe Harold-like mystery. He had at his side the beautiful and accomplished Jessie. He was as comfortable and confident mixing with men of power in the staterooms of Washington politics as journeying into the wilderness with such peerless frontiersmen as Kit Carson—who, as a result of the munificent praise in Frémont's books, had his own fame and following.

In June, 1845, within weeks of the meeting with the President in which he had spoken of the need for accurate maps of the trans-Mississippi West, Frémont left St. Louis for Bent's Fort.

The new expedition seemed conventional work for a captain of the Army Corps of Topographical Engineers. His mission was to explore the Great Basin, the vastness of mountain and desert running north to the Columbia Plateau, south to the Mojave and sandwiched between the Rockies and the Sierra range bordering California.

In truth, he had a greater purpose. He served as westward agent for his forceful father-in-law, and he served an even more puissant master, the President of the United States, who intended making facts of the hopes and prophesies of Benton and his followers in Washington.

Frémont's ostensible duties lay in the Great Basin, with the secondary work of surveying and mapping a wagon road between Missouri and Great Salt Lake, then over the mountain passes to the Pacific. But although it was not mentioned in his official orders from the Bureau of Topographical Engineers, his real destination was California, "the road to India," "the garden of the world," as the great senator dreamily called it.

❁

Frémont had most of his expedition members signed up by the time he reached Bent's Fort in August. Army lieutenants Theodore Talbot, James W. Abert, and William Guy Peck considered it an honor to accompany their celebrated captain, as did the civilian artist-cartographer Edward M. Kern of Philadelphia. Among the French-Canadian hunter-trappers gathered in St. Louis were Basil Lajeunesse, Raphael Prou, and Auguste Archambeau. The "free colored man," Jacob Dodson, was there, as were a gunsmith named Stepp; Denny, an Iowa half-breed; and twelve Delaware Indians recruited from a settlement near Westport Landing, on the Missouri River. The Delawares, remnants of the tribe that had been pushed ever westward since the 1750s, were led by chiefs Segundai and Swanok, who became Frémont's colorful personal bodyguards. In the East, their tribal name was Lenni-Lenape, "real men," and the explorer learned the truth behind the name in the months to come. Among Western tribes deemed enemies, the Delawares were killers and scalp-takers; at all times, they were utterly fearless and dependable trailbreakers and hunters.

"Broken Hand" Fitzpatrick had also signed the three-dollars-a-day contract, as had Lucien Maxwell, out of Kaskaskia, Illinois, a hunter-trader among the Utes and plains tribes, plus two other mountain legends, Joseph Reddeford Walker and Alexis Godey.

Joe Walker, a forty-seven-year-old Tennessean, had been in the West since 1819, tramping and trapping from the high Rockies to the Rio Grande. During his Santa Fé Trail days, he had even been a prisoner of the Mexicans for a time. He had also served as the first sheriff of Jackson County, Missouri, and in 1833, with a party of forty free trappers, made a three-week crossing of the Sierra Nevada, and in November of the same year, discovered Yosemite Valley.

In the twelve years since his first trek to the Pacific, Walker had become a hardened California hand, leading many parties to the Mexican province to trade horses and mules, and serving as guide for California-bound parties out of Fort Bridger, on the Green River of Wyoming.

Walker had been with Frémont in '42, as had Alexis Godey, another of the explorer's prized trailsmen. Twenty-seven at the time, he came eagerly to join the new expedition. Godey had trapped with Jim Bridger in the Rockies and had made more than one trip as far west as the Mary's River in Nevada. He was a close associate and friend of Kit Carson's and earned Frémont's high praise for his dependability and cool courage. These words also applied to another Carson crony, Richard "Dick" Owens, an Ohio-born mountaineer, a proficient hunter-trapper and Indian fighter. He had a special knack for stealing horses from the Blackfeet and Shoshone, and on at least one occasion, from the Mexicans in southern California.

Frémont asserted that Carson, Godey, and Owens, had they served in Napoleon's army, would have all been field marshals. He wrote: "Carson of great courage; quick and complete perception, taking in at a glance the advantages as well as the chances for defeat; Godey, insensible to danger, of perfect coolness and stubborn resolution; Owens, equal in courage to the others, and in coolness equal to Godey, had the *coup d'œil* of a chess player, covering the whole field with a glance that sees the best move."

Carson, when he returned to New Mexico after the 1842 expedition, had gone into partnership with Owens, and the two set up a farming operation on the Little Cimarron River fifty miles from Taos, where Kit built a cabin for his beloved Josefa. But he had promised Frémont that if called, he would come, and when the message arrived from Bent's, he and Owens sold their ranch, for about half of what they had paid for it, Kit kissed Josefa good-bye, and the two men rode north to the Arkansas River.

❦

They rode northwest out of Bent's on August 16, 1845, Frémont and his sixty-two "experienced, self-reliant" men, heading a pack train of two hundred animals and a two-hundred-fifty-head cattle herd. In two months, this somewhat suspiciously overmanned and overarmed expedition crossed the Upper Colorado, trekked into the wastelands of eastern Utah, followed old Indian and trapper trails across the Green River, traversed the Wasatch Mountains, and arrived at the Great Salt Lake in October.

They rode across the salt plain and through gray seas of sagebrush until, in late October, they reached the sluggish Mary's River, which Frémont renamed the Humboldt after the German geographer Friedrich Alexander von Humboldt. At the camp on the river, on November 5, 1845, the explorer split his party into two topographical units, rendezvousing with them on November 27 at Walker Lake (named for Joe Walker). This stunningly pristine lake, a hundred miles northeast of the Yosemite Valley, was alive with cutthroat trout, the fish so abundant that the men could kick them ashore to be killed, cleaned, and roasted on the spot.

On November 29, Frémont again divided his expedition. Most of the men, commanded by Talbot and guided by Joe Walker, marched south along the eastern escarpment of the Sierras and crossed into the San Joaquin Valley. Talbot was to map the eastern flank of the range and its passes and rendezvous in the south after the rest of the party reached Sutter's Fort and reprovisioned. Frémont took Carson and fifteen men, including some of the Delawares, and struck out for the Truckee River. Six days were spent crossing the mountains through what later became known as Donner Pass to reach the south fork of the American River. From that point it was an easy march through the pine and manzanita country to the broad flatlands of the Sacramento Valley of Alta California.

Frémont led his men into Sutter's Fort on December 10, 1845.

✤

CHAPTER SEVEN

Hawk's Peak

1

Frémont and his men rode into the Sacramento Valley that winter in the wake of the latest efforts to stem the flow of American settlers in the province. Just a month before the exploration party arrived, the commanding general of Alta California, José Castro, had carried out orders from Mexico City by issuing a decree ordering all American emigrants in the northern province to proceed to Sonoma. There, at Colonel Vallejo's direction, they were to swear an oath to obey Mexican laws and apply for a license to settle in the province. Those whose applications were denied would be banished from the country.

In 1845, there were about eight hundred Americans in California, most of them distributed on small farms and homesteads in the north, within a horseback ride to New Helvetia. Some of the earlier arrivals had become Mexican citizens; the more recent emigrants had not bothered to take the oath and had not been pressured to do so.

Castro's procrustean orders produced little but dissension and anger among the Americans, only twenty of them showing up in Sonoma to apply for the settler's license. The general and an escort rode north from Monterey to Sonoma to visit Vallejo on November

11 and to reinforce the decree demanding that the Americans come forth.

Given the war clouds darkening over the Rio Grande, Castro's orders from Mexico were a wise if belated attempt to identify the Americans who had entered California without sanction—which meant virtually all of the newcomers—and who might represent a threat in the event of war with the United States.

Californios drew little distinction between them, these Americans being sorted out, but they were a disparate lot.

William Brown Ide, a Massachusetts man, came to the Sacramento Valley to see if he could succeed at something. He had worked as a carpenter and farmer in New England, and even as an occasional schoolteacher in Ohio and Illinois. None of these endeavors proved very successful and at age forty-seven, a skinny, pious teetotaler with a wife and five children, he joined an emigrant train in Independence, Missouri, bound for Oregon. Near Fort Hall, Idaho, Ide, a Tennessean named John Grigsby, and several others turned their wagons south and made a harrowing crossing of the Sierra Nevada to Sutter's lands.

Ide may have failed in the East, but he was an industrious man, no stranger to hard work, and he soon found a tract of rich land north of New Helvetia, built a cabin, and began clearing and plowing.

Besides Grigsby, there were several other squatters a day or two by horse from Ide's place. Robert "Long Bob" Semple was a six-foot-eight Kentucky dentist and printer. Granville Swift, also from Kentucky, claimed descent from Daniel Boone and worked for the Swiss as a hunter. Peter Lassen, the Danish blacksmith, became a trusted Sutter lieutenant and a Sacramento Valley hunter and rancher. Moses Carson, older half-brother of Kit's, was a veteran fur trader and Indian fighter who had become a Mexican citizen in 1836 when he settled in the Russian River area. Trappers in the waterways off the Sacramento included Henry L. Ford of New Hampshire, a twenty-four-year-old army deserter; William O. "Le Gros" (Big) Fallon, a burly Irishman who had followed beaver streams from New Mexico to California; John Neal, an Irish sailor and likely another fugitive from justice; and Samuel J. Hensley, a Kentuckian whom Sutter regarded as "of strong will and well-balanced mind, generous, temperate, and brave."

Another resident in the valley, William Todd of Illinois, had the distinction of being the nephew of Mary Todd, who in 1842 married a Kentucky-born lawyer named Abraham Lincoln. Todd had been in California only a few months when, in April, 1846, he wrote home:

> If there are any persons in Sangamon who speak of crossing the Rocky Mountains to this country, tell them my advice is to stay at home. There you are well off. You can enjoy all the comforts of life—live under a good government and have peace and plenty around you—a country whose soil is not surpassed by any in the world, having good seasons and yielding timely crops. Here everything is on the other extreme: the government is tyrannical, the weather unseasonable, poor crops, and the necessaries of life not to be had except at the most extortionate prices, and frequently not then. . . .

He added a prescient note: "The Mexicans talk every spring and fall of driving the foreigners out. . . . They must do it this year or they can never do it. There will be a revolution before long. . . . If here, I will take a hand in it."

Among the most volatile of the emigrants, one who had shown up at Sutter's doorstep in 1841, was a big, stuttering, excitable frontiersman with a bushy, tobacco-juice-stained beard, a mane of graying hair, and fierce bloodshot eyes. This specimen of a mountaineer, Ezekial Merritt by name, had a shadowy history. He hinted that he had been with Joseph Reddeford Walker in 1833 during the expedition that discovered Yosemite Valley. Historian Hubert H. Bancroft described him as "a coarse-grained, loud-mouthed, unprincipled, whiskey-drinking, quarrelsome fellow, well adapted to the use that was made of him in promoting the fili-busters' schemes." And John Charles Frémont, who may have known Merritt before 1845, said he was "a rugged man, fearless and simple; taking delight in incurring risks, but tractable and not given to asking questions when there was something he was required to do."

Both Bancroft and Frémont were correct in their varied descriptions of this obstreperous man. In making a point of Merritt's unquestioning nature, the explorer was describing the perfect Frémont man, and as events to come were to prove, Merritt became just that.

2

On December 10, 1845, Frémont and Kit Carson led fifteen men, including some of Chief Segundai's Delawares, into New Helvetia and camped on the American River three miles above Sutter's Fort. Frémont had made vague arrangements to rendezvous in a month or two with Ted Talbot, Joe Walker, and the bulk of the party, nearly fifty men, in the San Joaquin Valley east of Monterey. The Talbot contingent was slowed by their mapping assignment on the eastern flank of the Sierra Nevada, and in the waiting, Frémont had to gather pack animals and provisions before making his way south.

The explorer grew restless. He had arrived at one destination and needed to move on. He had business in Monterey, an expedition to re-form and its work to finish. California, for all its isolation and putative independence, was Mexican, and perhaps, given the war fever that had been gripping Washington six months ago when he had met with the new President, he might soon find himself in enemy territory. Although it seems never to have daunted him, he was a military officer already in enemy territory, with a small, well-armed army and subject to internment.

At the fort, Frémont learned that Sutter had departed on a business trip to Yerba Buena. In his absence, John Bidwell, the faithful majordomo, dealt with the impatient explorer and the two were quickly at odds. Bidwell, a twenty-five-year-old farmer who had come to the Sacramento Valley in 1841 with a pioneer train, was a somewhat prim, utterly honest factotum whom Sutter trusted to manage his affairs. He greeted Frémont and his men affably and listened as the explorer demanded to buy sixteen pack mules, six packsaddles, and provisions. Bidwell explained that the fort's foodstuffs and animals were in short supply. He could not provide the mules but had some good horses and said he could make the packsaddles and come up with some flour and other edibles.

Frémont was annoyed by the man's inability to meet his demands and rode off in a huff. He had figured out why he did not get what he requested: he represented one government, Sutter and Bidwell another, and the two governments were having "difficulties." There was some truth in this. Sutter had a foot in both the Mexican and American camps and was having problems keeping his balance.

In a few days, the problems were solved. Bidwell rode out to the explorer's camp, needlessly apologized and explained that he was only an employee following instructions. Soon thereafter, Sutter returned to the fort and Frémont had fourteen of the sixteen mules he wanted, plus the packsaddles and supplies, and even a few head of cattle to provide beef for his men. The Swiss also gave the captain use of his schooner *Sacramento* to sail down to San Francisco Bay and to Yerba Buena to visit the American vice consul, William Leidesdorff.

Frémont moved his camp several times, from the American River to tributaries of the San Joaquin—colorful streams such as the Calaveras, Merced, and the poppy-covered banks of Mariposa Creek, the marshes loud with ducks and geese, rich with elk and antelope—before heading south in late January for the rendezvous with Talbot. He led his men in at least three Indian raids against the Miwoks and other "horsethief tribes" in the valley. These swift and merciless strikes were in retribution for ancient thefts of white men's horses dating back to Ewing Young's trapping expedition in 1830, in which Carson had been learning the mountain trades. The Delawares were particularly adept at the raids, and took scalps. The killing of these natives rated little more attention in the memoirs of Frémont and his men than did the shooting of geese or elk. Lucien Maxwell, Dick Owens, and Kit Carson are mentioned as "deftly shooting" Indians; Carson would later say: "We came on a party of Indians, killed five of them, and continued on to the Fort."

In January, 1846, six weeks after he entered California, Frémont and his men crossed the San Joaquin Valley to Monterey. The old capital, on the headland south of the bay seen by Cabrillo in 1542, was a cosmopolitan place by California standards, a seaport, a hub of commerce. Its whitewashed and red-roofed adobes were nestled between green hills and a white ribbon of beach lapped by ocean waters running from dark blue to turquoise and green as the sun set. On January 27, Frémont paid a visit to one of the most beautiful of Monterey's dwellings, the two-story, New England-style home of Thomas O. Larkin, and sat with the consul on a veranda overlooking the pine-circled bay.

They were a study in contrasts even though such a mix of men was common to Monterey, its path and byways a-jostle with wealthy Californios, traders, sea captains, merchant sailors, government men, Mexican soldiers, street urchins, and Indians. Even so, it must have been amusing for the urbane, mutton-chopped Larkin, in starched shirt, coat, collar, and cravat, to sit face-to-face with the scraggy-bearded explorer wearing a wide-brimmed sombrero, trail-worn boots, grimy buckskins decorated with beads and porcupine quills.

There is no record of their meeting, but it is clear that they discussed the worsening relations between their native country and Mexico and their duties should news of war arrive on the Pacific coast. Frémont told of his expedition and its purpose and asked Larkin for a loan, to be billed to the Topographical Corps headquarters in Washington, to buy supplies. The consul agreed to supply the money and took Frémont to visit two of Monterey's leading dignitaries, Commandante José Castro, and the town's prefect,

Manuel Castro. Frémont told these wary men of his peaceful mission, assured them that his party was not military but comprised of civilian explorers, mapmakers, and guides under the command of army officers. He asked the commandante for permission to buy supplies and to "winter in the valley of San Joaquin." Castro, probably out of respect for Larkin, agreed to these requests with the proviso that Frémont and his men stay inland, outside the settled coastal areas.

3

By mid-February, Frémont had rejoined Talbot, Walker, Ed Kern, and the others who had crossed the Sierra Nevada farther south. Now, with his full sixty-two-man complement, he moved the party north toward the southern extremity of San Francisco Bay and camped in a meadow about fifteen miles from the San José Mission, where almost immediately he ran into trouble.

Sebastián Peralta, who owned a large rancho outside the village of Santa Clara, a short distance from the mission, registered a complaint with the *alcalde* of San José. Peralta said that some of his horses were missing and had turned up in the herd being kept by the Americans. He said he had ridden out to the American camp to claim his animals and had been ordered away. On February 20, he had addressed a letter to the leader, Frémont, and had received an antagonistic response. The explorer, Peralta reported, claimed that all his animals had been purchased and paid for, and that Peralta "should have been well satisfied to escape without a severe horse-whipping" for having the temerity to attempt to gain horses that did not belong to him.

Peralta, vastly insulted by the American officer, showed the *alcalde* Frémont's letter and fulminated over the arrogance of it. The letter ended: "Any further communication on this subject will not, therefore, receive attention. You will readily understand that my duties will not permit me to appear before magistrates of your towns on the complaint of every straggling vagabond who may chance to visit my camp."

Before this incident could be resolved, Frémont ensured that there would be trouble with Mexican authorities by moving his camp to the outskirts of the coastal town of Santa Cruz, on the north edge of Monterey Bay. Then, on March 5, the exploring party moved again, to a camp on the Salinas River, even closer to Monterey.

During this period when Frémont blatantly broke his pledge to keep his party inland and away from coastal settlements, some of his men were further testing the patience of Mexican officials. The Monterey customs official, Antonio María Osio, wrote in his 1851 memoir of the incident that ended all tolerance of the Americans.

Osio told of three of Frémont's "soldiers" who invaded a rancho near San Juan Bautista, a short distance from the American camp. The ranch was owned by Don Ángel Castro,* who reported that one of the drunken men held a gun at his head while another tried to rape his daughter. Don Ángel, a tough former soldier, resisted, even at the risk of death, and succeeded in wrestling the gun away and chasing the *Americanos* out of his home.

This act, Osio said, had infuriated General José Castro and convinced the commandante that Frémont and his "army" were purposely inciting a confrontation. The general reacted to the outrage by notifying Consul Larkin of his decision to expel the Americans—at least from the Monterey area—and by sending a courier to Frémont's camp to deliver the message demanding that he and his men leave Monterey forthwith. Castro wrote:

This morning at seven, information reached this office that you and your party have entered the settlements of this department; and this

---

There were many Castros in California. Ángel Castro, a former presidio soldier, was a judge and distinguished citizen of San Juan Bautista and uncle of General José Castro. The prefect at Monterey, Manuel Castro, does not appear to have been directly related to General José Castro.

being prohibited by our laws, I find myself obliged to notify you that on receipt of this, you must immediately retire beyond the limits of the department . . . it being understood that if you do not do this, this prefecture will adopt the necessary measures to make you respect this determination.

Frémont received the message in his customary high dudgeon and dismissed it and the courier, whom he considered offensively brusque, with a wave of his hand. He did not respond. Afterward, he wrote, "I peremptorily refused compliance to an order insulting to my government and myself"—thus assuming an attitude that was later cheered by Senator Thomas Hart Benton as a courageous act.

On March 5, Frémont and his men broke camp on the Salinas River and moved north a short distance to a wooded hill known locally as Gavilán (Hawk) Peak, just thirty miles from Monterey and overlooking the Salinas Valley and San Juan Bautista. The captain flouted Castro's orders by having his men chop trees and throw up a crude log fort, complete with earthworks, as if expecting a siege. A stripped sapling served as a staff from which the American flag flapped in the breeze.

From this hawk's eyrie, Frémont heatedly scribbled a note to be delivered under cover of darkness to Larkin. It was an extraordinary declaration for a man ostensibly leading a peaceful mission of exploration into a foreign country.

Frémont wrote the consul that "if we are unjustly attacked, we will fight to extremity and refuse quarter, trusting our country to avenge our death." He proceeded with a statement that Larkin, a salaried secret agent of the United States, must have found laughable: "We have in no wise done wrong to the people, or the authorities of the country, and if we are hemmed in and assaulted here, we will die, every man of us, under the flag of our country."

Unmoved by the captain's bravado, Larkin dispatched a return message patiently explaining Castro's order, what it meant and why it had been written. The consul also tried to placate the commandante, urging a more tempered approach to the Frémont problem and even suggesting that the two men meet and reach some kind of accord.

Castro was having none of this, and at San Juan Bautista on March 8, he called on the citizenry to assist him in expelling the "band of robbers commanded by a captain of the United States Army, J.C. Frémont." The leader and his "highwaymen," he said, had made their camp nearby, "from which he sallies forth committing depredations, and making scandalous skirmishes." He asked for volunteers to place themselves under his immediate orders to "prepare to lance the ulcer" that would "destroy our liberties and independence."

Castro, whom Frémont later admitted had "a fair amount of brains," put together a cavalry force of nearly two hundred men, regulars and volunteers, including a handful of local Indians, believed to have been plied with liquor, to engage the Americans. The general deployed his horsemen in plain view below Frémont's position and ordered three brass cannon dragged into the brush beneath the hill and aimed at the summit.

On Hawk's Peak, Frémont anxiously watched all this activity through his spyglass. He had practically begged for a confrontation and now had one, was outnumbered three to one and unsure of what to do next. He had a log fort and primitive siegeworks, a good high defensive position, plenty of wood, water, powder, and shot, and men—especially his Delawares, who had already smeared paint on their faces—anxious for a fight.

But what business did he have in fighting the Mexicans? Or in provoking a fight? He did not know that on the day after he occupied Hawk's Peak, Polk's minister extraordinary to Mexico, John Slidell, had reached Jalapa and was denied an audience with the government in Mexico City. He did not know that on the day General Castro issued his "band of robbers" proclamation, General Zachary Taylor had moved his army across the Nueces River in Texas, headed for the Rio Grande. He did not know as he watched Castro's cavalrymen through his glass that Polk's other secret agent, Lieutenant Archibald Gillespie, had reached Honolulu en route to rendezvous with Commodore Sloat, Consul Larkin, and Captain Frémont, and bearing important messages for each.

All Frémont knew in the three tense March days he occupied Hawk's Peak was that he had gotten into something that far superseded his authority and that was potentially quite dangerous. He had learned that General Castro was not to be trifled with and that the Mexicans, despite talk of their indolence and cowardly obsequiousness, seemed willing to defend their country and capable of doing so.

The closest the two forces came to a fight occurred when the Americans spotted a cavalry patrol winding its way through the trees and brush toward the peak, apparently reconnoitering the position. Frémont gathered forty of his men and started down the trail to engage the Californians. They waited off-trail to ambush the patrol, heard the men's voices and saw them approach and stop, holding some kind of consultation. Then the patrol rode back down the slope.

Larkin meantime got messages to the explorer that he must abandon any plans to oppose Castro, and on March 9, Frémont led his men off Hawk's Peak and aimed them north toward Sutter's Fort. He wrote Jessie that he left the hill "slowly and growlingly" and he inflated the number of Castro's cavalry to "three or four hundred men."

Joe Walker, a faithful Frémont man up to the Hawk's Peak retreat, wanted a fight and was so disgusted at the turn of events that he quit the expedition. The Tennessean, mountain legend, and discoverer of Yosemite Valley, would later call his old chief "morally and physically . . . the most complete coward I ever knew . . . timid as a woman if it were not casting unmerited reproach on that sex."

In Washington, Thomas Hart Benton saw no cowardice or timidity in his son-in-law's performance. "To my mind," he later wrote, "the noble resolution which they took to die, if attacked, under the flag of their country, four thousand miles distant from their homes, was an act of the highest heroism, worthy to be recorded by Xenophon."

4

News of Frémont's exploit in the Gavilán Mountains preceded him upcountry. John Marsh, a Harvard-educated physician who had a cattle ranch near Mount Diablo in the northern San Joaquin Valley, was in the Monterey area during the March dust-up between Castro and the Americans and sent a courier to Sutter's Fort with the news. Marsh was a veteran of the Blackhawk War in the Midwest, a one-time post surgeon and trader in the Sioux country of Minnesota who had grown wealthy among the Californios and saw the province as a Texas in the making. He wrote letters back East encouraging emigration to California. He may have seen Frémont as the vanguard of an American takeover—which he favored—but the *filibustero* appearance of the explorer's ruffian-like band disturbed him.

Not so James Clyman, a Virginia-born mountaineer of the Joe Walker stripe. Clyman had fought Arikaras with Jedediah Smith and Tom Fitzpatrick while Frémont was still in knee pants in Savannah. Now the frontiersman, newly arrived at California and hearing of the Americans' "defense" of Hawk's Peak, wrote the explorer a letter offering him a company of emigrant volunteers to help fight the Mexicans. Frémont answered Clyman's inquiry:

> I have received information to the effect that a declaration of war between our government and Mexico is probable, but so far this news has not been confirmed. . . . If peace is observed, I have no right or business here; if war ensues, I shall be outnumbered ten to one, and be compelled to make good my retreat, pressed by a pursuing enemy. . . . Under these circumstances, I must make my way back home, and gratefully decline your offer of a company of hardy warriors.

Frémont and his men, after camping among the lupin, poppies, and oaks of the San Joaquin Valley, moved north to the American River. On March 21, 1846, he reached Sutter's Fort to refit his expedition to continue north to the Oregon Territory and, perhaps, to turn east for home.

❈

Klamath Lake

1

In June, 1845, Commodore John Sloat, the elderly, cautious commander of the United States Pacific Squadron, received orders from the Navy Department to proceed from the Peruvian coast to Mexican waters. Aboard his sixty-gun flagship *Savannah,* after delays in provisioning, he led his seven-vessel squadron northwest and in November was joined off Mazatlán by the sloop-of-war *Cyane,* which carried more recent instructions.

Sloat's orders were a reflection of the Polk administration's belief, reinforced by Larkin, Leidesdorff, and other Americans in California, that the citizens there were friendlier to the United States than to their home country. The commodore was thus instructed that if he learned with certainty that war had begun between Mexico and the United States, he was to seize San Francisco Bay and blockade the other California ports, while attempting to preserve friendly relations with the people.

In an odd choice of words to send to an officer assigned to blockade and seize foreign territory, Sloat was told to be "assiduously careful to avoid any act which could be construed as an act of aggression."

Larkin in particular had advocated that a deft and delicate touch would be necessary to win over the Californios, and Frémont's ham-handed little drama at Hawk's Peak had greatly upset him. So much so, in fact, that he sent a panicky message to Sloat, then poised off Mazatlán, asking that one of his ships be dispatched to Monterey. Even after Frémont had abandoned Hawk's Peak and disappeared into the San Joaquin Valley, Larkin apparently feared that the explorer's defiance of General Castro might lead to bloodshed.

Sloat responded to the consul's request by sending Commander John B. Montgomery's twenty-four-gun sloop *Portsmouth* to Monterey Bay, ostensibly to discover "the designs of the English and French" in California—an old bugaboo given credence by Larkin's worried messages to Washington. More important, Sloat wanted Montgomery to discover "the temper of the inhabitants" and to demonstrate the "friendly regard" for them held by the Americans. In a more overt act, one that might have been seen as openly fomenting rebellion, the *Portsmouth* skipper was also to distribute among the people of Monterey copies of the constitutions of the United States and the new State of Texas, translated into Spanish.

The *Portsmouth* anchored in Monterey Bay on April 21, 1846, four days after Larkin had had a long, private conversation with a young marine lieutenant named Archibald Gillespie. This emissary, sent by Navy Secretary George Bancroft, had made his way overland from Vera Cruz to Mazatlán bearing important messages from Washington.

Another of the consul's visitors on this eve of war was Lieutenant Charles Warren Revere, patriot Paul Revere's grandson, who had transferred from the *Cyane* to Montgomery's *Portsmouth*. He had permission from Larkin and local authorities to take horseback rides around the Monterey hills, hunting and sightseeing, and was captivated by the place. He predicted that the land "will yet prove one of the brightest stars in the American galaxy."

Sloat and his squadron were patrolling between Mazatlán and the Sandwich Islands; the impetuous Frémont, who had come close to starting a war from his eyrie in the Gavilán Mountains, was still in the province, up in the north with sixty well-armed and restless men; and now an American warship lay at anchor off Monterey. Three weeks passed before war was declared against Mexico, and several more weeks went by before news of the war reached the Pacific rim, but Washington had already placed its agents in California on a war footing.

2

After buying supplies at Sutter's stores, Frémont led his men north, following the Feather River to a horse-and-cattle ranch on Butte Creek run by Samuel Neal, a blacksmith who had served with Frémont in '43 and who had asked for his discharge at New Helvetia. On March 30, the Americans reached Peter Lassen's Rancho Bosquejo on Deer Creek, some two hundred miles north of Sutter's. Lassen, also a blacksmith by trade, was a forty-five-year-old Dane who had come west with a fur brigade in 1839. He had traveled from Vancouver Island to Sutter's lands and in 1841 built a sawmill at Santa Cruz, become a Mexican citizen, and received the twenty-six-thousand-acre Deer Creek land grant in 1843. Except for the Indians he hired to work his horses and cattle, he lived in isolation and at the time Frémont arrived, had not seen a white man for seven months.

Lassen was a hospitable man and he and Frémont became good friends; the explorer and his men rested in camp on the Dane's land for a week before moving on again, this time toward the western flank of the Cascades. There the tentative plan was to map a route across the Great Basin to link with the Oregon Trail and then head home.

The American settlers who saw or heard about Frémont's exploring party regarded it as a miniature army, perhaps presaging a full-scale military invasion of California. That spring of 1846 had brought threatening news, especially for the squatters in the Sacramento Valley who had ignored the requirement to report to Colonel Vallejo in Sonoma. This disobedience of orders from Mexico City, and Frémont's defiance at Hawk's Peak, seemed to have energized General José Castro.

At the end of March, three weeks after the Americans skulked off the mountain, Castro called a military *consejo* (council) in Monterey to formulate a strategy to answer the insults of Frémont and his men. In attendance were the most powerful leaders in the province: Castro, Vallejo of Sonoma, the newly appointed governor Pío Pico, who came north from Los Angeles, and former governor Juan Bautista Alvarado

News of the *consejo,* carried north by mocassin telegraph, gave rise to fresh rumors: Castro was arming Indian tribes to help expel the illegal emigrants; he was courting French and British officials to assist in the event of war with the United States.

On April 17, a *bando* (proclamation) was issued in Monterey that confirmed the settlers' worst fears: unnaturalized foreigners would no longer be permitted to hold or work land in California and were subject to expulsion.

By the time Lieutenant Archibald Gillespie met with Larkin in Monterey on April 17, 1846, many of the confidential messages entrusted to him had been memorized and destroyed. Instead of making his way to California by the common routes around Cape Horn or a portage across the Isthmus of Panama, he had spent five nerve-racking months traveling across Mexico in a stagecoach under the guise of a whiskey salesman. The overland journey had a purpose, and Gillespie was a resourceful and intelligent officer. He was fluent in the Spanish language; he read, listened, watched, and absorbed everything he could in a country seething with political chaos; he saw firsthand examples of the hatred of Americans over the annexation of Texas, and the preparations for war.

After meetings with President Polk, Secretary of State Buchanan, Navy Secretary Bancroft, Senator Thomas Hart Benton, and Jessie Frémont, Gillespie had departed Washington the previous November 16 and traveled to Vera Cruz by commercial steamer. He reached Mexico City by *diligencia* and spent a month there while one government fell and another, led by a military man, took its place. He read of the mission of the American minister John Slidell, who was coming to Mexico to attempt to buy the country's provinces north of the Rio Grande.

By the time he was able to leave the Mexican capital, his ears rang with *"¡Dios y Libertad!"* and *"¡Viva, Mexico!"* and anti-American speeches; his brain teemed with newspaper stories about the United States' attack on Mexico's honor and scenes of soldiers on the march.

He had reached Mazatlán in April, gotten word to Commodore Sloat, and after delivering oral messages and briefing the officer on his mission, had boarded the *Cyane* for a voyage to Honolulu, thence to Monterey.

Gillespie met with Larkin and upon learning of the Hawk's Peak incident and Frémont's probable whereabouts north of Sutter's Fort, he prepared to move upcountry to intercept the explorer. On the evening before his departure, he was invited to a ball at the home of former Governor Alvarado. The marine's mufti did not seem to fool the Mexican officials in attendance. Colonel Vallejo eyed the American with undisguised suspicion, and Commandante Castro seemed overly attentive, plying Gillespie with brandy and asking difficult questions.

With a servant and two horses provided by Larkin, Gillespie made his way north. At Yerba Buena, he visited Vice Consul Leidesdorff, then proceeded north to New Helvetia. Sutter recognized the lieutenant—they had met in Honolulu some years before when the marine had been assigned to the Pacific Squadron—and the Swiss knew that this man was no whiskey salesman.

On May 8, 1846, Frémont learned that a military man carrying some kind of dispatches was riding north to intercept him. Sam Neal brought the news from his Butte Creek ranch to the explorer's camp, sprawled among a stand of cedars in a meadow at Upper Klamath Lake in Oregon territory, a few miles above the northern limits of Mexican California. Neal said that the officer was about a day behind.

The next morning, Frémont gathered ten men—Kit Carson,

Alexis Godey, Lucien Maxwell, Dick Owens, Basil Lajeunesse, Denny the Iowa half-breed, Bill Stepp the gunsmith, and the Delawares Segundai, Swanok, and Crane—and by sunset, after a thirty-mile ride, found Gillespie. He, Peter Lassen, and a few other men from Sutter's Fort were camped at the lower end of the lake.

Although neither man left a detailed record of their meeting on the wilderness shore of Klamath Lake, Frémont's normally chilly demeanor must have been put to the test. It had been eleven months since he had seen Jessie and his baby daughter Elizabeth— little Lily—eight months since he and his party had ridden out of Bent's Fort. He was news-famished, had had no contact with any American fresh from the East, had heard no news since his visit with Larkin in Monterey the past January. He was supposed to be heading home, but war was imminent and he could not yet abandon California. He desperately needed orders, news, something to guide his movements, and now there were possible answers, carried by this military man who had come across Mexico bearing letters, perhaps instructions, and certainly news.

Gillespie must have been similarly anxious as he was greeted by a trail-weary gallant in buckskins who turned out to be John Charles Frémont, the celebrated Pathfinder, explorer, author, husband of Jessie Benton. And the others! Kit Carson, the shy little gray-eyed man Frémont had hailed in his famous reports as the very embodiment of the intrepid Western frontiersman; and the French-Canadians, sons of *voyageurs* and *couriers du bois*, and the grimly silent Delawares who seemed to be the captain's bodyguard.

The marine even saw a small delegation of Klamath Indians as they hesitantly visited the camp and gave Frémont's men some salmon from their strings. The Klamath chief personally handed one of the fish to Gillespie.

After a meal of salmon cooked over the roaring fire built to ward off the winter wind hurtling off the lake, the marine and explorer talked into the night. In his tent under hurricane-lantern light, with the men rolled in their frosty blankets beneath the cedars as the wind whistled, Frémont read the mail and messages Gillespie presented in an oilskin packet. There were letters from Jessie; a note from Secretary of State Buchanan dated November 1, 1845, introducing the lieutenant; cryptic letters from Senator Benton, and miscellaneous newspaper articles.

Gillespie had committed to memory certain confidential messages from President Polk, Senator Benton, and Larkin. It is certain that Benton and the President had something to say about the British navy's presence off California, a matter Larkin had reported to Washington in the winter of '45; something was relayed about the imminence of war with Mexico, and Gillespie certainly talked at length about his journey from Vera Cruz to Mazatlán, his month in tumultuous Mexico City, and what he had learned from Sloat and Larkin.

In his memoirs published forty years afterward, Frémont remarked only on the messages from Benton that Gillespie carried, these on the old John Bull fear, subsequently proven groundless, that the British were concocting some scheme to "steal" California from the Americans. "The letter of Senator Benton," he wrote, "was a trumpet of no uncertain note. Read by the light of many conversations and discussions with himself and other governing men in Washington, it clearly made me know that I was required by the Government to find out any foreign schemes in relation to California, and to counteract them so far as was in my power. His letters made me know distinctly that at last the time had come when England must not get a foothold; that *we must be first*. I was to *act*, discreetly but positively."

In a peculiar anachronism in his memoir, Frémont wrote that he learned from Gillespie that "my country was at war." He could not have learned this from the marine since their meeting at Klamath Lake occurred on May 9, 1846, four days before the war against Mexico was officially declared.

Years later in his own memoirs, Kit Carson also remembered learning of the war before it could have been possible for him to have heard of it: "A few days after we left [Lassen's rancho, on April 24], information was received from California that war was de-

clared. . . . Lieutenant Gillespie, U.S. Marines, and six men were
sent after us to have us come back."

Clearly, it was not the actual news of war that turned Frémont
south again; it was the certainty of war as borne out by Gillespie's
experiences and the intelligence he had picked up in Mazatlán and
Monterey. The explorer was a trailsman too experienced not to
have known of the impossibility of crossing the Cascade range in
winter. He knew that winter snows blocked the passes, that game
was scarce, his animals in poor shape. Common sense demanded
that if he did return east, he would need to do so from a southern
route. In a letter to Benton from Klamath Lake, he had laid the
groundwork for returning to California, writing that "snow was
falling steadily and heavily in the mountains," that "in the east, and
north, and west, barriers absolutely impassable barred our road; we
had no provisions; our animals were already feeble."

(Benton later added to the confusion as to why his son-in-law
turned back to California when he wrote that it was "in the midst of
such dangers, and such occupations as these, and in the wildest regions of the Farthest West, that Mr. Frémont was pursuing science
and shunning war, when the arrival of Lieutenant Gillespie, and
his communications from Washington, suddenly changed all his
plans, turned him back from Oregon, and opened a new and splendid field of operations in California itself. . . .")

The truth seems to be that Frémont's movements north of Sutter's Fort comprised a calculated delaying tactic and that he fully
intended to return to New Helvetia, there to bide his time and learn
what he could. If war was averted through some eleventh-hour
diplomatic legerdemain, he would head his men for Walker's Pass
and a southern route home.

3

That night of his meeting on Klamath Lake with Frémont gave
Archibald Gillespie his first taste of combat since he had entered
the Marine Corps in 1832.

Kit Carson remembered the long day's ride on May 9 and falling exhausted into his bedroll on "the only night in all our travels, except the one night on the island in the Salt Lake, that we failed to keep guard." He said that since Gillespie and his companions had strengthened their party, they anticipated no Indian attack and that "the Colonel," as he called Frémont, posted no night watch and sat up late talking with Gillespie.

"Owens and I were sleeping together," Carson wrote, "and we were waked at the same time by the licks of the axe that killed our men. . . ."

Deep into the night, the scout had heard a noise and wakened suddenly. He called out to Basil Lajeunesse, sleeping nearby: "What's the matter there? What's the fuss?" There was no answer. Lajeunesse was dead—"his head had been cut in, in his sleep," Carson said. Instantly, the camp had come alive with men scrambling for their weapons amid the yelping of the attackers—a Klamath band—and the frenzied stamping and snorting of hobbled horses.

As the Klamaths fell on the camp, the four Delawares sprang up, and one of them, Crane, who had failed to load his carbine, flailed at the attackers with the gun until he fell, bristling with arrows. The half-breed Denny was also killed in the first few seconds of the melee. Frémont burst from his tent and joined Maxwell, Godey, and Stepp, all of them running toward the Delawares at the center of the fight.

Carson, who found his rifle useless because of a broken cap-nipple, sprinted toward the others, firing his pistol.

"I don't know who fired and who didn't," the scout said later, "but I think it was Stepp's shot that killed the Tlamath chief; for it was at the crack of Stepp's gun that he fell. . . . When the Tlamaths saw him fall, they ran. . . ."

Maddened at seeing his friend Lajeunesse's head split open, Carson had taken an ax to the fallen Klamath chief's skull, after which Segundai's knife sliced expertly and he popped the scalp off.

Frémont recalled that his party had encountered some of the Klamaths the day before and that the slain leader, who had given a salmon to Gillespie, had worn an "English half-axe" hanging from his wrist. "Carson seized this and knocked his head to pieces with it," the explorer said. The arrows in the chief's quiver were "all headed with a lancet-like piece of iron or steel—probably obtained from the Hudson's Bay Company's traders on the Umpqua—and were poisoned for about six inches. They could be driven that depth into a pine tree."

The quick fight was over, "but we lay," Carson said, "every man with his rifle cocked, until daylight, expecting another attack."

None came and at daylight, the bodies of Lajeunesse, Denny, and Crane were wrapped in their blankets and buried in a laurel grove before Frémont gathered his men for a retaliatory strike.

On May 12, Carson and ten men found a Klamath village of fifty lodges and charged in, Frémont and the others following. Within minutes, fourteen Indians lay dead, the lodges and huts and stores of dried fish on scaffolds torched, the canoes smashed to kindling. The Delawares, determined to avenge the slaying of Crane, did particularly close work with knives and axes.

Carson, who commanded the raid, recalled, "Their houses were built of flag [a lakeshore plant with sword-shaped leaves], beautifully woven. They had been fishing and had in their houses some ten wagon loads of fish they had caught. All their fishing tackle, camp equipage, etc., was there. I wished to do them as much damage as I could, so I directed their houses be set on fire. The flag being dry, it was a beautiful sight."

Gillespie, goggle-eyed at the bloodshed, opined, "By heaven, this is rough work," and promised that his superiors in Washington would learn of the gallantry of Frémont and his men.

Before they returned to California, there were several isolated incidents when Indian arrows whispered out of the trees at them. On one occasion, Carson fell off his horse as an arrow missed him by inches. Frémont spurred his big mount, El Toro de Sacramento, into a gallop and ran the lone Indian down. Segundai finished the job and took the hair.

The Klamaths were suspected of being recruited, along with

Modocs and other tribes, by General Castro to harass the Americans. Carson said merely that "The Indians had commenced the war with us without cause and I thought they should be chastized in a summary manner. And they were severely punished." Frémont's view was somewhat different, writing that the reason for his brutal raids on the natives was to "anticipate" Indian problems and strike first to make them realize that "Castro was far and I near."

They reached Peter Lassen's ranch on May 24 and there learned that the sloop-of-war *Portsmouth* had anchored at Sausalito, on the northern headland of the Golden Gate. Gillespie, who had put himself under Frémont's command, was sent down to request supplies from Captain John B. Montgomery—rifle lead, percussion caps, gunpowder, and foodstuffs—and to ride on south to Monterey with a letter to Larkin assuring him that while Frémont and his expedition were back in California, they were heading home.

Writing almost a hundred years later, Bernard DeVoto asserted that Frémont returned from Oregon "to seize California for the United States and wrap Old Glory round him, to give a deed to the greatness in him." The historian maintained that the explorer needed honor and glory, "to seize the hour, take fortune at the full . . . to trust that the war which was certain to come would transform an act of brigandage into an act of patriotism, would transform the actor from a military adventurer, a freebooter, a filibuster, into a hero."

Frémont had written home that "The nature of my instructions and the peaceful nature of our operations do not contemplate any active hostility on my part, even in the event of war between the two countries." But forty-five years later, he contradicted himself, writing in his memoirs that he "knew the hour had come" before he turned south from Klamath Lake, even though he made a pretense of heading "home." He said he was "but a pawn, and like a pawn, I had been pushed forward to the front at the opening of the game."

CHAPTER NINE

War

1

When Gillespie and Frémont rendezvoused at Klamath Lake on May 9, 1846, four days remained before the United States and Mexico went to war, yet cannon smoke had already settled on one battlefield and was rising on another.

In Mexico City, Gillespie had witnessed the country's furious reaction to America's annexation of Texas and attempts to buy the provinces of New Mexico and California. Mexico's President José Herrera, after refusing to meet with the United States' special envoy John Slidell, ordered his top military man, General Mariano Paredes y Arrillaga, to organize an army and march north to subdue the Texans and reclaim the annexed territory. A rabid anti-American, Paredes stepped up his orders: he turned the army against Herrera, seized the government, and installed himself as president. His first act thereafter was to send a five-thousand-man army to Matamoros on the Rio Grande, and on April 23, 1846—while Frémont was heading his men north out of Sutter's Fort—he declared a "defensive war" against the United States.

The army Paredes sent north, commanded by General Mariano Arista, had some of Mexico's most experienced light-infantrymen and sixteen hundred lancers under a celebrated cavalry general,

Anastasio Torrejón. When the commanding general of this Army of the North arrived at Matamoros on April 24, his American counterpart, General Zachary Taylor, had been waiting with his expeditionary force of three thousand men for nearly a month. When Arista sent a lancer patrol across the Rio Grande twenty-four miles upstream from Matamoros and dispatched a polite message to the American camp that "hostilities have commenced," Taylor welcomed it and sent his own patrol of dragoons to meet Arista's lancers.

On April 25, the as yet undeclared war began.

2

The President chose Zachary Taylor to "defend the Rio Grande" because Taylor, as commanding general at Fort Jesup in Louisiana, was closer to the river than any other of the army's senior officers. Ever the political man, Polk the Democrat despised Taylor's Whig politics but hated even more the idea of appointing the army's top general, Winfield Scott, to command the expeditionary force. Polk considered Scott, also a Whig, a political intriguer and a man who, when not preening in his spotless blue uniform with its braided gold epaulettes and yellow sash, was preparing for a run at the presidency. Moreover, Scott wanted to take time to train and equip an army before moving it into battle. The President had no interest in such time-consuming matters. Quickness interested him—quick victories if diplomacy failed, a war ended quickly.

Scott was sixty-one, six-foot-four in height, a wounded veteran of Lundy's Lane in 1814, a scholar of war, and a tireless, inspirational officer always in the thick of a fight. But because of his politics, his insistence that men should be trained before sent into battle, and his well-known vanity (his men bestowed the "Old Fuss and Feathers" sobriquet on him), he was temporarily left in the capital. There, while waiting the appointment he knew would eventually come to him, he said sagacious, presidential-sounding things such as, "I do not desire to place myself in the most perilous of all positions, a fire upon my rear from Washington and the fire in front from the Mexicans."

Meantime, it was left to Zachary Taylor to start the ball, and no officer in the army stood in sharper contrast to the impeccable Scott than "Old Rough and Ready." Born in Virginia and raised on the Kentucky frontier, he had a rudimentary wilderness education, but in his nearly forty years in the army, he had fought in the War of 1812, in the Blackhawk War in the Midwest in 1832, and against the Seminoles in Florida. He was sixty-one, short, solid, and as powerful as a bullock, with a face furrowed with deep lines, unruly gray hair, and big knotty hands. In the field, he commonly wore a filthy oilskin or straw hat mashed on his head, a long, mud-spattered linen duster, rumpled shirt, and baggy trousers. He was often taken to be a camp follower or sutler as he sat under a shade tree, an ammunition box for desk, gnawing a lump of salt pork or chewing a huge quid of tobacco.

He hated pomp, was quickly bored with paperwork—Scott thought him "slow" of pen and speech—and knew little of strategy or tactics. He had a perfect correlative in the British army, General Hugh Gough, a Tipperary Irishman who was fighting Sikhs in the Punjab region of northern India while Taylor was fighting Mexicans on the Rio Grande. Like Taylor, Gough knew little of grand designs in war. Once, on a battlefield against the Sikhs, he was informed that his artillerymen were running low on powder and shot. "Thank God," Gough said. "Now I can be at them with the bayonet!"

Zachary Taylor and a certain dragoon general-to-be, Stephen Watts Kearny, had the same battle philosophy.

Taylor's officers loved to tell stories of his perfect calm in battle, of how he slouched on his horse "Old Whitey," chewing and spitting and growling orders amid musket balls, round shot, shrapnel, and cannon smoke. His men loved him.

Taylor brought his expeditionary force to the Rio Grande on March 28, 1846, and raised the Stars and Stripes on the bank of a horseshoe bend of the river. There he ordered the building of a fort from which his gunners could rake Matamoros with artillery fire. This pentagonal structure, its walls nine feet high and fifteen feet thick, with a bastion at each corner holding a cannon battery, was completed by the time General Arista came north to command the Mexican army of five thousand men opposing Taylor's three thousand.

The fighting began on April 25 when an American patrol marched through the chaparral to some abandoned ranch buildings twenty-five miles upriver from their fort opposite Matamoros. In a skirmish with Mexican lancers, sixteen Americans were killed, several others wounded and taken prisoner.

Taylor sent a message by courier to Washington, two weeks away from the Rio Grande: "American blood has been spilled."

More was due to be spilled before the President received the intelligence. On May 8, as the Americans were returning to their besieged fort from their supply base at Port Isabel on the Gulf Coast, Taylor met Arista's army, spread out in the saw grass on the treeless prairie, blocking the road at a place called Palo Alto. The Mexican cannons opened fire at two-thirty that afternoon, their range too short, the round shot bouncing and ricocheting like croquet balls and rolling into the American lines so slowly that the ranks opened to let them pass. Taylor's own big guns, eighteen-pounders loaded with grapeshot, were better manned and more accurate, and his "flying batteries" of small brass six-pounders and cast-iron twelves did murderous service among Torrejón's advancing lancers.

The artillery duel ended at nightfall, and as the cook fires were lit and the surgeons in their bloody aprons sawed, cauterized, and wound dressings around stumps and torn flesh, the casualties were counted: Taylor had lost five dead, forty-three wounded; Arista, over thirty killed.

The next day, the day Gillespie and Frémont met at Klamath Lake, Arista's battered army made a stand in a shallow ravine that formed an arc facing the road from Port Isabel to Matamoros. This roadway, called Resaca de la Palma, required more than cannon-shot to vanquish the enemy, and Taylor warned his infantry, Gough-like, that their "main dependence must be upon the bayonet." His flying battery advanced on the road, his infantry plunged through the tangle of chaparral, and as enemy grape and canister shot raked them, his dragoons charged Arista's cannons with Taylor shouting through the din, "Take those guns, and by God, keep them!"

The Fourth and Fifth Infantries charged into the Mexican line and after firing their muskets once, and with no time to reload, began the furious hand-to-hand bayonet killing the old general had predicted would be necessary.

The attack routed Arista's troops; they fell back south toward the river, leaving four hundred wounded behind.

The Americans lost thirty-three dead and eighty-nine wounded at Resaca de la Palma, but Taylor's army had won the first two battles of the war with Mexico, the first battles against non-Indian forces since 1815.

On May 18, the army was ferried across the Rio Grande and after occupying Matamoros, Taylor began laying plans to move deeper into Mexico.

3

President Polk received the general's "blood has been spilled" message on May 9, and with his *casus belli* in hand, sent his own message to Congress two days later. He asked that the legislators acknowledge that a state of war existed and provide "the means for prosecuting the war with vigor, thus hastening the restoration of peace." He asserted that "the cup of forbearance had been exhausted" and that Mexico, by entering Texas, had invaded American territory and opened hostilities.

Despite Whig opposition, in which Polk was accused of fomenting war by sending Taylor to the Rio Grande in the first place, a war bill passed empowering the President to raise fifty thousand troops to serve for the duration of the war—said troops to furnish their own uniforms and horses—and appropriating ten million dollars to bring the "existing war" to conclusion.

On May 13, 1846, the war became official by a vote of 42 to 2 in the Senate, 174 to 14 in the House. The declaration was filled with high-minded words but many, especially Polk's Whig opposition, saw the war as a plot by Southerners to spread the evil of slavery into the West. Others saw it as blatant aggression and a landgrab. In a Senate debate, Senator Thomas Corwin of Ohio said that greed alone had created the war. "If I were a Mexican," he said, "I would tell you, 'Have you not enough room in your own country to bury your dead men? If you come into mine, we will greet you with bloody hands and welcome you to hospitable graves.'"

In the House of Representatives, Abraham Lincoln, the young Illinois Whig, called the President "a bewildered, confounded, and miserably perplexed man" and spent much of his single term demanding that Polk prove his allegations that the Mexicans had provoked the war by attacking Americans on American soil.

But in the *Brooklyn Eagle,* poet Walt Whitman spoke for the political expansionists of the Polk and Benton stripe, and for a sizable portion of American citizenry, as he echoed the doctrine of Manifest Destiny in writing: "Let our arms now be carried with a spirit which shall teach the world that, while we are not forward for a quarrel, America knows how to crush, as well as how to expand."

❖

Soon enough, General Winfield Scott would plan and command the campaign to the Halls of Montezuma. In November, 1846, the President reluctantly appointed the man he considered "rather scientific and visionary in his view" to command the Vera Cruz expedition. Scott assembled his army at Tampico, engineered an amphibious landing at Vera Cruz, and captured the city in May, 1847. Then, without a dependable supply line, he led fourteen thousand men against superior forces into the mountainous gateway to Mexico City, emerged from the passes, and stormed Chapultepec Castle, said to be impregnable, on September 14, 1847, to crown one of the most brilliant campaigns in American military annals.

(In the process of trying to identify a Democrat who could lead the army into Mexico, Polk had been visited by Thomas Hart Benton of Missouri. The senator, who had no military experience whatever, had offered to command the American force if the President would appoint him lieutenant general—then the highest rank in the army, held by only one man: Winfield Scott. The President let this preposterous idea die.)

The seventeen months of warfare cost thirteen thousand American lives (seventeen hundred were killed in battle or died of wounds, the balance dying of "other causes," mainly disease). It cost a hundred million dollars and changed the map of the United States more radically than any event after the Louisiana Purchase.

On the day of the war's declaration, while Captain Frémont and his men were riding south from above the forty-second parallel and seeking out Klamath Indian villages to burn, the War Department made its first overt move toward capturing the biggest prize of the war. On May 13, 1846, War Secretary William Marcy sent orders to Colonel Stephen Watts Kearny, commanding the First Dragoon Regiment at Fort Leavenworth, Kansas. Kearny was to prepare to march west, conquer and occupy the province of New Mexico and its capital at Santa Fé, and continue on to California.

❀

CHAPTER TEN

Los Osos

1

A week after the war officially opened, Frémont and his men, with the marine courier Lieutenant Archibald Gillespie and his escort riding with them, were camped in the low hills known as the Buttes, sixty miles north of Sutter's Fort. During the ride down from the Oregon border, still smoldering over the murder of Basil Lajeunesse and the others in the Klamath attack, the Americans had fallen on several small Indian villages, burning lodges and scattering the inhabitants. "The number killed I cannot say," Kit Carson wrote later. "It was perfect butchery. Those not killed fled in all directions. . . ."

At Peter Lassen's place and beyond, Frémont heard gossip and settlers' tales claiming that the attack on his men on Klamath Lake was but a precursor of planned massacres and burnings of fields. This strategy, it was said, had been authored by General Castro and other Californios to drive the Americans from the valley. Furthermore, it was rumored, Castro was issuing *bandos,* arming the Indians, and organizing a huge army that would soon march north from Monterey.

The settlers were banding and they looked to Frémont, the man who had defied Castro at Hawk's Peak, for guidance.

Everything came together, and fell apart, in June.

In the first week of the month, Frémont appears to have thrown in with the squatters while managing to keep up a pretense of neutrality. During that week, he later said, he had "decided on the course which I would pursue," but as late as June 16, he wrote to Commander Montgomery of the sloop-of-war *Portsmouth*: "It is therefore my present intention to abandon the further prosecution of our exploration and proceed immediately across the mountainous country to the eastward . . . and thence to the frontier of Missouri." Montgomery must have thought it remarkable that this return home would require the supplies Frémont requested through his emissary to the *Portsmouth*, Lieutenant Gillespie: eight thousand percussion caps, three hundred pounds of rifle lead and a keg of powder, along with flour, coffee, tea, tobacco, salt pork, and similar ordinary provisions.

What triggered Frémont's decision to join the Sacramento Valley rebels, however furtively at first, is not clear. One important factor was the request by Kit Carson and others in his party to release them from service so that they could join the "Osos," the name the rebels had adopted, inspired by the grizzly bears in the area whose "fighting spirit" they much admired. The explorer had instructions of some kind. He had them when he left St. Louis with his men and others had been brought to him by Gillespie. War, he knew— from Gillespie's experiences and from information Benton and others had relayed to him—was a virtual certainty. The Californios were attempting to expel American emigrants from the province, and these settlers were rising. He could not leave California, could not overtly lead the rebels, but he could encourage and advise them in a silent partnership until his path became better defined.

He wavered, waited, talked with Sutter and listened to the couriers and news- and rumor-bearers who beat a path in and out of New Helvetia.

Sutter himself was in a vise. The pinch was not so much a matter of divided loyalties—he was Swiss, not American—as his trying to find a footing amid the tremors of war between an impending American takeover and his loyalty to those who had trusted him. He was a Mexican citizen, had been given an enormous, profitable land grant, and the trust, to the degree that any foreigner was trusted, of Mexican authorities. He had been warranted as a departmental official. He had encouraged American emigration, employed many of the Americans who had made their way to the Sacramento Valley, and he foresaw the end of Mexican California and the old way of life, knowing that he had had a hand in ending it.

In June, 1846, the twilight of his loyalty to Mexico and, more specifically, to his immediate superior, José Castro, Sutter, in one last act of loyalty to his adopted country, notified the general that the whiskey salesman named Gillespie was in fact an American military officer carrying secret dispatches and urged Castro to consider sending a "respectable garrison" north in the event of trouble with the settlers.

Frémont, while enjoying Sutter's hospitality and depending on him for supplies and mounts, did not trust him, knew of the empresario's divided loyalties, but also knew where the teetering man would fall when California fell.

The man none of the Americans could gauge, the most influential personage in northern California, and to Frémont's thinking, the most dangerous, was Don Mariano Guadalupe Vallejo of Sonoma. This thirty-eight-year-old aristocrat, former commanding general of California, had the peculiar distinction of being at once a respected Californio patriot and a man known to favor the United States' intervention in California. At least he favored it over Mexico's ruinous rule, and over other rumored contenders for annexation such as England.

Born in Monterey in 1808, Vallejo had earned the respect of Californios, north and south, and of men such as Sutter, the consuls Larkin and Leidesdorff, and the occasional visitors to his home in Sonoma and his rancho, named Lachryma Montis (Tears of the Mountain) after the springs in the surrounding hillsides. He was a portly, handsome, well-educated, somewhat fatalistic man, frustrated in his administrative duties by Mexico City's neglect of his beloved land, and especially of its northernmost outpost.

He was also a man with a keen sense of justice, a trait illustrated in a story told by a contemporary Californio, Antonio María Osio of Monterey, who knew Vallejo well.

At Yerba Buena in the 1830s, a soldier named Francisco Rubio was condemned to die for raping and killing two small children. This man, holding a crucifix, said at his execution, "I shall presently account for my actions to this Divine Redeemer I hold in my hands. I tell you—He is my witness—that it was not I who killed Ignacio Olivas's children. Someday you will realize this. But I have committed other offenses, and I should resign myself to the decrees of Providence."

Vallejo, who was *ayudante de plaza* (adjutant of the town), refused to take charge of the execution detail, although he witnessed Rubio's death. He was apparently convinced that the soldier had told the truth—"virtually all the inhabitants of that area believed that Rubio was not guilty," Osio said.

Vallejo decided to inquire into the case and kept the investigation going for six or seven years, during which time he was appointed a commandante and moved to Sonoma.

Eventually he received convincing information that an Indian named Román, from Mission San Rafael, was the actual killer of the Olivas children. "When he had verified this," Osio said, ". . . he ordered Sergeant Lázaro Piña to go there [Mission San Rafael] with a detachment of soldiers. He ordered Piña to shoot the Indian four times as soon as he found him, to leave the Indian lying there on the ground, and to return straightaway to report that he had fulfilled his duty. Two days later, the order was carried out."

Larkin, who described Vallejo as "stiff, pompous and exacting . . . pleasant and condescending," believed this *jefe político* would support American annexation if for no other reason than because neither Mexico nor Alta California could prevent it.

But others were not so trusting of Don Mariano, especially after it was learned that Castro had visited Vallejo at Lachryma Montis on June 5, 1846. The general, it was widely believed, had sought the eminent Sonoman's assistance in enforcing the new restrictions on American emigrants and in preventing any new flow of them into the Sacramento Valley. Castro also had collected horses and supplies for his men from Vallejo's rancho.

Three days after this meeting, William Ide, the Massachusetts carpenter who farmed north of Sutter's Fort, was visited by another American of the area, William Knight, a Marylander who operated a ferry on the Sacramento. Knight reported that "armed Spaniards on horseback" had been seen in the valley burning homes, destroying crops, and driving off horses and cattle. Ide grabbed his carbine, said good-bye to his wife and children, and mounted up, riding with Knight to Frémont's camp north of New Helvetia. When the two men arrived, they found others already talking to the captain, among them Ezekial "Stuttering" Merritt, and Henry Ford, the New Hampshireman and army deserter who worked for Sutter as a trapper.

The tale Knight had reported had no foundation in fact, but as it happened, a real Castro matter was being reported to Frémont. A Lieutenant Francisco Arce, Castro's secretary, and a militia officer named José María Alviso, with an armed squad of eight men, had crossed the Sacramento near Sutter's with a herd of 170 horses, said to have been obtained from Colonel Vallejo in Sonoma. Arce, it was reported, was taking the herd to Santa Clara, near the southern shore of San Francisco Bay, where General Castro was organizing a cavalry force to drive the American settlers out of California.

On June 10, Merritt, Ford, "Long Bob" Semple the Kentucky giant, and sharpshooter Granville Swift, descendant of Daniel Boone ("in a fight, worth a dozen men," Frémont said of him), took six volunteers, picked up four more en route, and rode out to intercept Arce. They surprised the lieutenant in his camp on the Cosumnes River south of Sutter's Fort, forced his surrender and seized the horse herd. The Americans returned the swords to the two officers and left one horse each to Arce, Aviso, and their men.

Arce was told to deliver to his commander the message that if he wanted the rest of the *caballada,* he would have to come get them.

The Americans drove the herd north to the Buttes camp the next day.

Frémont's role in this escapade is not known, although there is evidence that he encouraged the raid, if not actually directed it. One of his men, a twenty-two-year-old Tennessean named Thomas Martin, later claimed that the captain "called us together and told us that we were going to take the country and called for volunteers to go and capture this band of horses." But William Ide's recollection differed. He said that Frémont "in my hearing, expressly declared that he was not at liberty to afford us the least aid or assistance; nor would he suffer any of his men to do so . . . that he was able, of his own party, to fight and whip Castro if he chose, but that he should not do so unless first assaulted by him. . . ."

H. H. Bancroft, four decades after the fact, wrote that Frémont "instigated and planned" the horse raid as a continuation of the insolence he had demonstrated at Hawk's Peak and that the explorer "spoke guardedly" to the Sacramento Valley settlers, "inciting them indirectly to revolt, but cautiously avoiding remarks and promises which might in certain contingencies be used to his disadvantage later."

Thomas Hart Benton gave an orotund rationale to the press for his son-in-law's behavior, saying that Frémont had found his progress north in the Klamath Lake area "completely barred by the double obstacle of hostile Indians, which Castro had excited against him, and the lofty mountains covered with deep and falling snow." He said that General Castro had been assembling troops "with the avowed object of attacking both Frémont's party and all the American settlers." The formidable Missourian, known for bellowing "The *facts*—what are the *facts*?" in the halls of Congress, said: "I could add much more to prove that Captain Frémont's private views and feelings were in unison with his ostensible mission— that the passion of his soul was the pursuit of science and that he looked with dread and aversion upon every possible collision either with the Indians, Mexicans, or British, that could turn him aside from his cherished pursuit."

Benton's "facts" notwithstanding, before the June 10 horse raid, the Sacramento Valley settlers were looking for a leader; after it, they seemed to have found one.

2

For a few days following the capture of the horses, Frémont managed to remain in the shadows. He could not be identified as the leader of the Osos and their now open rebellion. He was an army officer with an ostensible scientific mission, as yet uncertain that California had become enemy territory. His act of belligerency the past March, from which he had narrowly escaped, had produced a modicum of caution. He had to walk heel to toe like an acrobat on a swaying wire, advising and directing while giving the impression—to whom, it is not clear since no one was fooled—of his neutrality.

Zeke Merritt, who appears to have been Frémont's handpicked leader, had gathered a dozen new volunteers in his ride back from the horse raid and had thirty eager Osos in the Buttes camp when the next stage of the miniature revolution began. This step, a far more ambitious and potentially dangerous scheme than a mere horse raid, was directed against the most powerful man in northern California and the seat of his governance. The strategy was to seize the town of Sonoma, force the surrender of Colonel Vallejo and his military garrison, and thus forestall General Castro's plans to harry the settlers and force them from the country.

This plan, which many thought in the aftermath was designed and directed by Frémont, had little of military thinking behind it, but at least it depended on more than blind luck. Sonoma's primitive defenses were no secret to anyone who passed through the village, and no one doubted that even a tiny armed force could occupy the town without bloodshed.

On June 13, one month after war was declared against Mexico, Ezekial Merritt and thirty-three men rode southwest from the

Buttes, crossed the Sacramento River, and headed for Sonoma, thirty-five miles north of San Francisco Bay. In the party were William Ide, John Grigsby, Bob Semple, Henry Ford, William Todd, Le Gros Fallon, William Knight, Granville Swift, and three recently arrived settlers, Sam Kelsey, Thomas Cowie, and George Fowler.

Frémont himself did not saddle up, nor would he allow any of his men to take part in the raid, although many of them, notably Kit Carson and his friend Dick Owens, were anxious to join the Osos.

The village of San Francisco Solano de Sonoma was squalid and flyblown, its spacious plaza littered with rubbish and the bones of slaughtered cattle and surrounded by caved-in *jacales* and weed patches. More important to the Osos, the town's defenses, never remarkable, had deteriorated to ruin since the time they were set up by Colonel Vallejo in 1835 as protection against possible incursions by Russians out of Fort Ross. These defenses consisted of a *cuartel,* a windowed wooden barracks on the north side of the town's central plaza adjoining Vallejo's two-story Casa Grande home; a *torreon,* a four-story adobe tower with loopholes for riflemen; nine brass cannons stationed around the plaza; and an armory, located in the barracks building, holding 250 muskets, some lead ball and iron shot, and a hundred pounds of gunpowder.

But even the *cuartel* was a sham. Sonoma had no garrison, no one to lay the cannons or load the muskets. The soldiery had been removed during the Micheltorena troubles in '45 and never replaced. Mexico City had been of no help—the home country insisting that all its colonies be self-supporting—nor was Governor Pico in Los Angeles of any assistance; he provided no finances for a Sonoma garrison despite the problem of the unauthorized settlers in the north.

These matters were known to the Osos as they clattered across the bridge between the Napa and Sonoma valleys at dawn on June 14, entered the town from the north, rode past the Misión San Francisco de Solano, reined up in front of Vallejo's Casa Grande, and banged gun butts on the door.

Don Mariano came to the door in his nightshirt. Arrayed before him, bathed in the yellow lantern light, some still on horseback, some afoot, stood a crew that might have come north from San Pablo Bay off a ship flying the Jolly Roger. This motley nightmare consisted of "about as rough looking a set of men as one could well imagine," Kentuckian Robert Semple later said. Some wore bandannas, pirate-fashion, on their heads, others coon, fox, and coyote-skin caps; most favored buckskin hunting shirts and trousers, and Indian mocassins. All were armed—rifles, muskets, pepper-box pistols, tomahawks, hunting knives—and all were tired and agitated.

After a few words at the door, Vallejo invited the ringleaders into his *sala*. As they lounged on his mahogany furniture and eyed the piano and paintings, the colonel dressed. His wife Doña Francisca begged him to escape from these banditti through the back of the house, but he rejected this idea; he would not desert her and their six children. He sent a servant to fetch his brother-in-law, the Ohio-born merchant Jacob Leese, to serve as translator.

"To what happy circumstances shall I attribute the visit of so many exalted personages?" Vallejo asked Merritt with a witty irony lost on the ruffian with the tobacco-juice beard.

"We mean to establish our own government in California, an independent republic, and are under arms to support it. You are under arrest, General, as the responsible head of the Mexicans hereabouts," Merritt stuttered. He added a point, useful and perhaps even true, asserting that he and his men were acting under orders from Captain Frémont of the United States Army.

Frémont's name must have convinced Vallejo that these "white Indians," as he later called them, were not mere bandits. He handed over the keys to the town arsenal and offered the men food and brandy. One eyewitness reported that after hearing of their mission, he went to his room and, "following the usages of war," retrieved his ceremonial sword, which he offered to his captors. None of the Osos seemed to know what to do with it and so Don Mariano returned it to his room.

After sunrise, Vallejo's brother, Salvador, a captain in the Mexican army, and the colonel's secretary, a French emigré named Victor Prudon, came to Casa Grande and were also placed under arrest. Now, the buckskinned Osos and their prisoners enjoyed the repast the general's servants brought into the *sala.* William Ide later recalled that the "generous spirits gave proof of his [Vallejo's] usual hospitality as the richest wines and brandies sparkled in the glasses, and those who had thus unceremoniously met soon became merry companions. . . . The bottles well nigh vanquished the captors."

Meantime, with the town now awake, the rebels still lounging outside Casa Grande were growing restless. They had found a few villagers willing to sell them food and wine but were tired of the waiting, and some of then drunkenly surveyed shops and homes with looters' eyes. John Grigsby volunteered to find out about the delay and disappeared into the casa. William Ide followed some time later.

At last documents were drafted by Robert Semple, written in both English and Spanish, in which Vallejo agreed to surrender Sonoma to the Americans with the provision that the townspeople would not be molested and personal properties would be respected.

Three hours had passed since Merritt and the others had entered Vallejo's home. Those outside listened as the capitulation paper was read aloud. To several of the Osos, primed with *aguardiente,* everything was too easy—no fight, no booty, no reward for their efforts—and there was loud talk of abandoning the revolt. Grigsby, under the clear impression that Captain Frémont had ordered the capture of Sonoma and its leading citizens, said he would "resign and back out of the scrape." Others talked of tearing down Casa Grande and ransacking it and the town before riding back to the Buttes.

Semple was furious over such talk and threatened to shoot any man who tried to turn the revolution into a "looting expedition," and was backed up by Grigsby and Sam Kelsey.

It fell to the schoolteacher-farmer William Ide to bring the rabble under control. In a theatrical speech to his fellow insurgents, he said, "Saddle no horse for me. I will lay my bones here before I will take upon myself the ignominy of commencing an honorable work, and then flee like cowards, like thieves, when no enemy is in sight. In vain will you say you had honorable motives. Who will believe it? Flee this day, and the longest life cannot wear off your disgrace!"

He closed his peroration by shouting like a backwoods Bible-thumper: "Choose ye this day what you will be! We are robbers, or we *must* be conquerors!"

The exhortation had its effect. Twenty-four Osos voted to stand with Ide and elected him their leader and spokesman.

The raiders "seized and held in trust for the public benefit" the armory, the nine cannons and 250 "stands of arms," shot and powder, estimated to be worth twelve hundred American dollars, and 140 horses that were handed over to the Americans by Vallejo and Leese.

Next, ten men, Semple, Grigsby, and Merritt among them, were selected to escort the prisoners—Vallejo, his brother Salvador, and Victor Prudon, with Leese as interpreter—to the American camp on the Sacramento, eighty miles northeast. Ide apparently confirmed to Don Mariano that Captain Frémont had ordered the raid, and Vallejo was relieved to learn it. He felt that he would be treated justly by an officer of the Army of the United States.

Ide and twenty-five Osos controlled Sonoma. The still-terrified Doña Francisca and her six children remained at Casa Grande under guard.

The escort and prisoners spent a night on the trail and arrived at Frémont's camp at noon on June 16. Vallejo's hope of cordiality and fairness from the explorer was quickly dashed. Frémont denied responsibility for the raid, denied even that the colonel was his prisoner, yet lectured the stunned Californio on the complaints of the

Americans in the Sacramento Valley. Vallejo shrewdly assessed the captain as having "a very elastic conscience."

Merritt and the others, with Frémont's approval, removed the prisoners to Sutter's Fort, where the empresario treated them with kindness, leaving them unguarded, sharing meals with them, and permitting them walks outside their quarters to escape the stifling heat. (Frémont, when he visited the fort sometime later, sternly reprimanded Sutter for trying to make Vallejo's cell more comfortable.) The prisoners' cubicles were infested with mosquitoes rising from a slough behind the fort, and the colonel soon developed malarial symptoms, lost weight, and presented a haggard appearance. This disturbed Sutter and after he sent a message to Montgomery of the *Portsmouth,* anchored off Yerba Buena, a ship's surgeon came to the fort, escorted by Lieutenant Charles Warren Revere, to treat the prisoners.

By the time he was released from captivity on August 1, Vallejo's frayed and shabby clothing hung on his six-foot frame as on a bone rack. After being reunited with his wife and children, he toured his Lachryma Montis estate and sadly estimated that during his six-week imprisonment, more than a thousand head of cattle and six hundred horses had been stolen from his lands. His entire untended wheat crop was also lost.

During his absence, Doña Francisca treated the Americans with Californio courtesy and hospitality and earned their respect and admiration. The surgeon from the *Portsmouth,* who tended her husband and visited her at Casa Grande, described her affectionately as "*muy gorda* [very fat], but still has the evidence of much beauty. She seems to be femininely passive and voluptuous, contented and happy."

Months after the event, Thomas Hart Benton reported on the "capture" of Sonoma to his Senate colleagues. He treated the event as a military enterprise of considerable tactical effort and gave the impression that a siege had been required to force the surrender of the town, which he described as "a fortified, well-garrisoned presidio." He based his information on letters received from his son-in-law, on the scene.

In truth, of course, the decrepit, soldierless village had been conquered by dint of a rifle rap on the door of Colonel Vallejo's home by a coonskinned company of Frémont-inspired freebooters. Sonoma, as Bernard DeVoto put it, "could have been captured by Tom Sawyer and Huck Finn."

Even so, the buckskin rising needed a symbol, and the duty to come up with one fell to William L. Todd (whose aunt Mary in Illinois, just four years past, had married a frontier lawyer named Abraham Lincoln). With the help of Ben Dewell, an Ohio saddler, and rebel Thomas Cowie, Todd fashioned a flag—a white field with a red-flannel stripe at the bottom—from a petticoat and chemise contributed by the wives of the Osos. On the white material, using a chewed stick as a brush, Todd daubed a figure of a passant grizzly bear (someone said it looked more like a "big fat Berkshire") and a large, red five-pointed star above the words "California Republic," lettered, DeVoto says, "in pokeberry juice."

This rude banner was fixed to the flagpole in the Sonoma plaza and raised on June 14 to the cheers of the gathered rebels. One shrewd observer, Antonio María Osio, said of the Osos and the occasion, ". . . they decided to camouflage the flag of stars and stripes with a temporary flag which depicted a brown bear on a white field. . . ."

3

Two days after the capture of the town, John Montgomery of the *Portsmouth,* now anchored off Sausalito, sent a small landing party up to Sonoma. The commander's sixteen-year-old son accompanied the sailors and officers and recorded later that "on arriving we found a party of 24 men, mostly dressed in Buckskins . . . [led] by a plain man about 50 years old in his Shirt Sleeves . . . Capt. Ide welcomed us to Sonoma."

Ide was actually sixty years old as he performed his first acts as commander in chief of the California Republic. With the Bear Flag newly snapping in the breeze above the Sonoma plaza, he reappointed José Berreyesa, the town's *alcalde,* to continue as local magistrate under the "new regime." He also organized his three dozen men somewhat ambitiously into two military units, designated the First Artillery (presumably in charge of the six captured cannons) and the First Rifles.

Another duty all revolutionary leaders must perform, the drafting of a grandiloquent proclamation, Ide zestfully accomplished. On June 15, he issued his, declaring that the aim of the rising was to overthrow "a military despotism" that "shamefully oppressed the laboring people in California." He and the Osos promised that all Californians who surrendered their arms would "not be disturbed in their persons, their property or social relations." The arduously phrased document declared the rebels' intent to establish a "republican government" that would ensure "civil and religious liberty . . . encourage industry, virtue and literature . . . leave unshackled by fetters commerce, agriculture and mechanism."

As this Bear Flag manifesto, mostly by word of mouth, made its way south, Americans everywhere who learned of it flocked to Sonoma, swelling the Bear Flagger ranks to over a hundred men within a week, many of them sunshine patriots attracted by the prospect of the square league of land offered as an enlistment enticement.

Of Ide's effusion, H. H. Bancroft said sourly, "As a whole, in truthfulness and consistency, as in orthography and literary merit, it was below the plane of Castro's and Pico's proclamations. In respect to bombast and general absurdity, it stood about midway between the two. . . . As a product of filibusterism, pure and simple, it deserves praise not to be awarded from any other standpoint."

Castro and Pico did not delay in issuing responses to the Osos' declaration. On June 17, from his headquarters in Santa Clara, the general condemned "the contemptible policy of the agents of the government of the United States," which he said had induced a number of "adventurers" to invade the province and capture Sonoma. And in Santa Barbara, Governor Pico declared that "a gang of North American adventurers, with the blackest treason that the spirit of evil could invent, have invaded the town of Sonoma, raising their flag, and carrying off as prisoners four Mexican citizens."

❀

CHAPTER ELEVEN

Olómpali

1

On June 14, the day the Bear Flag was raised in Sonoma plaza, Frémont and his band, as yet knowing nothing of the outcome of the raid, rode into Sutter's. Lieutenant Gillespie and sailors from the *Portsmouth* were waiting for him on the American River with a launch loaded with the gunpowder and supplies the explorer had requested. Among the bags, boxes, and barrels was a gift from Commander Montgomery, a hogshead of whiskey, which the men fell upon with a will.

On the sixteenth, Merritt, Semple, and Grigsby rode into the fort with Colonel Vallejo and the other prisoners, turned them over to Sutter, their reluctant jailer, and provided endless embroidered details of the capture of Sonoma.

Nearly a month passed before Frémont learned with certainty that the United States and Mexico were at war, but he seemed to regard Merritt's news as the act requiring him to exert his leadership. He began signing his letters "Military Commander of U.S. Forces in California" and proceeded to alienate John Sutter by commandeering his supplies. Ned Kern, the civilian artist-cartographer from Philadelphia, who got along well with Sutter, was placed in command of the fort and its prisoners.

In Sonoma meantime, Captain William Ide of the Republic of California's hundred-man army sent William Todd on a mission to the *Portsmouth* to notify its skipper of the horse raid, the surrender of Colonel Vallejo and the town, and, in effect, of the Osos' independent declaration of war. Unlike Frémont, Ide was hesitant to ask Montgomery for gunpowder and supplies since the naval officer, with no assurance that his country was at war, could not legally arm and provision a rebel force. Instead, Todd was given a second assignment and, with another man, rode north toward Bodega Bay to find American settlers who had stores of arms and powder. Ide also dispatched two other Osos toward the Russian River below Fort Ross for the same purpose. These men, Thomas Cowie and George Fowler, were to locate Moses Carson, who could help them find arms and gunpowder. Carson had been a Mexican citizen since 1836 and now served as majordomo at the Sotoyomi rancho owned by Henry D. Fitch, a former trade-ship master from New Bedford, Massachusetts.

Two days passed and when the parties failed to return from the short ride north, Ide's chief lieutenant, Henry L. Ford, organized an eighteen-man search team to comb the countryside between Sonoma and the Russian River. Moses Carson reported that he had seen neither Cowie nor Fowler, but during the return to Sonoma, Ford and his party spotted a small body of Californio soldiers and after exchanging a few gunshots, captured a man who told them of the awful fate of the two Osos.

The prisoner, one Bernardino "Four-Fingered Jack" García, whom Vallejo described as "the wickedest man that California had produced up to that time," said that the two Americans had been captured near Santa Rosa by a patrol of "irregulars" led by Castro lieutenants Juan Padilla, a barber, and Ramón Carrillo, brother of Francisca Vallejo. García, who was present during the horrors he described, and probably participated in, said that Cowie and Fowler were tortured for two days—tied to trees, stoned, mutilated with knives, and disembowled—before being shot.

(Writing in the *New York Evening Post* in October, 1856, the faithful Frémont man Alexis Godey, who saw the corpses, said ". . . their bodies presented a most shocking spectacle, bearing the marks of horrible mutilation, their throats cut, and their bowels ripped open; other indignities were perpetrated of a nature too disgusting and obscene to relate." He said that Cowie "was well known to many of our men, with whom he was a favorite, and the sight that his lifeless remains presented, created in the breasts of many of his old friends a feeling of stern and bitter revenge. . . .")

After delivering García to the *calabozo* in Sonoma and giving Ide the details of the murders, Henry Ford and Granville Swift gathered eighteen volunteers and, on the morning of June 23, rode northwest toward Santa Rosa. They hoped to pick up the trail of Padilla and his irregulars and determine the fate of the still-missing Bill Todd and his companion.

Near the village of San Antonio, Ford's men captured four Californios and after camping the night and acting on information the prisoners provided, the searchers turned south on a trail toward San Rafael. At mid-morning, near the mouth of the Petaluma River, they found a corral of horses at a place known locally as Olómpali, named after a Miwok Indian village that had been visited by Drake's freebooters in 1579. It was also known as Camilo's Rancho for its owner, Camilo Ynita, an Indian wheat grower and one-time business partner of Colonel Vallejo's.

Ford and his men dismounted after spotting a number of uniformed Californio lancers milling around Ynita's adobe ranchhouse eating a late breakfast. The horsemen, about fifty in number, were commanded by Captain Joaquín de la Torre, a veteran officer from Monterey. He had been sent north by Castro after the American attack on Sonoma, and with him at the rancho was the Cowie-Fowler culprit, Juan Padilla.

The Californios ran for their horses after Ford's men opened fire on them from the brush and trees bordering the rancho. They managed to make a ragged cavalry charge toward the brush, but the American volley fire killed one lancer, wounded one, and scattered the others, forcing them to kick their mounts out of rifle range.

After some desultory firing on both sides, De la Torre and his men, Padilla among them, escaped downtrail toward San Rafael.

During the volley from Ford's men, William Todd and his gun-powder-searching partner, both captured by De la Torre some days earlier, ran from the ranchhouse to the American line and reached it unscathed. Todd said he was saved from execution by the Californios by telling his captors that if they killed him and his partner, the Americans would execute *their* prisoners—presumably alluding to Vallejo and the others in Sutter's cells.

Ford did not pursue the lancers. None of his men had been scratched in the encounter, he had rescued the two missing Osos, and he feared that his tiny force might ride into a trap if he chased De la Torre's already superior numbers, so he gathered his men and rode on to Sonoma to report to Captain Ide.

The "Battle of Olómpali" was the only fight of the Bear Flag Republic.

2

Frémont, in camp with his ninety men near Sutter's, learned of the fate of Cowie and Fowler, and of Ford's patrol, from an express dispatched from Bear Flag headquarters in Sonoma. Days earlier, he had learned from various Sutter men that General Castro had called for a *levée en masse* and had sent a force of lancers north from Mission Santa Clara preparatory, it was believed, to an attack on Sonoma. The informants said that Castro was determined to chase the rebels out of Sonoma, but considered it his real duty to rid California of all Americans—Frémont and his men first among them.

On June 25, the explorer and his men (among them a new recruit named James Marshall, a thirty-five-year-old New Jersey wheelwright and carriage-maker), with Archibald Gillespie, Kit Carson, Segundai, and his Delawares in the van, rode into Sonoma, where they learned of the skirmish at Olómpali. The next morning, joined by Lieutenant Ford and a detachment of Osos, Frémont rode out of Sonoma south to San Rafael, hoping to intercept De la Torre and Padilla. Upon reaching the village and discovering that the Californios had vanished, the Americans set up camp at the old mission, situated on a hill overlooking San Pablo Bay. In the waiting, scouting parties fanned out toward Sausalito to see if there was any activity among Castro's forces.

Across San Francisco Bay, Castro had yet to learn the whereabouts of his lancer patrol, and on June 28, he sent a boat into San Pablo Bay with a message to Captain De la Torre. In the small launch were an oarsman and three others: the twin brothers Francisco and Ramón de Haro, age twenty, of Yerba Buena, and their uncle, José de los Reyes Berreyesa, father of the *alcalde* of Sonoma, who hoped to visit his son, whom he believed had been taken prisoner by the Americans.

From his perch on the mission hill above San Rafael, Frémont trained his telescope on the launch as it crawled across the bay toward the landing at Point San Pablo and ordered three of his men, Kit Carson, Granville Swift, and the Pennsylvania blacksmith Sam Neal, to ride down to the beach and ascertain the business of the boatmen.

Precisely what occurred after the oarsman rowed across the bay and the old man and the twin brothers slogged ashore with their saddles and gear is not known, but it is indisputable that the three, apparently unarmed, were murdered in cold blood.

In his memoirs, Frémont dismissed the incident in a few lines and seemed to forget whom he had sent to intercept the boat—or perhaps he wished to protect Carson, Swift, and Neal—especially Carson—from blame. He also reduced the number of murders by one, neglecting to mention there were two De Haros killed. "Both the settlers and the men of my command were excited against the Californians by the recent murder of the two Americans [Cowie and Fowler]," he wrote, "and not by the murder only, but by the brutal circumstances attending it. My scouts, mainly Delawares, influenced by these feelings, made sharp retaliation and killed Berreyesa and de Haro, who were bearers of intercepted letters."

A man named Jasper O'Farrell, an Irish resident of San Rafael at the time, reported in the *Los Angeles Star* in September, 1856, that he was in the village when Captain Frémont and his "troops" arrived and when the boat landed the three men at the Point San Pablo estuary. O'Farrell wrote that Kit Carson and two other men were detailed to intercept the boat and that Carson soon returned to where Frémont was standing in the corridor of the mission "in company with Gillespie, myself, and others, and said, 'Captain, shall I take those men prisoners?' In response, Frémont waved his hand and said: 'I have got no room for prisoners.'" Then, according to O'Farrell's account, Carson and the others "advanced to within fifty yards of the three unfortunate and unarmed Californians, alighted from their horses, and deliberately shot them."

In a highly improbably postscript to the story, the Irishman claimed to have talked with Carson in 1853 about the incident, "and he assured me," O'Farrell said, "that then and since he regretted to be compelled to shoot those men, but Frémont was bloodthirsty enough to order otherwise, and he further remarked that it was not the only brutal act he was compelled to commit while under his command."

O'Farrell concluded, "I must always look upon [Frémont] with contempt and consider [him] as a murderer and a coward."

Many years later, Archibald Gillespie, by then alienated from the man he once considered his hero, placed responsibility for the murders on his former chief. In Gillespie's recollection, when Carson returned from the estuary, Frémont asked, "Where are your prisoners?" And when Carson said, "They lay out yonder," the captain replied, "It is well."

(Bernard DeVoto's version of the incident, lifted from O'Farrell's with customary sarcasm added, was that "Kit reported to Napoleon and asked for instructions. The Conqueror's mind swarmed with enemies, this was war, and he must be stern. 'I have no room for prisoners,' he said, possibly thinking of biographers unborn. So Kit Carson and his corporal's guard killed them.")

Alexis Godey, in the *New York Evening Post* story in which he described the savage mutilations of Cowie and Fowler, claimed that Berreyesa and the De Haros were "carrying letters to the commander of the enemy's force" and that they "resisted efforts to seize them as prisoners." Godey said, "Had they submitted, and not attempted to escape, they would have received no harm, but they furnished a pretext which, to the friends of Tom Cowie, was, perhaps, not unwelcome."

Bancroft called the incident "cowardly vengeance," the time when "the only blood of Frémont's campaign was spilled, and that under such circumstances as to leave a stain of dishonor upon the commander and some of his men."

Ten years after the event, José S. Berreyesa, the Sonoma *alcalde,* recounted in a Los Angeles newspaper a sad footnote to the murder of his father. After the capture of Sonoma and his imprisonment before being reinstated as magistrate, Berreyesa said that Don José had embarked from Santa Clara for San Pablo to determine his son's condition and fate. The *alcalde* said that on the day after the event at the estuary, as he was held prisoner in a room in Sonoma, he saw a soldier pass by with a scrape that had belonged to his father. He made a request of Frémont: "I told him that I believed my father had been killed by his orders and begged that he would do me the favor to have the article restored to me that I might give it to my mother . . . to this, Col. Frémont replied that he could not order its restoration as the serape belonged to the soldier who had it, and then he retired without giving me any further reply. I then endeavored to obtain it from the soldier, who asked me $25 for it, which I paid, and in this manner I obtained it."

3

After the estuary murders, Frémont moved his camp from San Rafael south to Sausalito, still hoping to encounter Captain De la Torre and his lancer patrol and prevent them from ˉejoining General Castro in Santa Clara. (De la Torre, meantime, had escaped; he and his men had been ferried from the southern shore of the Marin Peninsula across the strait to Yerba Buena some days before.)

At the end of June, the merchant barkentine *Moscow,* which had made a run around Cape Horn from Worcester, Massachusetts, anchored off Sausalito and its master, Captain William D. Phelps, a veteran in the California trade, paid Frémont a visit. Phelps described the celebrated explorer as a "slender and well-proportioned man, of sedate, but pleasing, countenance," and said that the captain was dressed in a blue, open-collared flannel shirt covered by a deerskin hunting jacket, blue cloth pantaloons, moccasins, and a cotton handkerchief tied around his head. Phelps said the outfit "might not appear very fashionable in the White House or be presentable at a Queen's levee; but to my eye it was an admirable rig to scud under or fight in."

The two men struck up a friendship, and on July 1, Phelps provided passage on the *Moscow* to Frémont, Gillespie, Carson, and several other of the explorer's men for a small venture. The bark ferried the party from Sausalito across the strait—which Frémont felicitously named "the Golden Gate"—to Castillo de San Joaquín, just south of the entrance to San Francisco Bay. This vacant, horseshoe-shaped fort, built in 1794, had ten rusty cannons on its battlements that Frémont believed could be used by the Californios to harass American ships attempting to enter the bay. Bill Stepp, a blacksmith and an old wilderness hand, had come along on the mission to end even the remote possibility that the cannons could be used. With a maul and a handful of rattail files, Stepp plugged the cannons' touchholes with the iron shafts and snapped them off.

The next day, Long Bob Semple and a small force of Osos crossed the Golden Gate to Yerba Buena, took a few Mexican officials prisoner, and occupied the village without resistance.

On Independence Day, 1846, with new volunteers arriving every day, the Bear Flaggers held a celebration in Sonoma. The Declaration of Independence was read loudly in the town plaza, cannons banged salutes, whole beeves were roasted, tubs of tamales and chiles, and bottles, jugs, demijohns, and kegs of wine, brandy, and whiskey were consumed. The festivities ended on the night of the Fourth with a fandango held in Salvador Vallejo's big adobe home, now serving as Frémont's headquarters, with waltzes and quadrilles, mountain-men stomps, and Delaware war dances performed to whoops and loud chatter, and the music of fiddles, guitars, mouth harps, and concertinas.

The next day, Captains Frémont and Ide and their officers met to discuss new strategy. Ide's rebels now numbered nearly three hundred men, but it seemed clear that the Bear Flaggers' day was ending. Although explicit news that the United States and Mexico were at war had yet to arrive in Sonoma, few doubted it would be long in coming. Frémont hedged and contradicted himself, telling the group he was determined to find and defeat Castro and his forces but that until war was a certainty, he was not aiming at conquering all of California. He pledged support of the Osos and said he would supply them from stores he had commandeered at Sutter's Fort. In return, he asked the Bears to pledge to "conduct the Revolution honorably," to "abstain from the violation of the chastity of women" and to "obey properly constituted officers."

He also announced, to the confusion of all, that the time had come to form a disciplined army, which he volunteered to command, to meet the exigencies of real war; a force that could march south, engage Castro and any other force of Californios, and conquer the entire province in the name of the Government of the United States. The Osos did not resist this move; Ide, ever the orderly minded, practical leader, even seems to have anticipated it: he resented Frémont's usurpation of his command (and wrote vehemently of it in the years to come), but knew that his Bear Flaggers had started something they could not finish.

Frémont set out to organize what he came to call the "California Battalion," with Gillespie as his adjutant. His original exploring party served as the veteran core of the force, and over two hundred of Ide's rebels, Sutter workers, and a handful of local Indians signed pledges to serve. In all, Frémont had close to three hundred men, whom he organized into four companies. Dick Owens, the Rocky Mountain trapper, Indian-fighter, and friend of Kit Carson's, was named captain of Frémont's men; John Grigsby, Granville Swift, and Henry L. Ford were named to lead the other three companies. Grigsby and fifty men remained in Sonoma; the rest of the battalion marched out with Frémont on July 6 for the American River camp near Sutter's. There they planned the campaign against Castro and the Californios fifty-five days after the war against Mexico had been officially declared, twenty-nine days after the official news of the war had reached California, and three days before the official news of the war reached Frémont.

✶

Commodore John D. Sloat and his Pacific Squadron had been patrolling between the Sandwich Islands and Mazatlán, on Mexico's west coast, for many months, awaiting a message from the Navy Department on the war. Sloat had spent a lifetime at sea, an eternity awaiting orders from Navy Secretary George Bancroft. He was sixty-five years old, ill, and dreaming of retirement; indeed, in early May, he had requested that he be replaced in his command. While he waited for that eventuality, he had no orders and no initiative. For months after he reached Mexican waters, he knew only that when he learned "beyond a doubt" that the war was on, he was to sail north, seize San Francisco Bay, blockade the other main California ports, and "preserve, if possible, the most friendly relations with the inhabitants" of the province.

On May 18, after detailed news of General Zachary Taylor's army fighting on the Rio Grande reached him, Sloat sent the *Cyane,* under Captain William Mervine, to Monterey to inform Consul Larkin of the increasing rumors of war, and Commander John B. Montgomery's *Portsmouth* to San Francisco Bay to be in a position to occupy the harbor. With Mervine, the commodore sent a confidential letter to Larkin in which he revealed his tentativeness. Despite admitting to Larkin "it appears certain that hostilities have commenced on the north bank of the Rio Grande," he said it was his "intention to visit your place immediately, and from the instructions I have received from my government, I am led to hope that you will be prepared to put me in possession of the necessary information, and to consult and advise with me on the course of operations I may be disposed to make on the coast of California."

After asking a civilian for guidance in his anticipated military operations, the commodore dallied at Mazatlán. He may have mistrusted the information he had received on May 18 from overland travelers, and may have been given contradictory information. But on May 31, he received reports that he knew were trustworthy, telling of Taylor's battles at Palo Alto and Resaca de la Palma and the capture of Matamoros.

But was there a war? On June 6, he wrote at length to Secretary Bancroft that he had, "upon more mature reflection," concluded that in the absence of news of an actual declaration of war, he felt no justification in "taking possession of any part of California, or any hostile measures against Mexico (notwithstanding their attack upon our troops)." In referring to his original orders, he advised Bancroft that he would "be careful to avoid any act of aggression" and would proceed to California "to await further intelligence." He said that the "want of communication" from Washington "renders my situation anything but pleasant; indeed it is humiliating and mortifying in the extreme, as by my order I cannot act, while it appears to the world that we are actually at war on the other coast."

By the time the secretary received this message, all had been rendered moot, but on August 13, Bancroft reacted with barely restrained fury: "The department willingly believes in the purity of your intentions," he wrote, "but your anxiety not to do wrong has led you into a more unfortunate and unwarranted inactivity." The secretary, referring to Sloat's request to be replaced, and "other reasons," which were unnamed, relieved the commodore of his command.

While his fatal latter to Bancroft was en route by courier to Washington, Sloat had sailed north from Mazatlán on the *Savannah* on June 8, a day after he received news that an American squadron had blockaded Vera Cruz. He reached Monterey harbor on July 1, seventeen days after the Bear Flag had been raised in Sonoma. The *Cyane* and *Levant* had preceded him and were awaiting orders.

He remained in a funk; instead of being inspired by the news of Taylor's battles and the Vera Cruz blockade—in effect, a war confirmation—he seemed inert with uncertainty. What to do now? Spread out between Mazatlán, the Sandwich Islands, Monterey, and San Francisco Bay, he had six warships, an armed schooner, and a transport vessel. Mexico had no warships in California waters, and the British were the only potentially hostile foreign power Sloat had sighted in all his months in the Pacific. Admiral Sir George Seymour's flagship *Collingwood* was, in fact, a nettlesome presence in its seemingly aimless patrolling of the Mexican coast from Mazatlán to San Francisco Bay. Moreover, there was a persistent fear among the Americans in California that the Mexican populace favored British intervention and that England had designs on the province.

And Larkin, ever cautious, influenced the dithering Sloat with his ideas that Pico and Castro would eventually raise the Stars and Stripes voluntarily if courted with fine diplomacy rather than insulted by the rash tactics of Captain Frémont and the Bear Flaggers.

And finally, the commodore allowed himself to be haunted by the mistake of 1842, when Captain Thomas ap Catesby Jones had "captured" Monterey because he acted on false information.

Sloat took his gig ashore on July 4 and met at length with Larkin to hear the consul express his hope that California could be annexed to the United States without bloodshed. During this meeting, the officer bared his muddled state of mind to Larkin when he exclaimed, "I shall be blamed for doing too little or too much—I prefer the latter."

Still he delayed in occupying Monterey, and might have wavered longer had he not received a message from Commander Montgomery in San Francisco Bay telling of the developments in Sonoma and Frémont's involvement with the Bear Flaggers. The news galvanized the ailing commodore. Frémont's actions *must* have been sanctioned by Washington, he must be acting on *orders,* something Sloat desperately sought. His return message said he was "very anxious to know if Captain Frémont will cooperate with us," and he told Montgomery: "If you consider you have sufficient force or if Frémont will join you, you will hoist the flag . . . at Yerba Buena . . . and take possession . . . you will secure the bay of San Francisco as soon as possible."

On July 6, he summoned Larkin aboard the *Savannah* and spent the day with the consul preparing dispatches to Washington, messages to his officers, and a lengthy and carefully worded proclamation.

The next morning he sent a party ashore under Captain Mervine to demand the surrender of Monterey. In his yellow stone presidio headquarters, Captain Mariano Silva, an artillery officer in command of the virtually nonexistent garrison, told Mervine he was not "authorized to surrender the town." Silva was let off the hook and kept under guard.

At mid-morning, after reading orders to his sailors on the conduct expected of them, Sloat sent boats from the *Savannah, Levant,* and *Cyane* and landed 225 sailors and marines on the beach. Within minutes of the landing, the American flag was hoisted over the two-story frame customshouse, and after a twenty-one-gun salute from the three warships offshore, Sloat's expert, conciliatory proclamation was read. It announced the existence of war and the annexation of Monterey and the department of Alta California to the United States: "I declare to the inhabitants of California that, although I come in arms with a powerful force, I do not come among them as an enemy to California; on the contrary, I come as their best friend, as henceforward California will be a portion of the United States, and its peaceful inhabitants will enjoy the same rights and privileges as the citizens of any other portion of that territory. . . ."

He promised a fair and permanent government, improved commerce, reasonable duties, guarantee of titles to real estate, payment for provisions and supplies, no confiscation of property or goods. He touched on such familiar grievances as governmental neglect, corruption among officials, high prices for imports, and high duties on exports.

Messages from Sloat and Larkin were sent to General Castro, then located at San Juan Bautista, notifying him of the surrender of Monterey and asking him to a parley. Castro responded on the ninth: he intended to spare no sacrifice in defending his country and said he would consult with Governor Pico to plan this defense. The general added some lines condemning the activities of Frémont and his "gang of adventurers" and demanded to know whether these men were part of Sloat's invading force.

Sloat also dispatched a message to Pico in Los Angeles: "I beg your Excellency to feel assured that although I come in arms with a powerful force, I come as the best friend of California; and I invite your Excellency to meet me at Monterey, that I may satisfy you and the people of that fact."

By July 12, Sloat had three hundred officers and men ashore, had armed the presidio with two eighteen-pound carronades (short-barreled, muzzle-loading cannons that sailors called "smashers") mounted on trunnions as fieldpieces, and had ordered construction of a stockade and blockhouse.

Captain Mervine, appointed commander of the American garrison in Monterey, took up office in the customshouse and established a curfew, closed stores and shops for two days, and forbade the sale of liquor. He organized a company of horsemen to patrol the countryside and to confiscate arms.

There were no untoward incidents; not a shot had been fired accidentally or in anger. Larkin was overjoyed at the wise proclamation authored by Sloat and the gentlemanly ease with which the war had come to his beloved California.

Sloat himself could now relax. He had begun the annexation of this vast and priceless land for the United States and had done it fairly, democratically, and without violence. His dispatches on the occupation of Monterey and San Francisco Bay were en route to Washington, and his replacement in command of the Pacific Squadron, Commodore Robert Field Stockton, was due in Monterey within the week.

He had made a mighty capstone for his military career, a thing for which he would be remembered in history.

Robert Field Stockton.

❀

CHAPTER TWELVE

Stockton

1

Lieutenant Charles Warren Revere had been commissioned a midshipman in the navy in 1828 at age sixteen. Promotion and command were the stuff of dreams in the peacetime navy, but his assignment to the Pacific Squadron in the summer of 1845 seemed to offer a rare opportunity: wartime service. He had shipped aboard the *Cyane* out of Norfolk, Virginia, made the passage around the Horn, and joined Commodore Sloat's squadron off Mazatlán in November. He had been assigned to Commander John B. Montgomery's sloop-of-war *Portsmouth* in time for its visit to Monterey in April, come to know Consul Larkin, and taken horseback rides into the piney hills above the bay. He fell in love with California and predicted that it would become "one of the brightest stars in the American galaxy."

When Sloat had ordered the *Portsmouth* north in May, Revere had resumed his horseback outings, visiting San José village and the old Santa Clara Mission, near which General Castro would later have temporary headquarters. After the capture of Sonoma on June 14, he had visited the town, met the Oso leaders, and escorted the ship's surgeon to Sutter's Fort to attend to the ailing General Vallejo.

He was the senior lieutenant on the *Portsmouth* and now, on July 9, 1846, two days after Monterey's forced surrender, he had the honor of claiming San Francisco Bay for the United States.

At eight that Thursday morning, the handsome, gregarious Revere led a landing party of seventy sailors and marines ashore at Yerba Buena and raised the American flag—twenty-seven stars (Texas too new to be included)—over the customshouse. After a twenty-one-gun salute offshore, he read Commodore Sloat's proclamation, with Vice Consul Leidesdorff translating it into Spanish. There was not a single Mexican official in Yerba Buena to surrender the town.

Later in the day, Lieutenant Revere carried out his second flag-raising duty. In Sonoma plaza, before a gathering of cheering Osos and warily silent townsfolk, he again read Sloat's words and had them posted in both English and Spanish. Afterward, the grandson of Paul Revere watched as the passant grizzly banner, fashioned by the nephew of Abraham Lincoln, was lowered and the Stars and Stripes raised in its place.*

The twenty-five-day Bear Flag Republic had ended.

On July 10, in his camp on the American River, Frémont was visited by the purser of the *Portsmouth* carrying a message from Montgomery on the navy's occupation of Monterey and Yerba Buena. Now, at last, there was a war on and the word had spread that General Castro had retreated south to Los Angeles, seat of Pío Pico's government and of whatever resistance the Californios would muster against the Americans. Even the British, whose warships Sloat had seen patrolling the sea-lanes between Mazatlán and Monterey, seemed to know something was brewing. The sloop *Juno* had sailed past the Golden Gate on July 11 and the HMS *Collingwood*, Rear Admiral Sir George F. Seymour commanding, arrived on July

---

Revere is said to have tucked the original Bear Flag in his pocket. Years later, it was donated to the Society of California Pioneers in San Francisco but was destroyed in the earthquake and fire in 1906. The flag design became the official state emblem in 1911.

16. These visitors caused Montgomery to take some steps to defend Yerba Buena, but after courtesy calls by Seymour and his officers, the Americans became convinced that the British were mere observers and posed no threat.

On July 12—with the American flag now run up at Monterey, Yerba Buena, Sonoma, Sutter's Fort, and Bodega Bay on the coast north of the Russian River—Frémont, with his original exploration party, and the Bear Flaggers who had followed him from Sonoma, rode into New Helvetia. A letter from Sloat was awaiting him there, giving details of the capture of Monterey. The commodore said he expected General Castro to surrender but asked Frémont to bring in at least a hundred "well mounted" men to prevent Indian depredations against the Californios in the area.

The request seemed specious to the explorer, but he had received orders from a superior officer and prepared to march. He sent Gillespie ahead and after provisioning his hundred and sixty men and requisitioning cattle, horses, pack mules, and two small fieldpieces at Sutter's, he led his battalion down the Sacramento Valley. He expected that his meeting with Sloat would include plans to pursue Castro to Los Angeles.

The Americans reached San Juan Bautista on July 16, raised the flag there, and entered Monterey three days later.

The placid and picturesque town, accustomed to strangers strolling its pathways and bayfront trading posts, had seen nothing in its history like the entrance of the Americans that bright July day, and the citizenry, Californio and outlander alike, lined up to witness it.

The Americans were preceded by their beef herd and horses and mules, three hundred animals kicking up an immense cloud of dust. Some yards behind them rode Frémont and his praetorian guard of Lenni-Lenape "real men," the Delaware Indians, their faces painted, hair braided and strung with feathers, their big skinning-knives strapped at their waists, heavy muskets held across their saddle pommels. Next, two by two, rode Kit Carson, Alexis Godey, Lucien Maxwell, Dick Owens, Jacob Dodson, gunsmith

Stepp, the French-Canadians, army lieutenants Talbot, Abert, and Peck, former Bear Flaggers Ide, Swift, Merritt, Ford, Semple, and others, most of them sunbaked, trail-fouled, bearded apparitions in grimy deer-skin trousers and coats, and high moccasin-like boots lashed with rawhide thongs.

Admiral Seymour's *Collingwood* had preceded Frémont's battalion to Monterey, and his officers and sailors were ashore to watch the spectacle. The British were particularly interested in catching a glimpse of Kit Carson, whose name and exploits were almost as legendary in England as Horatio Nelson's. Frémont, too, was an object of special interest by the British seamen. One midshipman wrote of him as "a middle-sized man with an aquiline nose, very piercing eyes and hair parted amidships." Another officer described him as a "spare, active-looking man, with such an eye! He was dressed in blouse and leggings, and wore a felt hat." The middies viewed the Delawares admiringly, likening them to characters from a James Fenimore Cooper novel.

A copse of fir trees on the outskirts of town served as a camp. Once the animals were secured and under watch, the men were free to visit the town, to pass their time, one unimpressed observer recalled, "in drunkenness and debauchery."

2

A navy launch took Frémont and his adjutant, Gillespie, out to the *Savannah* at midday on July 19 and Sloat greeted them cordially, questioning the explorer at length on his role in the rebellion in Sonoma and his subsequent actions. Sloat particularly wanted to know by whose orders Frémont and his men had aided the rebels, imprisoned General Vallejo, spiked the guns at Castillo de San Joaquín, and organized the force he now had camped at Monterey. After a month of inertia, Sloat had taken Monterey only after he had learned of Frémont's work among the Bear Flaggers in the north, and he now needed to know the source of the explorer's authority.

Had Lieutenant Gillespie brought orders from Washington? From Secretary of War Marcy? From President Polk himself?

When Frémont casually explained that he had acted on his own authority to assist the settlers who were facing a fight with Castro and expulsion from the province, Sloat paled and retired to his cabin.

Frémont was livid. He had expected to talk to this officer about amalgamating his men into official service, thereby receiving a sort of ex post facto sanction for all his filibustering work over the past four months—Hawk's Peak, his encouragement of the Bear Flaggers, the imprisonment of Vallejo, the murders at San Pablo estuary, his commandeering of Sutter's Fort. He also had hoped to talk to the commodore about pursuing Castro south to San Luís Obispo, Santa Barbara, and Los Angeles. Instead, he learned that the navy had no shore operations planned other than holding actions, and that the highest-ranking American officer in California was old, ill, and timid.

What Frémont did not know was that his rescuer, Commodore Robert Field Stockton, had arrived in Monterey Bay. He had sailed for California from Norfolk, voyaging the customary route—the Horn, Valparaiso, Chile; Callao, Peru, and the Sandwich Islands—and on July 15, 1846, made his way into Monterey roads from Honolulu on the sixty-gun frigate *Congress*.

Stockton's sealed orders were dated October 17, 1845, the precise date of Secretary of State James Buchanan's orders to Thomas O. Larkin appointing him a "confidential agent" and instructing him to "conciliate" the Californios and urge them to support annexation.

Bernard DeVoto calls Stockton the d'Artagnan of the conquest of California, and there are similarities. Both the commodore and the swashbuckling Gascon were ambitious, vain, bombastic, and excitable, and both hungered for glory. But in contrast to the Dumas character, who rode penniless into Paris on a yellow pony, Stockton was a fifty-one-year-old blueblood who had arrived in Monterey on the biggest warship of the Pacific Squadron to the shrilling of a bosun's pipe and a cannon salute.

Born in Princeton, New Jersey, his grandfather had been among the signers of the Declaration of Independence, his father a lawyer and politician, serving in both houses of the Congress of the United States. Robert attended Princeton briefly but in 1811, at age sixteen, a perfect time for active service in far-flung stations, he earned a warrant as a midshipman in the navy.

He served in the war of 1812 on the frigates *President* and *Gurriere* at Chesapeake Bay, the defenses of Baltimore, Washington, and Fort McHenry. As a schooner lieutenant in the Mediterranean, he took part in the capture of Algerian warships, which brought an end to the Barbary Wars. In 1821, on the schooner *Alligator* off the West African coast, he directed the capture of four French slavers, and on the return voyage from Liberia, fought a successful engagement with a Portuguese pirate vessel. In the West Indies in 1822, the *Alligator* destroyed three pirate ships and captured their loot.

Stockton had retired from the navy in 1828 upon the death of his father and his inheritance of the family estate in Princeton. For ten years, he concentrated on improving the family's already substantial fortune in New Jersey railroads and ship canals. He married, became a celebrated horse-breeder, traveled in Europe, and dabbled in politics, first as a supporter of John Quincy Adams, later as an ardent backer of Andrew Jackson and John Tyler.

Upon reentering the navy in 1838, he was promoted to captain of the warship *Ohio* and studied naval architecture and marine engineering in England, where he became a disciple of John Ericcson, the steam-and-screw propulsion pioneer. When he returned to the United States, he promoted the idea of a screw-driven warship and used his wealth and political influence in supervising construction of the Ericcson-designed man-of-war *Princeton*. It was this ship, Stockton in command, that in February, 1844, had taken President John Tyler and four hundred Washington dignitaries—including Senator Thomas Hart Benton—on a cruise of the Potomac. The pleasure cruise had ended in unutterable tragedy when, during an ordnance demonstration, one of the *Princeton*'s massive guns, ironically called the Peacemaker, exploded, killing Tyler's secretary of state, secretary of the navy, and four other onlookers.

Stockton, who had been burned by the gun explosion, was cleared of any responsibility for the catastrophe. The next year, President Polk ordered the captain and a small squadron, including the *Princeton,* from the Mediterranean to patrol in the Gulf of Mexico and prevent any Mexican intervention during negotiations over the annexation of Texas. Stockton overstepped his authority in conducting talks with Texas officials and whipping up the idea of military intervention in Mexico, but since this notion was not unknown in the White House, its main tenant did not censure the officer for his arrogance. In fact, soon after his Texas coast duties, he was promoted to the rank of commodore and given command of the Pacific Squadron with orders to proceed to California.

He had not changed much in character over the thirty-five years since he entered the navy. His natural impertinence and tactlessness had flowered as he climbed the command ladder. He was obedient to his superiors as long as they remained in Washington and he far removed; he gave orders with alacrity, took them reluctantly, was protective of his rank and command, brooking no dissenting opinions among his officers.

He was also zealous, patriotic, and energetic. He did not avoid decision-making, did not let his rank interfere with his love of a fight.

He was a smallish, handsome man, long-nosed, dark-haired, clean-shaven, with piercing dark eyes and a cutlass slash of a mouth.

He had so much in common with John Charles Frémont that the two became fast friends at once.

The two commodores met for the first time on July 15 when Sloat took the preliminary step toward retirement by naming Stockton commander in chief of all the land forces in California.

Frémont and Gillespie, meantime, had also met with the new commodore and were greatly encouraged by Stockton's eagerness to pursue Castro and finish the conquest of California with land forces—including Frémont's 160 men.

On July 23, Stockton mustered the former Bear Flaggers and Frémont's men into the military service of the United States as the "Naval Battalion of Mounted Volunteer Riflemen"—soon known as the California Battalion—with Frémont as major in command, Gillespie as captain and second. Within a few weeks following, some 428 other volunteers were engaged, most of them at Sonoma and Sutter's Fort, to be paid twenty-five dollars a month. Fifty Walla Walla Indians from Oregon enlisted at Sutter's.

Commodore Sloat transfered his pennant to the *Levant* on July 29 and headed home. Among his last acts before turning the Pacific Squadron command over to Stockton was the ordering of the release of General Vallejo and the other prisoners at Sutter's Fort.

On the day of Sloat's departure and before sailing south to San Pedro on the *Congress,* Stockton issued a hammering proclamation annexing California to the United States, vowing to drive Castro and all Mexicans opposing the measure out of the province. He said he would march "against these boasting and abusive chiefs" who had "violated every principle of international law and national hospitality by hunting and pursuing with several hundred soldiers, and with wicked intent, Capt. Frémont of the U.S. Army, who came here to refresh his men, about forty in number, after a perilous journey across the mountains, on a scientific survey." The document named Castro as a "usurper" who "has been guilty of great offenses, has impoverished and drained the country of almost its last dollar, and has deserted his post now when most needed." Stockton wrote that "reports from the interior" told of "rapine, blood and murder" at the hands of the Mexican general and his soldiers. He went on, "I must therefore, and will as soon as I can, adopt such measures as may seem best calculated to bring these criminals to justice, and to bestow peace and good order to the country."

H. H. Bancroft called Stockton's declaration a "pronunciamento filibustero," found the remarks on Castro's "hunting and pursuing" Frémont particularly amusing, and said of it as a whole, "The paper was made up of falsehood, or irrelevant issues, and of bombastic ranting in about equal parts, the tone being offensive and impolitic even in those inconsiderable portions which were true and legitimate. . . . It should have borne the signatures of Frémont and Gillespie, who managed to gain for the time being complete control over the commodore. . . ."

Commodore Sloat, who took a copy of the proclamation with him on the *Levant,* wrote to the secretary of the navy, "It does not contain my reasons for taking possession of, or my views or intentions toward that country; consequently it does not meet my approbation."

3

Following Stockton's manifesto, General Castro, in Santa Clara, began his move south to Los Angeles to join forces, such as they were, with his old rival, Governor Pío Pico. At the time of the Olómpali skirmish with the Osos, Castro had close to two hundred men in his command, mostly local militiamen; now, with many of them deserting, drifting toward home rather than abandoning their families for a real and potentially deadly campaign against the Americans, his force had dwindled to about a hundred. He hoped—but probably knew the impossibility of it—to raise an army to "rise en masse irresistible and just" to crush the invaders and announced, "Duty leads me to death or victory. I am a Mexican soldier and I will be free and independent or die with pleasure for those inestimable blessings."

Governor Pico, doting on classical references, was even more emotional in his response to the Monterey takeover and subsequent American flag-raisings. "Fly, Mexicans, in all haste in pursuit of the treacherous foe," he wrote in his message to the populace. "Follow him to the farthest wilderness; punish his audacity; and in case we fail, let us form a cemetery where posterity may remember to the glory of Mexican history the heroism of her sons, as is remembered the glory won by death of that little band of citizens posted at the Pass of Thermopylae under General Leonidas."

On July 16, as Frémont and his men were en route to Monterey, Pico issued a more formal proclamation on the American invasion. He promised to "make every possible effort to repel this the most unjust aggression" and issued a conscription order for all Mexican citizens of the department of California between the ages of fifteen and sixty to "defend the country when as now the national independence is in danger." The governor called a special meeting of his legislators and gave the assembly a report on the invasion. "He and the others," historian Bancroft said, "made patriotic speeches."

But the speeches rang leadenly: the legislators were apathetic, and few among the citizenry saw any hope in defending California— neglected by its motherland throughout its history and now, in war, utterly abandoned—against so mighty a foe as the United States. There was no money to finance an army, no appreciable stock of weapons to arm it. Further, many influential Californios welcomed the American invasion and many others were secretly sympathetic to it. Thus few flew to pursue the treacherous foe; Pico's hope of raising a force with his conscription order produced about a hundred men to combine with Castro's hundred from the north.

❦

Stockton knew nothing of the precise numbers opposing him when he determined to mass his men at Los Angeles to locate, confront, and defeat Castro in battle. On July 26, he ordered Frémont and his battalion from Monterey downcoast on the *Cyane* to San Diego, there to gather cattle, oxen, horses, and a pack train of mules, preparatory to a march north to the capital. Stockton, meantime, planned to land his force from the *Congress* at San Pedro, thirty-five miles south of Los Angeles, and rendezvous with the explorer.

The California Battalion, about 120 weak-kneed, seasick men, landed at San Diego on July 29 and raised the flag there without opposition. A week-long search produced only a few horses and pack animals.

On his move south, Stockton dropped off a small garrison at Santa Barbara, and on August 1, the *Congress* dropped anchor in San Pedro Bay and landed the commodore and his 360 sailors and marines armed with muskets, pistols, cutlasses and boarding pikes, and four six-pounder cannons.

Thomas Larkin, who had accompanied Stockton on the *Congress*, came ashore at San Pedro with hopes high that he might negotiate a peaceful annexation of California. These hopes rose even higher on the day after the landing when two representatives from Castro arrived at Stockton's camp. The commissioners, Pablo de la Guerra and Captain José María Flores, delivered a letter to the commodore in which the Mexican general expressed a willingness to negotiate for peace provided that "all hostile movements be suspended by both forces."

This gentlemanly proffer seemed eminently reasonable to Larkin but not to Stockton, who did not believe negotiations with Castro would be valid without sanction from Mexico City and so rejected the terms of the letter out of hand. His return message to the general, dated August 7, said, "I do not wish to war against California or her people; but as she is a department of Mexico, I must war against her until she ceases to be a part of the Mexican territory. This is my plain duty." He ended the letter with a proposal he knew would be rejected: ". . . if, therefore, you will agree to hoist the American flag in California, I will stop my forces and negotiate the treaty."

Castro eloquently and indignantly rejected this proposal. "Never, never, never!" he proclaimed, and called the commodore's ultimatum "humiliating," "shameful," and "insidious." "Never will I consent that [California] commit so base an act . . . And what would be her liberty with that protection offered at the cannon's mouth?"

Two days after Stockton's truce-ending message was written, Castro held a war council at La Mesa, just south of Los Angeles, and dispatched a letter to Governor Pico. He said that he had been able to muster only a hundred men and these "badly armed, worse supplied, and discontented by reason of the misery they suffer." He notified the governor, "I have reason to fear that not even these few men will fight when the necessity arises." He had resolved, he said, to journey to Sonora, there to report to the supreme government in Mexico City the plight of their people in California, and he invited Pico to join him. He included in the letter his farewell address to the people of California, in which he said, "With my heart full of the most cruel grief, I take leave of you. I leave the country of my birth, but with the hope of returning to destroy the slavery in which I leave you; for the day will come when our unfortunate fatherland can punish this usurpation, as rapacious as unjust, and in the face of the world, exact satisfaction for its grievances."

Pico read Castro's messages to the legislature in Los Angeles. He announced that he agreed with Castro that it would be impossible to defend the department against the American invaders and told of his intention to join the general in leaving California to notify Mexico City of the latest occurrences. He proposed that the assembly adjourn *sine die,* and this was done.

"My friends, farewell!" Pico wrote in an open letter, an echo of Castro's, upon departing Los Angeles. "I abandon the country of my birth, my family, property, and whatever else is most grateful to man, all to save the national honor. But I go with the sweet satisfaction that you will not second the deceitful views of the astute enemy; that your loyalty and firmness will prove an inexpungable barrier to the machinations of the invader. In any event, guard your honor, and observe that the eyes of the world are fixed upon you."

On the night of July 10, Castro and Pico left Los Angeles separately. The general and twenty men rode toward the Colorado River. With him was his secretary, Francisco Arce, who precisely one month earlier had lost a horse herd after encountering Ezekial Merritt and other Bear Flaggers on the Cosumnes River. Early in September, Castro and his party reached Sonora, where he sent dispatches to Mexico City explaining his flight and urging that forces be marched to the defense of California.

Pico hid out with friends in San Juan Capistrano for a month before making his way to Mulegé on the eastern Baja California coast, thence across the Gulf of California to Guaymas and subsequently to Hermosillo, the Sonoran capital. He too urged, unavailingly, the Mexican government to defend its Pacific department.

4

On the day these two highest-ranking political officers departed the capital, Thomas O. Larkin rode into Los Angeles, sent ahead by Stockton with messages, now undeliverable, to General Castro. On August 13, with the news that Castro had fled, the commodore rode into the town of fifteen hundred inhabitants, a clamorous brass band from the *Congress* in the vanguard, followed by the trudging force of marines and sailors, the baggage train, bullock carts, and ox teams pulling the ponderous artillery caissons. Stockton's force was followed by Major Frémont and his scary, scruffy California Battalion of mountaineers, Indians, and former Osos.

The invaders were unopposed; the ship's band attracted many cheering Angelinos to the procession route.

At La Mesa, on the way to the capital, ten pieces of artillery were found at Castro's abandoned camp, only four of the guns spiked.

On August 17, Stockton, by this time referring to himself as "Commander-in-Chief and Governor of the Territory of California," issued a new proclamation, announcing that California was now a part of the United States, the people of California American citizens. He promised that a civil government would soon be established and that elections would be held. The document imposed a 10:00 P.M.-to-sunrise curfew, and warned that any person found armed outside his home during those hours without permission would be treated as an enemy and subject to deportation. Thieves would be punished, life and property would be protected.

This proclamation read and posted in two languages, Stockton ebulliently reported to Secretary of State Bancroft on August 22 that "The Flag of the United States is now flying from every commanding position in the Territory, and California is entirely free from Mexican dominion." In a burst of fantasy, he said that in under a month he had "chased the Mexican army more than 300 miles along the coast, pursued them 30 miles into the interior of their own country, routed and dispersed them, and secured the Territory to the United States, ended the war, restored peace and harmony among the people, and put a civil government into successful operation."

The commodore deemed the conquest at an end, and it had been a bitter disappointment. He was a man of action, seeking the exhilaration, the promise, of glory—and promotion—that "active service" offered. These emoluments had been denied him since 1812, the Barbary Wars, the pirate pursuits off the African coast and in the West Indies. The California command had been a bright hope, but in a month he had seen little more than the ashes of the enemy's campfires. He had grown tired of writing proclamations, was anxious to remove his sailors and marines from the now-conquered territory—"to leave the desk and camp and take to the ship and sea"—and find something worthy of his energy and talents.

One matter beckoned. Stockton had studied his maps and begun to fear the possibility of attacks on American commercial vessels in the Pacific by Mexican privateers based in Acapulco. He had alerted American ship captains on the availability of San Francisco Bay as a sanctuary harbor, and he began making plans to sail south to put an end to the privateer menace. Acapulco, he reasoned, would give him a base of operations for an even more ambitious plan that would put his name on the forefront of the war's heroes: he would raise a force of a thousand men and make an overland march "to shake hands with General Taylor at the Gates of Mexico."

Stockton took Frémont into his confidence on his scheme and

said that upon his departure from California, the explorer would assume the governorship of the territory.

On September 2, 1846, the commodore divided California into three military districts. A few days earlier, he had named Frémont military commandant of the new territory and had installed Gillespie as *alcalde* of Los Angeles. He assigned the marine a garrison of fifty men and issued instructions that until further notice, Gillespie would continue imposing martial law, enforcing the curfews, and overseeing the other regulations that had been imposed.

Stockton also authorized Frémont to enlarge the California Battalion to three hundred men to provide both a mobile field force and garrisons for the main California settlements. The two officers made arrangements to meet at Yerba Buena on October 25 to make further plans for the governance and protection of the territory.

Among his last duties before departing Pueblo de los Angeles on September 2, 1846, Stockton ordered Kit Carson to Washington with a full report to President Polk and Secretary Bancroft on the conquest. Letters to Jessie Frémont and Senator Benton were included in the dispatch pouch, and Carson was authorized to take a pack train of mules and handpick fifteen men to ride with him. Kit estimated that he could get the job done in sixty days—and that included a brief visit with his wife Josefa in Taos, New Mexico.

❈

On September 5, the commodore ordered his sailors and marines back aboard the *Congress* at San Pedro and set sail for Monterey. There, as Frémont and his men were making their way north toward the Sacramento Valley, the commodore had time to further study his grand scheme to shake hands with Zachary Taylor in Mexico City. He decided that he needed more men and sent word ahead to Frémont to raise seven hundred volunteers in the north to join him.

Finally, he sailed and arrived in San Francisco Bay in the last week of September. At Yerba Buena, where an official greeting had been arranged for him by Colonel Mariano Vallejo, Stockton—

resplendent in full uniform—came ashore in a barge to meet the erstwhile Bear Flagger prisoner, himself elegantly arrayed and wearing his medals. A large welcoming committee lined the wharf to see the conqueror of California and to follow his procession along the rutted streets of the village. The parade ended at the home of Vice Consul Leidesdorff, where a speech was made by William "Owl" Russell, a Kentuckian, veteran of Seminole battles in Florida, former U.S. Marshal, Frémont crony, and major of artillery in the California Battalion. He spoke generously of the commodore's illustrious career.

But Stockton had only a few days in which to enjoy the accolades. His plans to meet with Frémont, recruit men for his overland march, and sail for Acapulo were abruptly halted on October 1 with the arrival in Yerba Buena of a courier named John Brown. This man, known as "Juan Flaco" (Skinny John) had made the ride from Los Angeles—a distance of five hundred miles—in six days to carry the news that a force of armed Californios had risen in the capital and was besieging Gillespie's garrison.

Stockton treated the news dubiously but ordered Captain Mervine to sail for San Pedro on the *Savannah* and dispatched an express to Frémont's camp near Sutter's Fort ordering the explorer to bring his men down to Yerba Buena.

His plans gone awry, the commodore told his officers that if harm came to Gillespie or his men, he would "wade knee-deep in blood to avenge it."

✾

Conquest

Stephen Watts Kearny.

✤

CHAPTER THIRTEEN

Kearny

1

On the Congress, the conqueror of California pored over his sea charts and maps. At last he had time to perfect his plan to make a sensational sortie against privateers off the Pacific coast of Mexico and an overland march to the enemy capital. He would take a thousand men—a full regiment of marines, sailors, and volunteers—down Baja California, sail around Cabo San Lucas, take on supplies at Mazatlán, and proceed south by southeast around the elbow of Mexico, past San Blas and Manzanillo to Acapulco. There he would disembark his men and lead them the two hundred and fifty miles north to Mexico City. The idea of merging his force with Zachary Taylor's for a march into the ancient heart of Mexico—it was something a lesser man might find too daunting to contemplate.

Robert Field Stockton dreamt of a glorious apogee to his career as his flagship butted through blue-green Pacific swells on that splendidly clear September day of 1846. The *Congress* made its passage north from San Pablo roads to San Francisco leisurely. The commodore was at ease, if not at peace, thinking of what the future held for him, while outside his comfortable cabin, momentous events were unfolding in Mexico, New Mexico, and, just behind him, in Los Angeles.

Between September 20 and 25, as the *Congress* neared the Golden Gate, General Zachary Taylor's army of six thousand was fighting a Mexican army of similar strength in Monterrey* just two hundred miles south of the Rio Grande. It would be a full year before General Winfield Scott, leading a force of fourteen thousand, reached Mexico City.

In Los Angeles, meantime, Lieutenant Archibald Gillespie and his fifty-man garrison were under attack by an unorganized, angry band of Californios who had quite suddenly decided not to yield to conquest as docilely as expected.

And in the province of New Mexico, another military officer had begun a march down the valley of the Rio Grande, a thousand miles out of Fort Leavenworth, leading three hundred dragoons and an enormous wagon and pack-animal train, headed south to the Gila River.

❁

Of the triumvirate of conquerors of California, Stephen Watts Kearny was the last to arrive at the seat of conquest. Frémont had entered Sutter's Fort in December, 1845; Stockton had sailed into Monterey Bay in July, 1846; but it was Kearney's fate to be the first of the three to engage in battle on California soil and to throw a handful of grit into the well-oiled machinery set running by his predecessors. Between the time he arrived in California in December, 1846, and left six months later, Kearny annexed and secured the territory for the United States once and for all and placed his own reputation and career, and those of Frémont and Stockton, in peril.

Ninety-five years after Kearny's California adventure, Bernard DeVoto said of him: "In the vaudeville show of swollen egoism, vanity, treachery, incompetence, rhetoric, stupidity, and electioneering which the great generals of the Mexican War display to the

---

Spelled with two r's in Mexico, one in California. Either way, it means King's Mountain.

pensive mind, Kearny stands out as a gentleman, a soldier, a commander, a diplomat, a statesman, and a master of his job, whose only superior was Winfield Scott."

A newly appointed brigadier general with thirty-three years of army service at the time he led his dragoons toward the Gila, Kearny was the youngest of thirteen children of a prominent lawyer and landowner in Newark, New Jersey. As a lieutenant in the Thirteenth Infantry, he had fought his first (and until California, only) battle on October 13, 1812, at Queenston Heights on the Niagara frontier, where he was wounded and taken prisoner by the British. In 1819, then a captain, he had joined a regiment in Iowa and begun his long tenure in the Western territories—Council Bluffs, Iowa; Fort Smith, Arkansas; Fort Atkinson, Nebraska; St. Louis—with brief service in Detroit and in Baton Rouge, Louisiana, and expeditions across the Missouri River to the Yellowstone.

Except for minor skirmishes against Winnebagos in Wisconsin, Poncas and Mandans on the Missouri River, and Choctaws on the Texas border, he had seen nothing of the "active service" career that officers had pined for since 1812. In 1836, however, he did receive an important promotion, to the colonelcy and command of the First Dragoon Regiment at Jefferson Barracks in St. Louis.

He knew the great city on the Mississippi, had been assigned there before, and had married there. His bride was a lively eighteen-year-old named Mary Radford Clark, and Kearny had fallen in love with her the instant they were introduced. She was the stepdaughter of the great soldier-explorer William Clark, who with Meriwether Lewis had led the first expedition across the trans-Mississippi west to the Pacific in 1804. They were married in September, 1830, at Clark's Beaver Pond estate, just outside St. Louis.

In 1842, Kearny had been elevated to command of the Third Military Department of the Army, headquartered in St. Louis, and made responsible for guarding a thousand miles of frontier with little more than six hundred infantry and cavalry to patrol it. His duties were to keep the tribes at peace, inspect the reservations, and oversee escorts, patrols, and expeditions into troubled areas. In St.

Louis, he came to know Missouri's foremost citizen, Senator Thomas Hart Benton, his vivacious teenage daughter Jessie, and in May, 1843, Jessie's husband, John Charles Frémont of the army's Topographical Corps. Colonel Kearny, probably out of his friendship with Benton and Jessie, had magnanimously authorized the issuance of some Hall carbines and a twelve-pounder brass cannons to the young lieutenant, then en route to Oregon on his second expedition into the far West. He never saw the gun again, but he would see the explorer later, under the most trying of circumstances, in California.

In 1845, Kearny took five companies of the First Dragoons on an expedition along the Oregon Trail to the South Pass of Wyoming, holding a council with the Lakota tribes near Fort Laramie and returning to Fort Leavenworth by way of Bent's Fort and the Arkansas River.

The expedition had been particularly timely, giving his dragoons a long march, experience in the daily travails of the wilderness, and familiarity with the Santa Fé Trail. In under a year, he and his heavy cavalry would retrace the trail to Bent's great rest-and-outfitting oasis on the Arkansas.

On May 13, 1846, on the day President Polk declared hostilities against Mexico, Secretary of War William Marcy ordered Kearny to ready his three hundred First Dragoons for travel and be prepared to accept a thousand volunteers for the purpose of organizing an Army of the West. This army was to march to Santa Fé, capture the capital, and annex the province of New Mexico to the United States.

Kearny, soon to receive his brigadier general's star, had earned it and the command. Bernard DeVoto's assertion that he was "not only a practised frontier commander but one of the most skillful and dependable officers in the army" would be sorely tested in California—and his skill, at least, called into question.

Now age fifty-two, his physical appearance had not changed much since the time he had courted Mary Clark in St. Louis. He had a long, noble head with a fine crown of reddish-brown hair shot through with gray and combed forward, Roman-like, at the temples. His blue eyes retained their fire—his officers were often withered by his stare. He was clean-shaven, slim, and walked and sat erect—"tall, straight, bronzed, lean as a sea cusk," a contemporary described him.

In over three decades of army service, he had evolved into the prototypical "by-the-book" soldier and had a reputation as a martinet, this perhaps having had its origin among the volunteers in his army. These men, many of them hardscrabble farmers and ungovernable wanderers, could not abide Kearny's standard that they receive the same exacting discipline that kept his regular troops in order. One of his officers said of Kearny's iron disciplinary policies: "During the whole time he commanded the First Dragoons, no soldier ever received a blow [from flogging] except by the sentence of a general court-martial for the infamous crime of desertion . . . though the strictest disciplinarian in the service, there was less punishment in his corps than any other." And Ulysses S. Grant, who as a young lieutenant saw the dragoon commander in St. Louis in the early 1840s, called him "one of he ablest officers of the day" and said that his disciplinary measures were "kept at a high standard but without vexatious rules or regulations."

But while Kearny's twenty-five years on the windswept prairies of the Western frontier had browned and toughened him, it had also scoured him clean of humor and afflicted him with a certain plodding grimness like that of a blindered plow horse in a furrow. Kearny knew survival in lands unrelentingly hostile to humans; he was a gritty, demanding commander and had a righteous sense of duty. But his imagination, whatever there had been of it, had eroded, and occasional Indian skirmishes had not educated him in the skills of war.

And as a proconsul-in-the-making in New Mexico and California, he demonstrated considerable adeptness in dealing with conquered people when operating without specific direction from his superiors. But in an arena that required political delicacies among peers who held differing views, he saw no nuances, wielded his authority sullenly, and entertained no argument.

Kearny's original May 13, 1846, orders from Secretary of War Marcy were supplemented on June 3 to make clear the objective of the Western campaign: "It has been decided by the President to be of the greatest importance, in the pending War with Mexico, to take the earliest possession of Upper California," Marcy wrote. He advised Kearny that "in case you conquer Santa Fé," it was expected that New Mexico would be garrisoned before the march continued to California. Kearny was to have "a large discretionary power" in conducting the campaign: choosing the route to the Pacific, taking on volunteers, organizing supplies, and procuring animals to carry them. Marcy said that the President was desirous "that the expedition should reach California this season" but should the President be "disappointed in his cherished hope," Kearny was assured that he would be "left unembarrassed by any specific directions in this matter."

Significantly, Marcy's "Confidential Instructions," written one month before Commodore Sloat occupied Monterey, contained the news that "it is expected that the naval forces of the United States which now, or will soon be, in the Pacific, will be in possession of all the towns on the sea coast, and will co-operate with you in the conquest of California." In addition to making clear who would "co-operate" with whom, the secretary added, "Should you conquer and take possession of New Mexico and Upper California, or considerable places in either, you will establish temporary civil governments therein. . . ."

Kearny was notified that his promotion to brigadier general would take effect "as soon as you commence your movement towards California."

The secretary's "instructions" were similar in vagueness to those sent to Commodores Sloat and Stockton in California. The War Department's knowledge of New Mexico was sketchy—there were no dependable maps of it—and critical questions were unanswerable in Washington or anywhere else. It seemed unlikely that

Mexico would deliver without a fight a province of a hundred thousand square miles that had been held for three centuries, but how defiantly would the Mexicans defend New Mexico? What manpower and arms lay awaiting an invading force?

At least it was clear to Kearny that he would command the entire conquest of Mexico's western territory and that the navy would cooperate with him as he took charge of all military and political efforts once he reached the Pacific.

❅

Kearny's organization of his Army of the West turned out to be a logistical masterpiece. Working with the quartermaster general in St. Louis, arms, munitions, 1,556 wagons, 459 horses, over four thousand mules, and fifteen thousand head of cattle and oxen were massed at Fort Leavenworth. Supplies were sent ahead in small pack trains to Bent's Fort, rendezvous point for the invasion of New Mexico.

Answering the call sent out into Missouri and along the Santa Fé Trail to Bent's, volunteers began pouring off Missouri River steamboats and into the fort in the first week of June. The First Regiment of Missouri Mounted Volunteers came in under the command of Colonel Alexander W. Doniphan, a handsome six-foot-four Clay County lawyer. He had his ragged assemblage of 860 shag-bearded farmers, hunters, and drifters under control—a fact not lost on the discipline-minded Kearny, who overlooked the Missourians' tendency to call him "Ol' Hoss" to his face. Soon after the arrival of Doniphan's force, the Laclede Rangers, 107 men who would be attached to the the First Dragoons, arrived, followed by two companies of volunteer infantry and two of artillery, all from St. Louis. Two additional companies of regular First Dragoons rode in from northern outposts.

An odd addition to Kearny's gathering army came from the Mormon colony, camped at Council Bluffs, Iowa. In February, 1846, Brigham Young, the prophet and leader of the Church of

Jesus Christ of Latter-day Saints, had led sixteen thousand of his people from Nauvoo, Illinois, across the ice-clogged Mississippi. In five harrowing months, during which six hundred "Saints" died, the congregation reached Council Bluffs on the Missouri River en route to founding the church's new "Zion" somewhere in the Western wilderness. The Mormons were offered a chance to enlist in Kearny's army and assured of quick discharges once they reached California. The "Mormon Battalion," while having no direct role in the conquest of California, accomplished an epic march that would rival Kearny's own.

With his army and supply train growing massively by the day, on June 6, Kearny sent two companies of the First Dragoons ahead on the trail southeast toward Bent's Fort, 537 miles distant, and parceled out other units on the trail over the following three weeks. Doniphan's eight companies of First Missourians departed Leavenworth between June 22 and 28; the bullock-drawn trade and supply wagons and eight hundred head of cattle followed along with them. On June 28, the balance of the six troops of First Dragoons moved out, together with a 150-man battalion of infantry, two companies of light artillery, the latter 250 men commanded by Major Meriwether Lewis Clark, General William Clark's son, who also happened to be Mary Kearny's stepbrother and former suitor.

The fragmenting of his force was Kearny's plan to conserve the enormous amount of firewood and forage required to fuel the Army of the West.

By June 29, the colonel notified his superiors in St. Louis: "I have started fifteen hundred and twenty men from here on the Santa Fé Trail. I will leave tomorrow to overtake them and will concentrate the whole near the crossing of the Arkansas." Then, on the morning of the thirtieth, he hugged his wife and children on the steps of his bungalow, mounted his bay horse, and rode with his staff officers out of Fort Leavenworth to rendezvous with his army.

In all, he commanded a force of over seventeen hundred men, counting a hundred or so civilian hunters and teamsters, sutlers,

Santa Fé traders, and Delaware and Shawnee scouts. He had a contract surgeon, a remarkable Virginian named John S. Griffin, who kept a meticulous diary of the march; a small topographical corps headed by Lieutenant William H. Emory of Queen Anne's County, Maryland, a West Pointer and former artilleryman; and an interpreter, Antoine Robidoux, a naturalized Mexican citizen who had until recently operated a trading post in the desolate Uinta River region of Utah.

Kearny's ordnance train consisted of four twelve-pounder and twelve six-pounder brass field howitzers.

The dragoons, Kearny's and the army's pride, rode as confidently, if less splendidly accoutred, as the British "heavies" under General George Yorke Scarlett at Balaclava ten years hence. They were big men on big horses—grizzled, squint-eyed veterans of the sun and wind of the Western plains. They wore blue-flannel shirts and trousers, broad-brimmed hats, huge skinning knives in sheaths cinched around their waists together with braces of cap-and-ball pistols, and carbines in leather boots strapped to their saddles. Except for their weaponry and ammunition pouches, the dragoons traveled light: all they needed—spare blouses, mess tin and utensils—they carried wrapped in a blanket roll behind their saddles.

3

Kearny and his officers swiftly caught up with the main body of the army, and despite the ponderous string of ox wagons, horse- and mule-drawn carts, and gun caissons—a dust-clouded tail miles long wagging the dog of the soldiery afoot and on horseback—managed to push an exhausting pace of twenty to thirty miles a day in the broiling summer heat. The column was slowed only in the tedious crossing of the Kansas River.

On July 7, while Commodore Sloat was forcing the surrender of Monterey, Kearny's army, a hundred miles out of Leavenworth, reached Council Grove, the Santa Fé Trail gateway. The trail, already a fabled trader's route, in its busy twenty-year history had never carried a multitude, military or civilian, close to the numbers of Kearny's army.

Over the years, traffic on the trail had nearly denuded the countryside around it of timber, and game was scarce enough to force the civilian hunters hired to accompany the army to travel far afield to find meat. Kearny forbade the slaughter of any of the army's beef herd as long as his hunters were able to bring in deer and buffalo to add to the meager rations each man carried.

At Pawnee Rock, after a march of 250 miles, hunters riding several hours ahead of the force found a buffalo herd, an undulating brown blanket of half a million animals spread out for miles before them, and solved the meat problem for the rest of the march to Bent's Fort. The buffalo also supplied tinder for cook fires as troopers learned the value of dried *bois de vache* (buffalo chips) and how to skewer them with their ramrods without dismounting.

Water plagued the army in both its scarcity and abundance. Torrential rains burst on the crawling column with little warning, and those lasting a half-day turned the trail into a black porridge, burying the heavy wagons to their wheel hubs, balking mules and bullocks and filling the air with the crack of bullwhips, the shouted curses of the freightmen and the bellowing of the animals struggling forward. But often the rains were harmless cloudbursts that did little more than settle the dust plumes and add a steaminess to the day's heat, frequently a hundred ten degrees and higher.

On July 22, three weeks out of Fort Leavenworth, a landmark came into view far to the northwest, shrouded by thunderheads. The Spanish Peaks, the Wah-to-yah (Breasts of the World) of the Indians, signaled to the jaded army that they were nearing the end of the first leg of their journey, nearing an outpost of civilization in the midst of the eternal plains, a place as fabled among Western travelers as Sutter's New Helvetia—Bent's Fort.

This outpost, built in 1833 by the fur-trading partners Charles Bent and his brother William of Virginia, and Cerán St. Vrain of Missouri, lay twelve miles upstream from the junction of the

Arkansas and Purgatoire rivers of Colorado. The fort, called the "Big Lodge" by the Indians who frequented it and camped along the river nearby, had the configuration of a rough rectangle about 180 by 130 feet in size. Its yard-thick walls rose fourteen feet high, and at opposite corners of the square were two crenellated, martello-like towers, the battlements equipped with small field cannons. On the north side of the packed-adobe fort were two-story buildings, their roofs providing wide walkways to the ramparts. Above the gateway into Bent's, a great iron bell was housed in a belfry above which the proprietors kept an American flag flapping in the breeze.

Inside the compound there were shady arcades of trading rooms, cooper, carpenter, and joiner shops, a wagon park, blacksmith's forge, hide presses, water wells, warehouses, corrals, kitchens, apartments, the proprietor's home—even an icehouse and a billiard room. Built expressly to take advantage of the growing Santa Fé trade, the fort was the only permanent post between the Missouri River and the New Mexico capital and commanded the trade routes north and south along the Platte River and east and west along the Santa Fé Trail.

Bent's traded in everything—furs, livestock, buffalo robes, blankets, nails, guns, galena, powder, spirits, knives and axes, wagon parts, saddlery, foodstuffs—and services for the broken wagon, the shoe-worn horse, the tired, hungry, and thirsty Indian, trapper, trader, and ordinary traveler.

On July 29, 1846, the day in which Commodore Stockton was issuing his first bellicose proclamation as conqueror of California, Thomas "Broken Hand" Fitzpatrick rode up from Bent's and joined Colonel Kearny and his officers for the last leg of their march to the fort. The colonel and this white-haired native of County Caven, Ireland, were well acquainted. Just a year past, Fitzpatrick had guided Kearny and five companies of his First Dragoons along the Oregon Trail to the South Pass of Wyoming and back to the Arkansas. They had developed a mutual respect. Kearny knew that no man had better scouting credentials—not even Kit Carson—than this steadfast mountaineer who for more than twenty years had roamed the rivers, mountains, passes, and landmarks of the far West, from Missouri to the Pacific and from the disputed northern border with Canada down through Mexican lands to the Gila River.

Fitzpatrick brought the news circulating at the fort that Governor Armijo had called a war council in Santa Fé and was amassing a force to defend New Mexico.

The next day, July 30, Kearny and the vanguard of the Army of the West arrived on the Arkansas within sight of the great adobe walls of Bent's Fort. As the teamsters and their ox wagons and pack mules straggled in, the tents of the big camp bloomed along the river east of the fort; Major Meriwether Lewis Clark set up his ordnance park, and Colonel Alexander Doniphan ordered the horses and pack animals to be turned loose to graze.

Captain Benjamin D. Moore, who commanded the advance party of dragoons in scouting the campsite, reported to Kearny the capture of four Mexican "spies" who admitted they had been sent up from Santa Fé to gather information on the advancing American army. The men were brought to Kearny's command tent and questioned. The colonel shrewdly ordered they be given a tour of the massive camp—Major Lewis's twelve howitzers were especially impressed on them—before being freed to return across Ratón Pass to report to Governor Armijo what they had seen.

Kearny was anxious to press on. At Bent's on the last day of July, he issued a proclamation to the people of New Mexico, stamped from the same template as that written by Sloat in California. "The undersigned enters New Mexico with a large military force," Kearny wrote, "for the purpose of seeking union with and ameliorating the conditions of its inhabitants." He "enjoined the citizens of New Mexico" to "remain quietly in their homes and pursue their peaceful avocations" and said that as long as they did this, they would not be "interfered with by the American army," but he warned that those who took up arms against him "will be regarded as enemies and will be treated accordingly."

The freed spies carried copies of the proclamation to Armijo.

Meantime, an important courier arrived at the fort with messages for Kearny from President Polk and Secretary of War Marcy. This was James Wiley Magoffin of Kentucky, an eminent figure in Mexico who had been trading north and south of the Rio Grande since 1825. He had served as United States consul at Saltillo and Ciudad Chihuahua, married into a prominent Mexican family, spoke fluent Spanish, and had a wide circle of influential friends, including Senator Thomas Hart Benton of Missouri. It was Benton, in fact, who had pressed on the President the idea of sending Magoffin from Washington to intercept Kearny at Bent's Fort. The messages delivered, which Kearny probably divined before reading them, urged him to do whatever was necessary to persuade Armijo to surrender New Mexico peaceably and said that Magoffin was to serve as emissary to the governor-general.

On August 1, Kearny assigned one of his favorite officers, Captain Philip St. George Cooke of Leesburg, Virginia, a thirty-seven-year-old West Point graduate and Black Hawk War veteran, with twelve dragoons to escort Magoffin to Santa Fé bearing a letter for Governor Armijo. The letter bluntly said that the United States Army was on the march to annex all of New Mexico north and east of the Rio Grande and that if Armijo and his people presented no opposition, their lives, property, and religious practices would be honored and protected.

Magoffin, Cooke, and the dragoon escort, carrying a truce flag, entered the capital on August 12. Armijo read Kearny's message and said he would not surrender.

❀

CHAPTER FOURTEEN

Santa Fé

1

In 1846, Santa Fé stood as isolated as the Australian outback and had once been as forbidden to outsiders as Mecca and Timbuktu. The town was founded as La Villa Real de la Santa Fé (The Royal City of the Holy Faith) in 1610 and lay on an abandoned Tanoan Indian village in the foothills of the Sangre de Cristos. Conscripted Pueblo Indians had built the mission-presidio there, and for 120 years it lay virtually unknown to the rest of the world, even to the Spanish authorities who governed it from fifteen hundred miles south in Mexico City. The mission-presidio population grew slowly and quietly in a vacuum of time and space as Franciscan fathers went about their work of converting the Indians of the region to Christianity and reducing the converts to the same agricultural serfdom as those in California.

Miscellaneous outsiders trickled into Santa Fé as the decades passed but were generally treated harshly—jailed, their possessions appropriated, ordered out of the province on instructions from the viceroy in Mexico City. Such a greeting met the explorer-soldier Zebulon Montgomery Pike. In an exploration of the lower Louisiana Territory, he set out from Belle Fontaine, Missouri, in July, 1806, with twenty-one men ("a Dam'd set of Rascals but very proper for such an expedition," he said of them), explored the Republican River and the headwaters of the Arkansas, then moved south to present-day Colorado and built a stockade on the Rio Grande. In February, 1807, a patrol of one hundred Spanish soldiers took Pike and his men into custody and marched them to Santa Fé, where the expedition's papers were confiscated. Pike was escorted to Chihuahua for questioning, then escorted back to United States territory near Natchitoches, Louisiana, after five months as a prisoner of the Spanish.

Not until 1821 was an American, by happenstance, welcomed to Santa Fé.

William Becknell, a thirty-three-year-old veteran of the War of 1812, migrated to Franklin, in far-western Missouri Territory, from his native Amherst County, Virginia. In September, 1821, he and four partners ventured westward on a somewhat daring expedition to trade among the Comanches. The party crossed the Little Osage and Verdigris rivers, picked up the Arkansas, and followed it across Kansas and into Colorado.

At some point in their journey, Becknell and his trading company learned, perhaps from trappers, buffalo hunters, or a Mexican patrol, that the "gates of Santa Fé" were open—Mexico had won its independence from Spain—and so changed directions, heading south across Ratón Pass and into the fabled town. He fully expected to be jailed there and his goods taken, but he and his partners were welcomed and treated cordially. Clearly, the new authorities in New Mexico were eager to make contact with Americans, particularly those who came to trade. Josiah Gregg, a chronicler of the Santa Fé Trail, said that up to Becknell's time, the province had received all its goods and supplies from the internal provinces of Mexico and at such exorbitant prices "that common calicoes, and even bleached and brown domestic goods, sold as high as two and three dollars per *vara* (a Spanish yard of thirty-three inches)."

Becknell returned to Franklin in January, 1822, with his saddlebags full of Mexican silver.

There was but a single route from Missouri to the capital during the first year or so after Mexican independence and that over the treacherous Ratón Pass. The trail presented an obstacle for the heavy, wide-tracked and big-wheeled Murphy wagons, which became the conveyance of choice in the Santa Fé trade, some of them carrying three thousand pounds of goods. They could not negotiate the steep and narrow trail Becknell had blazed with pack animals and so, armed with a pocket compass and the stars to guide him, he traced an alternate route, crossing the water-scarce and searing (120° in summer being common) Cimarron Desert to the headwaters of the Cimarron River. Ignorance of the hardships of the route nearly cost Becknell and his party their lives: a few days into the desert, their canteen water ran out and the traders were reduced to killing their dogs and scoring the ears of their mules for blood, a measure that only added to the madness of their thirst. Close to the Cimarron, the men found a wandering buffalo, its belly distended with water, killed it and drank from its stomach. Now sustained and having found the river, the party reached Santa Fé without further incident.

Although always perilous—heat, thirst, and raiding Indians foremost among the dangers—Becknell's new route, called the Cimarron Cutoff, was shorter and flatter, and by 1824, when traders began traveling in caravans, it became favored over the Ratón Pass route.

The caravan system virtually eliminated the incidence of Indian attack and enabled traders to carry sufficient water and provisions to cross safely the fifty miles of the Cimarron Desert. Elimination of this hazard was aided by a Congressional bill sponsored in 1825 by Senator Benton that appropriated twenty thousand dollars from the Treasury to negotiate a treaty with the Osage and Kansas tribes for right-of-way through their lands and another ten thousand dollars to conduct a survey of the trail.

By the 1830s, caravans as large as one hundred wagons and two hundred men were wending westward out of Missouri to cross the prairies, mountains, and deserts to the New Mexican capital. They carried goods similar in their eccentric variety to the trade ships soon to be visiting the California coast: knives, axes, traps, kegs of nails, farm implements, glassware, thread, buttons, spoons, scissors, bolts of bright cloth, clothing, hats, spices, rifles, whiskey—all seemingly commonplace items such as were avidly sought in Santa Fé. Goods worth $35,000 were commonly traded for $200,000 in gold, silver, furs, horses, and mules.

The town also naturally changed. From a somnolent mission of under a thousand priests, soldiers, and *Indios* in 1820, after Mexican independence and the opening of trade, Santa Fé grew to a thriving commercial center. Shadowed by the snowcapped Sangre de Cristos, it was gathered around a 250-foot-square plaza of packed dirt, had a scattering of cottonwood trees, and an *acequia* (irrigation ditch) ran along two sides of it. The plaza was dominated by the governor's *palacio*. This unprepossessing building was constructed of the same adobe as all the other town dwellings and places of business but roofed with pine and spruce logs. It formed part of a presidio that enclosed a garrison barracks, drill ground, chapel, and *calabozo*.

The plaza of Santa Fé also offered access to the great cathedral and several other smaller churches, a customshouse, a hotel, houses and shops of whitewashed adobe, and the La Fonda Inn. The latter did a thriving business in liquor, gambling, and "painted women" (who were actually painted—wearing a white flour paste on their arms and faces as protection against sunburn) who smoked corn-shuck *cigarillos* and lounged in the shade of the *portales* (arcades).

By 1830, the sleepy plaza had been transformed into a great open bazaar, a raucous, odoriferous square seething with horses, mules, oxen, wagons, babbling traders and buyers (*"Los Americanos! Los carros! La entrada de la caravana!"* the Mexicans greeted the American traders and their trains of wagons), gamblers with tables for faro, monte, and dice games, beggars, Pueblo Indians selling pots and blankets, watchful Mexican soldiers and town authorities, kids playing under the cottonwoods, and women cooking and baking in open-air ovens. At night, there were the *bailes*—fandangos and other dances to the accompaniment of fiddle, guitar, and drum; on Sundays and feast days, there were cockfights, and *vaqueros* chasing bulls in a wild game called the *coleo*, in which the horseman attempted to overturn a running bull by seizing it by its tail.

For a decade, Americans with their goods and money were welcome in the teeming capital and no frontiersman who visited the place in "the earlies"—before the war with Mexico—ever forgot the experience. In 1826, when he was seventeen, Kit Carson had run away from home and work in Franklin, Missouri, to join a Santa Fé trade train as a "cavvy"—horse wrangler. As he rode with his employers into the town for the first time, the Mexicans shouted at the small and frail figure, *"Un muchacho Americano! Mira!"*—"Look at the American boy!" He loved the town, and New Mexico, as no other place in his life of wanderings.

With its newfound prosperity and flow of American and Canadian traders, mountain men down from the Rockies, mule drivers and bull-whackers, business agents, speculators, smugglers, gamblers, and outlaws, Santa Fé's monied citizenry came to resent the raucous intruders in their once-placid, remote, church-oriented community. It naturally followed that the Americans began finding their own reasons for resentment, particularly over the fickle method of levying tariffs on trade goods brought into the town. In general terms, the Mexican method was to charge what the traffic would bear, send as little as possible to the ruling government in Mexico City, and pocket the balance.

One particular nemesis of the *gringos* in Santa Fé was Manuel Armijo, thrice governor and a man the Americans called "His Obesity." He was a huge, brusque, rapacious character, a former sheep-rustler who had clawed his way from obscurity, who wore a spectacular self-designed uniform with gold epaulets and a helmet with a white ostrich plume as he traveled about his town in a gilded coach. When afoot, he had a propensity for caning any citizen who failed to doff his hat quickly enough in the imperial presence.

Never averse to taking a bribe, Armijo levied outrageous tariffs—

often a flat five-hundred-dollar tax on each wagonload, large and small, of trade goods—and grew rich in the process.

As in the pattern of Texas and California, the Americans, at first welcomed in New Mexico, became worrisome in their numbers and defiant independence, and Mexico City, racked by its own internal tumult, gave scarce attention to its old, remote province and the encroaching dangers it faced.

And now, in the summer of 1846, Governor Armijo, commandante-general of New Mexico, faced the same crisis as his California brethren, José Castro and Pío Pico: the Americans were on the march and there was little he could do but plan his escape.

2

Doniphan's Missourians cleared their camp on August 1 and proceeded south in advance of the main army to the Purgatoire River, first leg of the hundred-mile march to Ratón Pass, gateway to Santa Fé. Kearny led the balance of the force past the walls of Bent's Fort the next day.

All made slow progress in the suffocating heat, which rose on several days to 120° as horses, pack animals, and wagon bullocks lumbered along the waterless trail through mesquite and prickly pear, a hot wind carrying a pumice-fine dust that scoured eyes and clogged noses and throats. Some of the animals collapsed, wagons overturned, and gun limbers fell off the trail, to be labored aright by cursing teamsters and soldiers, many of whom themselves fell, prostrated by heat and exhaustion.

As each sweltering day waned, water and forage parties fanned out into the scrub to find likely campsites; cook fires were lit, half-rations and half-cups of tepid water from dwindling casks were doled out, and sentries posted. At nightfall, the Army of the West fell into a fatigued sleep wrapped in their blankets in the welcome night chill. The wolves and coyotes, after following the army from afar during the day, came closer, brushes up, sniffing the edges of the camp, howling into the starry night, awaiting the time when they could scramble and scavenge among the scraps left behind.

A hundred hard miles out of Bent's, the army made its ascent of Ratón Pass, the rarified air at seventy-five hundred feet and the narrow, unstable trail slowing the march to as little as a mile a day. From the summit could be seen a brilliant panorama: the Wah-to-Yah to the northwest, and beyond it the peak named for its discoverer, Zebulon Pike; the white-capped Sangre de Cristos (Blood of Christ) mountains on the southwest; and directly below, where the pass debouched, piney hills, fields of wildflowers and corn, a sluggish stream or two winding through red earthbanks, and, visible through the officers' telescopes, the heat-shimmered, mirage-like outlines of old adobe villages.

The descent of the pass, only slightly less painstaking and dangerous than the climb, was accomplished on August 14, and on that day a Mexican officer and an escort of three lancers rode into Kearny's camp to deliver a message from the governor-general of New Mexico. Armijo acknowledged having received the colonel's demand for surrender but said he intended leading his people in arms to resist the invasion and suggested that he and Kearny meet in the village of Las Vegas to discuss there vital matters.

Kearny asked the officer to convey a message to the governor: "The road to Santa Fé is now as free to you as to myself. Say to General Armijo I shall soon meet him, and I hope it will be as friends."

They were never to meet.

❁

All manner of rumor—none of it dependable—had reached Kearny from the time he departed Bent's Fort to his march south to Las Vegas, sixteen miles from the foot of Ratón Pass. There were stories that two thousand Pueblo Indians were being armed to help defend Santa Fé—very reminiscent of the rumors of General Castro's enlisting Indians in California. Other tales said that the citizenry of the entire province was rushing to assist in repelling the

American invaders, that Mexico had dispatched a force of dragoons to reinforce Armijo's garrison, that the Americans would have to fight for every inch of ground on the road to the capital. The warnings became so alarming that several of Kearny's officers who had been left behind at Bent's rushed out to intercept him and offer their services. (One of them brought news of Kearny's official promotion to brigadier general.)

In fact, Armijo, who appealed to the military commanders of Chihuahua and Durango for reinforcements and was promised assistance, received none; as well, most of the citizenry of about sixty thousand—as in California—were either ignorant of the invasion because of their remoteness from the seat of government in Santa Fé, apathetic about it, or in favor of American intervention.

In Las Vegas, Kearny issued a blunt proclamation that was posted in two languages at every village on his route of march to the capital. "I have come amongst you by the orders of my government, to take possession of your country and extend over it the laws of the United States," he said. "We come amongst you as friends—not as enemies; as protectors—not as conquerors."

He "absolved" the citizenry of all allegiance to Mexico and General Armijo and announced that he, Stephen Watts Kearny, was now governor of the new United States territory of New Mexico. He promised religious freedom, protection against thievery and misconduct by his army and from Indian depredations, and pledged safety for all who did not take up arms against him and execution by hanging for all who did.

Captain Philip St. George Cooke, who had escorted James Magoffin to Santa Fé on August 1 to deliver the American ultimatum to Armijo, rejoined Kearny's force on August 15. He reported that the governor and his ninety-man bodyguard had fled the capital into Chihuahua, but, Cooke said, the militia Armijo had raised to defend the province was reported ready to oppose the Americans at Apache Canyon, twelve miles from the capital.

This defense never materialized, and on the morning of August 18, a man named Nicholas Quintaro rode into Kearny's camp astride a mule and shouted, "Armijo and his troops have gone to Hell and the canyon is all clear!" Quintaro, secretary of state in the new government, carried a letter from Acting Governor Juan Bautista Vigil y Alarid welcoming the Americans to New Mexico.

3

On August 18, 1846, fifty days and 850 miles from Fort Leavenworth and in a sudden squall of rain, Lieutenant Thomas C. Hammond of the First Dragoons led the vanguard of the Army of the West into Santa Fé.

The town, with its jumble of low, flat-roofed adobe *jacales,* seemed to fit the "more a prairie-dog village than a capital" description. A few townspeople gathered along the route to the governor's palace to witness the arrival of the Americans, the army and its train of equipage strung out for miles behind Hammond's advance guard. If the townspeople were awed by the spectacle, they made no outward expression of it. Except for the clop and snort of horses and the screech of wagon wheels on ungreased axles, the army rode in silence through the pelting rain.

At the one-story adobe Palace of the Governors, Vigil y Alarid had arranged a thirteen-gun salute to welcome General Kearny and his army and the raising of the American flag over the plaza. After the courtesies and *abrazos,* and wine and brandy served the general and his officers, Kearny read a notice to the governor, his staff, and the townspeople gathered at the entrance to the palace. In it, in proper monotone, he instructed the people of New Mexico to "deliver their arms and surrender absolutely to the government of the United States" and promised protection to the "persons, lives and property" of those who did so, "and in this manner I take this province of New Mexico for the benefit of the United States."

The governor responded, "In the name of the entire department, I swear obedience to the Northern Republic and I tender my respect to its laws and authority."

Kearny was eager to proceed to California but he had duties to perform as the first American governor of New Mexico, and five anxious weeks passed before he could gather his force for the march south and west. He ordered construction of a fort, named Fort Marcy for the secretary of war, above the Santa Fé plaza. He attended mass (he was an Episcopalian) in the St. Francis Cathedral. He conferred with the governor and his staff and met often with his own officers to plan the security of the vast province after he left it. He visited the sick troops at Dr. Griffin's improvised hospital. He pored over the primitive maps of Mexican territory, planning his forthcoming march. He attended to a vast correspondence, keeping his Washington superiors informed of his every plan and pronouncement. He sponsored a public fandango at the palace in which five hundred people attended, dancing what one American described as "a kind of swinging gallopade waltz," and feasting and drinking until dawn.

On August 22, the day another American conqueror, Commodore Robert F. Stockton, was setting up his civil government in California, Kearny issued a more formal proclamation. He declared New Mexico a territory of the United States, repeated his warnings to those who would oppose him and his promises to those who did not. Alexander Doniphan's lawyerly skills were put to work drafting a legal code and bill of rights for the newly annexed region.

Between September 2 and 11, the general, with an ostentatious seven-hundred-man escort, toured the southern settlements—the *Río Abajo*—of New Mexico. In the villages of Bernalillo, Albuquerque, Peralta, San Tomé, and others, he reiterated to local *alcaldes* and *jefes políticos* that he and his army came "as friends, protectors, not as conquerors," and that no one would be molested who tended his fields and herds and did not take up arms. "Not a pepper, not an onion, shall be disturbed or taken by my troops without pay or by the consent of the owner," he said, adding the grave warning, "But listen! He who promises to be quiet, and is found in arms against me, I will hang!"

❖

Last arrangements were made. Garrisons were set up in Santa Fé and several other towns; patrols were sent out to protect New Mexicans from predatory Indians; Charles Bent, a Taos lawyer and one of the founders of Bent's Fort, was selected to serve as the first civilian governor of the territory.

Two of Kearny's support forces—a second regiment of Missouri volunteers commanded by Colonel Sterling Price, and the Mormon Battalion under Captain James Allen—were en route to Santa Fé as the general prepared to leave the capital. He had promised to send surplus troops to Chihuahua to join Brigadier General John E. Wool's force two hundred miles south of the Rio Grande, and he picked Colonel Doniphan to lead the Second Missourians to a rendezvous with Wool. Another favorite officer, Philip St. George Cooke, stayed behind to take command of the Mormon Battalion and march the five hundred volunteers to California. Colonel Price, a well-connected, Virginia-born Missourian who had resigned his seat in the House of Representatives to serve in the war, was designated military governor of New Mexico.

(Three weeks after Kearny departed, Cooke marched his battalion out of Santa Fé with a dozen wagons and oxcarts and moved down the Rio Grande. He led his force along a route considerably south of Kearny's and reached Tucson on December 14 to find that the Mexican garrison there had abandoned the town. With replenished supplies, the Mormons marched north along the Santa Cruz River and in late December, struck the Gila. They struggled into San Diego in the last days of January, 1847, nearly naked and shoeless, but with most of their wagons.)

4

The general departed Santa Fé on September 25, 1846, with three hundred of the First Dragoons, now mounted on mules—he believed them better adapted to the southwestern desert terrain than horses, surer to make what Captain Cooke described as "a leap in the dark of a thousand miles of wild plain and mountain." With Tom Fitzpatrick as guide, the troopers and their pack train moved down the east bank of the Rio Grande to Albuquerque, then crossed to the west bank as they neared the town of Socorro.

The dragoon column made good progress in cool weather down the Rio Grande Valley despite the tendency of the mules to wander off into the lush cornfields and the time taken to haggle with wary villagers in buying food, forage, and spare pack animals. A band of Navajo marauders had recently raided some of the pueblos on the line of march and Kearny sent a patrol ahead to locate them, but to no avail.

On October 6, two hundred miles south of Santa Fé and ten miles below the village of Socorro, there occurred an astonishing coincidence, one that Kearny's biographer said recalled Clotho, Lachesis, and Atropos, the Greek Fates who spun, determined the length, and cut the tread of human destiny.

Kearny, several of his officers, and Fitzpatrick, riding ahead of the column, spotted what appeared to be a large dust devil in the distance, then heard a shout and watched as a band of horsemen galloped toward them. Broken Hand instantly recognized the lead rider as his old comrade of trapping days in the mountains, Kit Carson.

Thirty days earlier, with fifteen men, including six of Frémont's Delawares, and a small pack train, Carson had ridden out of Los Angeles, bound for Washington with dispatches from Commodore Stockton announcing the capture of California. The scout had estimated that the journey would take sixty days, and his "express" party had traveled eight hundred miles over dim or nonexistent trails through hostile country when it spied the dust cloud of Kearny's column.

The meeting between the general and the scout was to be fateful for each, far beyond the coincidental timing of their encounter below Socorro.

Kearny read the dispatches Carson carried and the news stunned him: California had fallen to Stockton and his naval force and Frémont's volunteers. The Mexican governor and commandante-general had fled the province. A civil government under Frémont was in the making. The war in the West was over.

This was crushing news, but Kearny recovered from it in old-army fashion: he had orders and he intended to follow through on them. Four months earlier, the War Department of the United States had instructed him that he was to have "a large discretionary power" in commanding the Army of the West, and that while it was expected that American naval forces would soon be in possession of the coastal towns of California, Secretary Marcy had been clear that the navy would "co-operate with you in the conquest of California." The secretary had stated unequivocally what he expected of the general: "Should you conquer and take possession of New Mexico and Upper California, or considerable places in either, you will establish temporary civil governments therein. . . ."

Half of that assignment had been accomplished. He had conquered New Mexico and organized the rudiments of a new civil governance under Charles Bent. Carson's news did not alter his essential plan to proceed to California to attend to the other half of his orders, to assume governmental responsibilities there. True, since Stockton and Frémont had already pacified the province, certain adjustments would have to be made, and in his command tent in a cottonwood grove on the Rio Grande, Kearny worked out the details.

He now needed only a modest escort to proceed to California. With fewer men, he could travel faster and worry less about finding game, water, and forage en route. Carson warned that the southern route into Los Angeles lay across harsh, arid terrain, pitiless to man and animal alike, and that heavy wagons could not negotiate the primitive trails.

Kearny trusted Carson's information and cut his force by two-thirds, sending two hundred of his dragoons back to Santa Fé to join Doniphan's force preparing to march into Chihuahua. He retained two companies, C and K, of the First Dragoons, a hundred men under Captain Benjamin D. Moore and Lieutenant Thomas C. Hammond, and two mule-drawn mountain howitzers. The supply and baggage wagons were sent back to Santa Fé, and the officers returning there carried orders that packsaddles and additional mules were to be brought down to join the line of march.

Kearny also ordered Kit Carson to guide him and his foreshortened dragoon force back to California. This order made perfect sense: Carson knew the lay of the land between the Rio Grande and Los Angeles, was familiar with it from times past, had, in fact, just traveled it. He knew the water, game, and forage sources, knew the hazards, knew the dangers of moving through Apache lands. What better guide than Kit Carson, who only a month ago had departed California, had been intimately involved in its conquest, knew the Californios and their vast province from Klamath Lake on the north to San Diego on the south?

Kearny had no dependable maps; he needed the maps, and the experience, in Carson's brain.

But the issue was weightier than these practical elements. In ordering Carson to guide him, the general made the first overt assertion that he commanded all the American military forces in the Mexican territories of the West. He had orders and believed they were explicit on this. Those orders did not mention Stockton or Frémont, or any other officer superior to or superseding him.

Nor did he give a moment's pause in nullifying Stockton's orders to Carson to carry dispatches to Washington. The answer to that was simple: Tom Fitzpatrick could deliver the papers to the capital.

Carson must have wished he had taken a slightly more northern route out of Los Angeles, thereby bypassing the Army of the West entirely. He had come eight hundred miles through lean and dry country, he and his men at the edge of starvation, subsisting on parched corn, before striking the Rio Grande Valley. He was 250 miles from his home in Taos, from seeing his wife Josefa, and his children, for the first time in fourteen months since he left her to join Frémont at Bent's Fort for the California expedition. He had intended to take his men to Taos for rest and recuperation before continuing on east. Now he was ordered to go west again.

He protested to Kearny, but while the general later admitted that Carson was "at first very unwilling to turn back," he said that the scout, after being told that Fitzpatrick would carry the dispatches, "was perfectly satisfied with that and so told me." John S. Griffin, the dragoon surgeon, recorded in his journal that Kearny's force turned west "with merry hearts & light packs on our long march—Carson as guide, every man feeling renewed confidence in consequence of having such a guide." Captain Abraham Johnston, regimental adjutant, commented in his diary: "It requires a brave man to give up his private feelings thus for the public good; but Carson was one such! Honor to him for it."

If he was angry, which is likely, Carson left no evidence of it in his own dictated recollections. He was never much of a protester even as a civilian attached to the army, when he might have given notice and simply quit when inconvenienced. In truth, when it came to the military, Kit was a born follower and now, as an officer of the California Battalion and officially mustered into the service, he could scarcely disobey the orders of a general. He said, "On the 6th of October, '46, I met General Kearny on his march to California. He ordered me to join him as guide. I done so and Fitzpatrick continued on with the dispatches."

On October 15, after Fitzpatrick and most of Carson's express party had headed east, the scout rode west with the general, his officers, and dragoons from the cottonwood-grove bivouac below Socorro. With the small force and pack train, the journey, for all the difficulties of the trail, would be swift. Everyone knew that California, like New Mexico, had been conquered and was at peace, but the general had his orders: he had work to do and was anxious to get it done.

❈

CHAPTER FIFTEEN

Los Angeles

1

A month passed before Kearny heard news of it, but as he led his dragoons west from Socorro, a counterrevolt in California had stalled the conquest. At the time Kit Carson and his express party had departed Pueblo de los Ángeles in early September, the reports he carried had assured President Polk and the War Department that the province had been annexed and pacified, and it had been on this intelligence that the general had reduced his Army of the West by two-thirds.

The pacification had lasted five weeks, from August 17, when Commodore Stockton read his proclamation declaring California a territory of the United States, until September 23, the day Kearny marched south out of Santa Fé with three hundred dragoons. On that day, a tiny band of insurgents had besieged the American garrison in Los Angeles.

At the root of the problem lay Stockton's insensitivity and inattention. California had fallen far too easily to the restless commodore and his lethargic predecessor, John D. Sloat. Calling the annexation a "conquest" was certainly hyperbolic; there had been no war, no battle, no "campaign" to win the land. Sailing up and down the coast, raising flags, firing salutes, and reading proclamations to the dumbfounded citizenry did not comprise an ambitious officer's idea of military glory. Stockton had quickly tired of California; he had no interest in serving as its military governor and he turned his attention to his splendid scheme of raising a thousand volunteers and marching to Mexico City.

Nor did the commodore attempt to understand the Californios. Unlike Sloat, whose public pronouncements were unthreatening and studiously diplomatic, and who listened to men such as Thomas O. Larkin, who knew the land and its people, Stockton's approach was that of an impatient patriarch toward unruly children. He sought no counsel, issued belligerent statements and harsh orders, and while paying lip service to the "rights" of the new American citizens, plainly regarded them simply as a conquered people meekly willing to toe whatever line he drew for them. He seemed ignorant of the essential key to their contentment: the Californios had no loyalty to Mexico and its age-old policy of benign neglect, and while Los Angeles was the center of what little anti-American feeling existed in the province, it was at best a lukewarm hotbed. There existed what H. H. Bancroft called a "turbulent, lawless, and hitherto uncontrollable" element among the *abajeños* but little interest in the internecine rivalry between their *jefes políticos* and those in the north. In general, the Californios were willing to abide American annexation—indeed, many influentials openly championed it—provided their way of life could proceed unchallenged by unnecessary American rules.

Stockton had assured that this simple requirement would be denied when he assigned Marine Brevet Captain Archibald H. Gillespie to succeed Frémont as military commandant of Los Angeles.

The career marine had qualities that attracted Stockton as they had Frémont, who had been impressed with Gillespie from the moment they had first met at Klamath Lake in May, 1846, and who had subsequently selected him as adjutant of the California Battalion. He had been the perfect courier for President Polk and the Secretary of the Navy. He was courageous and imaginative in carrying dispatches and orders across hostile Mexico to Mazatlán, Monterey, and to Frémont in northern California. He had fought Indians alongside Frémont's men, and had been successful in the several missions entrusted to him. He was fluent in Spanish.

Now age forty-three, with fifteen years of service and still only a lieutenant of marines, Gillespie's weaknesses emerged fully when he was left in command of Los Angeles with a garrison of forty-eight men. The taste of power seemed to infuse him with the Marine Corps spirit, which a century later was described as "gung ho." He took control with a will, became imperious, quick-tempered, and tactless. He regarded Mexicans in general as a cowardly, inferior people, and his ill-concealed contempt for the Californios fit perfectly the attitudes of Frémont and his men, and of Stockton and his. Gillespie, now commanding men who had served with both Frémont and Stockton, was as drunk on power as the men were drunk on *aguardiente*.

The instructions he had received were simple: he was to "maintain military rule" in accordance with the commodore's proclamation and to be lenient with citizens "well-disposed" toward the United States, exempting them from the burdensome rules directed at the more recalcitrant populace. But Gillespie ignored these niceties and from his Government House headquarters, wrote orders like a man accustomed only to taking orders. He issued directives on enforcing curfews, closing shops at sundown, searching homes for weapons, outlawing gatherings in private homes, forbidding even family reunions in homes. He made it illegal for liquor to be sold without his permission, illegal for two people to walk in the streets together, illegal to gallop a horse across the plaza. He ordered the breaking up of fandangos—which he apparently felt were opportunities for the gathering of malcontents. He presided over and decided petty lawbreaking cases instead of leaving them to local magistrates. He freely used the word "rebel" in his adjudications, imposed fines, jailed perceived offenders without hearings.

After five weeks of obnoxious regulations and frivolous arrests, Gillespie's satrapy succeeded in igniting the damp tinder of revolt in Los Angeles.

Rumors of an insurrection in the planning reached the marine and his men weeks before the first overt sign of it. A militia captain named Cérbulo Varela, described by Bancroft as "a wild and unmanageable young fellow, though not a bad man at heart," gathered around him a number of like-minded "irresponsible fellows" and announced that he and his friends would not submit to the American's police-like rules. Varela and his street toughs seem to have harassed Gillespie's enforcers, yet remained out of range of capture while stirring discontent among the Angelinos.

In mid-September, in response to the burgeoning trouble, Gillespie made a fatal mistake. He divided his meager force by sending a detachment of nineteen men under Ezekial Merritt to San Diego, which had been left ungarrisoned. Merritt and his men had been gone a week when, before dawn on September 23, 1846, Varela and twenty of his ruffians made a noisy assault on the barracks building housing the remainder of Gillespie's men. The insurgents were apparently hoping that by firing a few shots in the air, beating drums, and shouting, they could roust the Americans and force their surrender. The ploy did not work and Varela and his rebels were chased off with a rifle volley. When the smoke cleared, however, the comic attack on the barracks had produced the result Varela hoped for: a swelling of the rebel ranks from among the numerous Californios who had held their tempers in check during the weeks of what they considered a suffocating governance. People began digging up the guns they had buried, and within days of his first sortie Varela had three hundred men in his ragged command, divided into bands, each with a "captain" in charge, several of these veteran officers officially "under parole" and pledged not to serve against the Americans.

The growing rebel force gathered at La Mesa, one of José Castro's old camps east of the village, and soon other leaders emerged. Captain José María Flores, an intelligent, professional military man, was elected *mayor general* of the insurgent force; Flores' second in command was José Antonio Carrillo, former *alcalde* of Los Angeles and a veteran intriguer against several governors of the province; and a third man, destined to loom larger than the others in the events to follow, was Captain Andrés Pico, now *commandante de escuadrón* (squadron commander), age thirty-six and the younger brother of the departed Governor Pío Pico.

On September 24, the insurgents issued their own proclamation, addressed to the "Citizenry" of California and signed by Varela and over three hundred others. The rebels said that "we see ourselves subjugated and oppressed by an insignificant force of adventurers from the U.S. of N. America, who, putting us in a condition worse than that of slaves, are dictating to us despotic and arbitrary laws. . . ." The manifesto, redolent of Pico's exit oratory and somewhat more portentous than those written by Stockton and Gillespie, called for freedom from "the heavy chains of slavery" and warned that the American oppressors intended "barbarous servitude" for native Californians. "Shall we wait to see our wives violated, our innocent children beaten by the American whip, our property sacked, our temples profaned, to drag out a life full of shame and disgrace? No! A thousand times no!"

A call to arms followed, asking all citizens from age fifteen to sixty to join in repelling the invaders and branding as traitors those who did not take up the fight.

The issuance of this document was accompanied by a demand that the Americans surrender. Gillespie now busied his men with unspiking four old cannons they had captured in August and in gathering what ammunition and powder he could find while awaiting developments from among the rebels.

On September 24, Gillespie dispatched John "Juan Flaco" Brown to Monterey with urgent messages scribbled on cigarette papers that were balled up and placed in the express rider's hair. Brown stopped at Santa Barbara to warn Lieutenant Theodore Talbot of the trouble brewing in Los Angeles, then proceeded to Yerba Buena with Gillespie's message to Stockton that Los Angeles was under siege.

The Americans held their position for several days after slipping out of Government House to the nearby gun emplacements at Fort Hill, an unreconnoitered position that was found to be waterless. Meantime, General Flores renewed his surrender demands and generously offered to permit Gillespie and his men to march out of town unmolested, taking their small arms with them, and proceed to San Pedro Bay, where they could board a merchant ship to remove them from California waters.

On about September 29, Gillespie accepted Flores' offer and surrendered. Five days later, he embarked with his force on the merchant vessel *Vandalia*.

In Santa Barbara, a small band that had split off the growing insurgent force in Los Angeles demanded the surrender of Theodore Talbot and his nine-man garrison. The lieutenant, one of Frémont's trusted adjutants and original exploration-party members, escaped with his men and lurked in the mountains within sight of the town for a week, hoping that an American man-of-war might arrive to rescue them. When none appeared, they crossed into the interior valley and pushed on to Monterey, a patrol of Californios snapping at their heels. They arrived there exhausted, starving, their clothes in rags, on November 8 and rejoined Frémont and his men, who had entered the town a few days before on the American trader *Sterling*.

In the old hide-and-tallow depot of San Diego, Zeke Merritt and his dozen men were joined by Sutter's majordomo John Bidwell and a handful of other American sympathizers. They fled the town upon the arrival of a party of fifty of General Flores' insurgents and boarded the commercial whaler *Stonington*, at anchor in the bay.

3

Stockton's Acapulco—Mexico City scheme evaporated on October 1. That day, Skinny John Brown, after a ride of five hundred miles in seven days, reached Yerba Buena on the last of a string of blown horses and delivered the news of the impending fall of Los Angeles.

The commodore, poring over his charts in the cabin of the *Congress*, received Brown's report dubiously but cleared his table and called his officers to a war council. He dispatched Captain William Mervine of the *Savannah* to reinforce the Los Angeles garrison; he also sent a courier to Frémont's camp near Sutter's Fort ordering the explorer to bring his California Battalion down to San Francisco Bay.

The *Savannah* reached San Pedro Bay on October 6 and found Gillespie and his men still aboard the *Vandalia* awaiting rescue. The next day, Mervine landed 350 sailors and marines on the beach, was joined there by Gillespie and his men, and began the march north toward Los Angeles. The expedition was poorly planned and ill-equipped, Mervine apparently having been infected with the prevailing belief that the Californios would run for the hills upon the approach of an American force. The sailors were armed with an assortment of muskets, cutlasses, belaying pins, and boarding pikes; no cannons had been taken from the *Savannah*, although several light, manageable ones were available. Mervine had no horses, no ambulance wagons, no supply train, and knew nothing of the terrain or the numbers and deployment of the rebel force. Gillespie later said that the captain was "without reason," and indeed, the two officers were at instant odds, Mervine accusing the marine of unprofessional, even criminal, conduct in surrendering his garrison.

After a few hours' march from the beach, the Americans began spotting mounted men in the distance, watching their advance. A few random shots were exchanged but Mervine and his force reached the Domínguez rancho, an outpost about fifteen miles from Los Angeles, without serious incident.

General José Flores had been able to mount about two hundred men in the week since Gillespie's surrender and had taken a wise precaution in herding all horses and cattle inland to deprive the Americans of them. While his force, equipped with lances, swords, skinning knives, and old muskets and pistols buried or hidden during the American takeover, was nearly as poorly armed as Mervine's, it did have a cannon. This ancient brass four-pounder, used for ceremonial salutes, had been buried in the garden of one Inocencia Reyes, exhumed, and mounted on a makeshift, horse-drawn limber. Flores and his second in command, Colonel José Carrillo, rode out with an advance guard to harass the American advance, and on October 8, 1846, just north of Rancho Domínguez, the engagement known as the "Battle of the Old Woman's Gun" took place.

The rebel tactics were simple and effective: the four-pounder was placed athwart the road on which the Americans had to advance; long ropes were lashed to the limber by which the gun could be pulled into the brush for reloading. Flores and Carillo deployed their horsemen at a safe distance from the roadway on the flanks of the approaching enemy.

Mervine's force advanced in close columns on the narrow trail, with Gillespie and his men serving as skirmishers on the flanks, all the men bunched up and vulnerable, with no reconnaissance to determine the enemy number and whereabouts. When they came within four hundred yards of the rebel position, the old fieldpiece was fired and quickly yanked back into the brush, followed by a ragged volley of musket fire from Flores' flankers.

The first several cannon shots were ineffective because of the weak homemade powder used, but inevitably, with the Americans clotted along the trail, the four-pound balls did some damage, as did the rebels' musketry. Mervine, who had placed his troops in square formation—the classic defense against cavalry—was helpless with his men afoot against a virtually unseen and uncounted enemy. With a dozen serious casualties, no place to hide, and no chance to advance on Los Angeles, he turned his force back to San Pedro Bay and reboarded the *Savannah*. After a few days, the warship sailed north to Monterey.

The "battle" had lasted less than an hour; four of the twelve Americans struck by ball and bullet died of their wounds and were buried on a little island in San Pedro Bay, perfectly named Isla de los Muertos (Island of the Dead).

❁

Frémont meantime had gathered his 170 men and reported to Stockton at Yerba Buena. Many of the men were afoot. Horses were becoming scarce in the north and both officers counted on finding mounts once they reached Santa Barbara, seventy miles upcoast from Los Angeles.

Stockton needed to get to sea and retake what Gillespie had lost, and on October 12, the day after Frémont arrived, he took the *Congress* out through the Golden Gate, Frémont and his men following on the chartered trader *Sterling*. But a day out and in a heavy fog, the *Sterling* lost sight of the flagship and all plans went awry. Stockton went on to Monterey, learned that the small garrison there feared a rebel attack, and left reinforcements. He proceeded to San Pedro and reached the bay on October 23. Mervine had returned there on the *Savannah* a few days earlier and Stockton learned the details of the recent encounter with Flores' rebels. Over the next couple of days, eight hundred sailors, marines, and Gillespie's volunteers were landed at San Pedro. Stockton then moved on to San Diego to set up a base of operations for the campaign against Flores, to drill and train his sailors, and to scour the countryside and send patrols into Baja California to locate horses and livestock.

(Antonio María Osio of Monterey said that Stockton's efforts in San Diego were abetted by "corrupt Californios and some Mexican traitors" who offered supplies to the commodore "so that he could increase his ranks and resources in the war he was fighting against the men whom they should have regarded as their brothers." Osio said that these turncoats were blinded by ambition and that "if those men had been Americans, Señor Stockton, a patriotic and upright man, would have hanged them like bunches of grapes from every yardarm of his frigate's main mast.")

After the false start, Frémont and his men proceeded toward Santa Barbara on the *Sterling,* but en route met the *Vandalia,* the merchant ship on which Gillespie and his men had taken refuge upon surrendering the Los Angeles garrison. After learning from the merchant skipper of Mervine's failure to retake Los Angeles and that the rebels had run all horses and cattle inland, Frémont ordered the *Sterling* to reverse course for Monterey. There he hoped to gather horses and increase his volunteer force for an overland march to Los Angeles to join with Stockton, whose exact whereabouts for the moment were unknown.

Frémont's return to Monterey on October 27 and the three weeks he tarried there removed him and his men from the theater of operations between San Diego and Los Angeles, but he did not waste the time. Mervine's experience against Flores proved that the insurgents were perhaps more numerous than anybody had estimated.

From his headquarters in Monterey, Frémont, who received word there of his promotion to the brevet rank of lieutenant colonel of the army, sent express riders north with letters to Captain Montgomery of the *Portsmouth* in San Francisco Bay and to Ned Kern at Sutter's Fort. These messages requested that volunteers and horses be massed and made ready to join Frémont's force in Monterey. This recruiting effort, with Sutter's as the main depot, and with the efforts of Kern and Lieutenant Revere in Sonoma, produced nearly two hundred men, including a number of Paiute and Walla Walla Indians. These mounted volunteers and a remuda of spare horses and mules came south to Frémont toward the end of November.

While the explorer awaited reinforcements, Ezekial Merritt, John Bidwell, and two dozen men were landed from the whaler *Stonington* a short distance from San Diego and wrestled the three small cannons appropriated from the ship to the outskirts of the town. Flores' men discovered them and set up a desultory fire, but after the pieces banged a few times, the rebels vanished into the brush and Merritt and his tiny force reoccupied San Diego. They raised the flag in the town plaza and nervously held their position until the end of October, when Stockton and Mervine arrived in the bay with their warships and the town was secured once and for all.

The commodore's main order of business was to find horses, saddle-rigging, mules, and cattle; armed patrols fanned out into the countryside and others shipped to the Baja California coast to gather the animals and equipage. One of these expeditions succeeded in gathering a hundred forty head of horses and five hundred of cattle, but did not return until late December.

While Stockton was establishing his base in San Diego and preparing to march north and Frémont was gathering his force in Monterey for a march south, General José Flores was also regrouping. At an assembly convened in Los Angeles, he had been elected governor and military commander of California, but the added power did nothing to alleviate his problems. He had no funds with which to pay his men—regulars and unenthusiastic volunteers, about four hundred in all; he was running low on powder and ammunition and had to operate with an inadequate supply train. He had also divided his force into thin units, a hundred men under General José Castro at San Luís Obispo, between Monterey and Santa Barbara, to watch for the advance of Frémont's force, another hundred under Captain Andrés Pico to guard the eastern approaches to San Diego, and the remainder of the men—less than two hundred—in Flores' own command, camped near Los Angeles to counter, as best they could, either Stockton or Frémont, or both.

One significant encounter between the Americans and Californios occurred during this November regrouping period and involved the United States consul in Monterey, Thomas O. Larkin. He rode out of Monterey for Yerba Buena after receiving news that his four-year-old daughter Adeline was seriously ill there. He was aware of the danger of the journey, knew that he might be taken prisoner in retaliation for General Vallejo's capture in Sonoma, and during the night of November 15, while staying with friends in San Juan Bautista, his worst fears were realized. He was captured by Castro's troops and taken to the general's camp on the Salinas River, within view of Frémont's old battlements on Hawk's Peak.

As these events unfolded, there arrived in San Juan a force of California Battalion men out of Sutter's Fort, bringing five hundred head of horses and mules to Colonel Frémont in Monterey. As the advance guard of the battalion advanced toward the Salinas and reached a rancho called La Natividad, they were met by a patrol of 130 Californians—with their prisoner Larkin among them. The melee that ensued, later called the "Battle of La Natividad," cost the lives of five to seven Americans, two Californians, and several wounded on each side. Larkin was unhurt but was not released from captivity for a month. In that period, Adeline Larkin died in Yerba Buena.

Frémont got news of the skirmish as he prepared to depart Monterey; he took his men north the thirty miles to the San Juan Bautista outskirts to gather his new recruits and the horses and mules they had herded. He spent two weeks there as reinforcements continued to arrive from the Sacramento Valley, bringing with them more horses and pack animals.

At last, on November 30, in a thunderstorm that instantly turned the dirt trail into a muddy swamp, he was ready to strike out toward Los Angeles. He led an army of 430 men, three artillery pieces, and nearly two thousand horses and mules.

❧

Frémont and his cumbersome force were still slogging down the Salinas River Valley, three days out of San Juan Bautista, when Commodore Stockton, in San Diego, received a letter, brought in by an express rider, from Brigadier General S.W. Kearny of the United States Army. The general informed the commodore that he was approaching the city from the east and asked about the state of affairs in California.

Stockton sent for Gillespie, gave him quick orders to select a number of good horsemen and ride out to meet Kearny and his men. Gillespie led his patrol out of San Diego in the early evening of December 3, 1846.

CHAPTER SIXTEEN

❋

San Pascual

1

Stephen Watts Kearny received the news that California had been annexed with his customary stoicism, but it shocked him. The miraculous convergence of his path down the Rio Grande Valley with that of Kit Carson and his escort on October 6, a month out of Los Angeles, seemed a wicked trick of fate. He had come a thousand cruel miles at the head of an army and raised the flag of the United States over the old province of New Mexico. Now, the second half of his objective had been snatched from him by the navy, a gang of topographical explorers, and a handful of malcontents calling themselves Bear Flaggers.

Carson could be trusted. He told of the capture of Sonoma and the subsequent surrender of Monterey, of the occupation of San Francisco Bay and Los Angeles, matter-of-factly. The Californians had folded pitifully. Carson said they were cowardly, had no means to resist and, worse, no will.

Carson's news dictated a new course of action. The general still had responsibilities in California, now political rather than military. His orders were to take over command there, and with the navy's cooperation, establish a civil government and serve as proconsul. The War Department was shipping another army unit

around Cape Horn to California, commanded by Richard B.
Mason, colonel of the First Dragoons, and Mason would succeed
Kearny as military governor when the general was satisfied that the
entire territory had been pacified.

He now needed only an armed escort to travel through Indian
country and so sent back to Santa Fé two hundred of his three hundred dragoons and all but two fieldpieces, and cut his supply train
to the bone, trading his wagons for packsaddles. He retained
only the First Dragoon companies, under Captain Benjamin D.
Moore and Lieutenant Thomas C. Hammond, the latter married
to Moore's sister. His other officers were Captain Henry Smith
Turner, acting assistant adjutant general; Captain Abraham R.
Johnston, aide-de-camp; Major Thomas Swords, quartermaster;
lieutenants William H. Emory and William H. Warner, topographical engineers; Lieutenant John W. Davidson, in charge of the two
mountain howitzers; and assistant surgeon John S. Griffin. A dozen
assistants and servants were selected to accompany the escort,
and the French-Canadian Antoine Robidoux, a veteran tracker, remained the principal guide, with Kit Carson his associate.

On October 15, Robidoux and Carson led Kearny and his escort, most of them mounted on mules, and the pack train southwest
toward the Santa Rita del Cobre country, inhabited by Mimbreño
Apaches. The trail was an ancient one, used by Spaniards and Mexicans traveling to and from California, and it cut through wilderness both weirdly beautiful and forbidding: in the first few days, a
lushly green country of oaks, ash, and walnut trees, and aspens on
the higher ground, the Mimbres range and other mountains to the
north; then rock-strewn desert, countless bone-dry arroyos, great
canyons, mesas disappearing into the horizon, yucca and Joshua
trees and all manner of cactus, some hugging the ground with ten-
tacles spread seeking moisture, others squat and fat and decorated
with gorgeous flowers, still others tall and stately, like sentinels
with arms pointing skyward, their hides pocked with bird holes.
There were occasional grassy stretches along the old roadway, and
small streams and rivulets and great cottonwood copses, but these

were rare, and water and forage were daily problems for man and beast.

On October 20, five days out of the Socorro camp, the Americans crossed the Continental Divide and reached the southernmost branch of the Gila River, where they made camp, and watered their stock. Before starting out the next morning, Kearny and his officers were startled when a band of twenty Apaches—Mimbres men led by their great chief Mangas Coloradas (Red Sleeves)—rode into the camp. Through sign language and what Apache-Spanish Kearny's officers could understand, Mangas said that his visit was peaceful and assured them they could pass through his country unmolested. He knew that Kearny had captured Santa Fé and he was delighted—the Apaches and Mexicans were ancient enemies, slaughtering each other since conquistador times—suggesting to the general that he join forces with the Apaches and conquer all of northern Mexico. Kearny politely declined and after many hours of bartering with the band for a few mules, the march was resumed and Mangas led his men south into the hills.

❀

In early November, the trail threaded through scattered villages of the Pima and Maricopa tribes, some of them with irrigated patches of land growing corn, wheat, beans, melons, and squash. The Pimas were especially friendly and when Carson tried to barter with a chief, he was told that "bread is to eat, not to sell; take what you want." But there were no horses or cattle available and the Americans were able to gain only a few bony mules, these from a Coyotero Apache band.

They rode on, twenty or thirty miles a day, depending on water and graze and the state of fatigue of the men and animals, fording streams and arroyos—dismantling the guns and their carriages each time—climbing rocky hills, trudging across miles of deep sand that bogged the heavily laden mules and fieldpieces. Each day, men in advance of the main column searched for water, grass, and suitable campsites, and each night, after the animals were fed and picketed, the men ate their frugal meal and fell exhausted into their bedrolls.

The tedium of the march was broken on November 22 when the column reached a point ten miles from the confluence of the Gila and Colorado rivers. The advance guard had discovered near a pueblo ruins fresh remains of an abandoned camp. The size of the camp and the countless hoofprints around it seemed to indicate that a large number of horses had been there, tended by a few men.

After the two mountain guns were brought forward, Kearny dispatched Lieutenant Emory and a detail of riders to investigate, and ten miles downtrail, they discovered a dust cloud caused by a *caballada* of at least five hundred animals. Emory and his men took four Mexican herders prisoner with no resistance and brought them to Kearny's camp to be questioned. "Each gave a different account of the ownership and destination of the horses," Emory wrote, and while it appears that the animals were headed from California to Sonora to be sold, many of the dragoon officers were convinced that the horse herd belonged to General José Castro.

Of far more importance than the captured horses was the alarming news related by one of the Mexican prisoners that there had been a revolution in Los Angeles and the pueblo had been taken back from the Americans. This astonishing story was substantiated the next day when Emory captured a courier carrying dispatches to Castro in the Sonoran capital. The papers were unsealed, found to be dated October 15 and containing details of a counterrevolt that had "thrown off the detestable Anglo-Yankee yoke." Castro was informed that Pueblo de Los Ángeles, Santa Barbara, and other towns in the southern province were again in the hands of the Californians and that General Flores had defeated the American naval officer Mervine at San Pedro.

The news in the captured dispatches was five weeks old and Kearny had no idea of what might have happened in the interim, but one thing seemed clear: the Californians had been misjudged.

Kearny had no intention of taking prisoners and did not need five hundred wild horses. The captured dispatches had transformed his hundred-man dragoon force into a flying column and he was restless, fretting over every hour spent off the trail, desperate to discover the state of affairs in California. He freed the horse herders, even resealing and returning the dispatches to the courier, and in a gentlemanly and unwarlike gesture, purchased twenty-five of the tamest animals and a few mules and gave the Mexicans some tea, coffee, and sugar from his meager stores.

On November 25, the dragoons found a suitable ford on the Colorado, a place where the river, nearly a half-mile wide, ran less than four feet deep. Because Carson had advised that the grass and mesquite thinned out a short distance from the river, the mules were loaded with forage and bags of mesquite pods after the laborious crossing. Ahead lay desert country and within two days of the Colorado crossing, Kearny's men were digging deep into the sand in dry streambeds looking for water seepage. The four-day crossing of the desert cost the lives of several of the 250 mules and horses in the expedition, but the dragoons found water and graze at Carrizo Creek, struggled through a gap in the foothills of the Vallecitos Mountains, and in the mid-afternoon of December 2, reached Warner's Ranch, fifty miles northeast of San Diego, the first trace of civilization the Americans had seen since leaving the Rio Grande Valley on their "thousand-mile leap" fifty days ago.

The ranch and nearby springs lay on the Agua Caliente land grant awarded in 1844 to Jonathan Trumbull Warner of Lyme, Connecticut, who had served with Jedediah Smith's 1831 trading expedition to New Mexico (during which Smith was killed by Comanches). Warner was a naturalized citizen of Mexican California and had a fifteen-year history in the province. Carson knew "Juan Largo" Warner (Long John stood six-foot-three), and Kearny was anxious to meet the proprietor of the remote way station, but Warner was away on business when the dragoons reached the springs.

There they were greeted by Juan Largo's factotum, an American named Marshall. With men and animals watered and fed and the camp made, Marshall told Kearny and his officers all he knew: the Californians had taken control of much of the southern province; the Americans still held the ports of San Francisco, Monterey, and San Diego. A neighboring Englishman, a former sea captain named Edward Stokes, came to the Warner ranchhouse and confirmed this information. He said he was on his way to San Diego and offered to carry with him any messages Kearny wished delivered to Commodore Stockton.

On December 2, Kearny wrote to Stockton from "Headquarters, Army of the West, camp at Warner's":

> Sir: I this afternoon reached here, escorted by a party of 1st regiment dragoons. I came by order of the pres. of the U.S. We left Santa Fe on the 25th Sept., having taken possession of N. Mex., annexed it to the U.S., established a civil govt in that territory, and secured order, peace and quietness there. If you can send a party to open communication with us on the route to this place, and to inform me of the state of affairs in Cal., I wish you would do so, and as quickly as possible. The fear of this letter falling into Mexican hands prevents me from writing more. Your express by Mr Carson was met on the Del Norte; and your mail must have reached Washington at least 10 days since. . . . Very respectfully . . .

Kearny's letter, in announcing that his arrival was upon direct orders of the President of the United States, contained the hint that he now commanded the American forces in California. He made no mention of the strength of his "party," of the fact that he had given Stockton's dispatches to Tom Fitzpatrick "on the Del Norte," or that he had ordered Carson to turn back and guide the Army of the West to California.

Stockton's reply, dated on the evening of the third and reaching Kearny on December 5, said that Captain Gillespie, a detachment of mounted riflemen, and a fieldpiece were proceeding "without delay" to intercept the general and his force and that "Capt. G. is well informed in relation to the present state of things in Cal., and will give you all needful information." The note contained its own hint of who was in charge: it was signed "Robt. Stockton, commander-in-chief and governor of the territory of California, etc."

※

Kearny and his dragoons made their way south from Warner's ranch in a flogging rain on December 4, taking the entire day to snail along the swampy roadway the fifteen miles to Stokes' Santa Ysabel property, where a hot dinner was prepared for them by the Englishman's majordomo and Indian workers.

The thunderstorm had not abated the next morning when the march resumed toward some rugged hills in the west and the Indian village of San Pascual, but after a few hours on the trail, Stockton's promise was fulfilled: the dragoons, making their way through an oak grove, met outriders from Archibald Gillespie's detachment of thirty-five sailors, marines, and volunteers from the *Congress* and the California Battalion. The two American columns merged and camped—a short distance apart, as if Stockton, or Gillespie, wanted Kearny to be mindful of separate commands.*

As Kit Carson and Alexis Godey celebrated their reunion, Captain Gillespie and his two officers, Navy Lieutenant Edward F. Beale and Midshipman James M. Duncan, met with Kearny and his staff and Gillespie announced the most critical news: a force of lancers, perhaps a hundred men under Captain Andrés Pico, was posted at San Pascual village, about ten miles ahead on the direct route to San Diego. Stockton, who had learned of the insurgents' position from two captured deserters, suggested, via messages carried by Gillespie, that Kearny attack Pico and "beat up the camp if the

---

These camps were near the modern town of Ramona, a few miles from the San Pascual battlefield, today a state historic park lying eight miles southeast of Escondido on California Route 78.

general thought it advisable" in order to continue the march without harassment. One of the deserters, an Indian named Rafael Machado, had been sent along with Gillespie's party.

At a war council that night, Captain Benjamin Moore, one of Kearny's ablest officers, asked to lead a raid on Pico's camp and the general appears to have given this idea serious consideration. But he decided instead to send a patrol out under Lieutenant Thomas Hammond to reconnoiter the enemy position and return with as much detailed information as could be gathered in the dark of night. Moore opposed this decision, saying that a horseback reconnaissance might be discovered and thereby ruin the element of surprise. He preferred a full-blown night attack that would find Pico's men unmounted and unprepared—"To dismount them is to whip them," he said.

The captain was overruled, and on the night of December 5 Hammond, the deserter Machado, and six dragoons rode out in a sleety rain to find Pico and his insurgents.

3

Thomas Clark Hammond of Fort McHenry, Maryland, West Point class of '42, was age twenty-seven when he led the patrol that night. The second lieutenant had been married two years; his wife was the daughter of a prominent Platte County, Missouri, judge, and he was the father of a one-year-old son. He was a dedicated career officer, tough, uncomplaining, ambitious, eager for a fight. Kearny would not have entrusted the mission to a lesser man.

The patrol located San Pascual village with no difficulty, and as the dragoons huddled against the biting cold and needling rain in the brush at the foot of a hill, Hammond sent Machado into the scattering of huts to "bring an Indian out" who could tell of the strength of Pico's force. Gillespie, in recounting the events later, said, "Rafael went into the midst of the Enemy where they were sleeping, pulled out an Indian and ascertained that Andrés Pico was there with one hundred men." Lieutenant Edward Beale explained the ease by which Machado gained the critical information: "The Indians are very inimical to the Californians and always ready to betray them."

After waiting some anxious minutes for Machado's return, Hammond, fretting lest the Indian had run into trouble, led his dragoons to the outskirts of the village. According to Gillespie, the clank of the dragoons' sabers alerted Pico's sentries and instantly dogs began barking and the Californians, thrown awake, began shouting *"Viva California!" "Abajo los Americanos!"* and "a great variety of abuse."

Pico, it appears, could not at first credit that the intruders were Americans. The insurgents' spy network in San Diego, rudimentary but effective, had notified him of the hated Gillespie's departure from the town on December 3 with a small party of horsemen, riding east. Apparently no mention had been made of the brass cannon being pulled along at the rear of the American party, for Pico believed that the marine officer was merely leading a foraging expedition to find horses and stray cattle. He had taken his lancers— probably about a hundred men*—to San Pascual to keep an eye on Gillespie and did not know of Kearny's arrival nearby. He could not believe that a small foraging patrol would be so audacious as to challenge him and seemed to resist the idea that Gillespie was not alone in the area, even when a sentry showed him a dragoon jacket and a blanket stamped with the letters "U.S." that had been dropped on the trail. When Pico ordered his lancers to gather their horses, he did not know what to expect—a skirmish with the marine and his foraging party still seemed unlikely.

Not until dawn, when he saw Kearny's army for the first time, did he realize that he faced a full-fledged battle.

❀

Hammond and his horsemen returned to Kearny's camp at two on the morning of December 6 and the lieutenant reported Ma-

---

*Some sources put the number as high as 160.

chado's information and the unfortunate fact that Pico and his men had been alerted to the American presence. The general's reaction to the latter news is not recorded but his fury, and that of Captain Moore, who had warned of this danger in the reconnaissance, cannot be doubted. Gillespie, who was not present to witness it, placed the blame for the fiasco directly on the patrol commander: "Thus the Californians were warned of the proximity of the Americans. The blunder by Hammond lost for Kearny the powerful advantage of surprise."

Kearny had no time to lecture; he ordered the camp be awakened and the men mounted; he sent Alexis Godey and Lieutenant Beale to Gillespie with orders for the marine to gather his men and join the dragoons on the trail to San Pascual village.

The advance began before dawn on December 6. The rain had stopped, but in the bitter cold the men had to wrestle themselves from their frozen blankets and saddle up in the moonlight with no time for breakfast rations. They were exhausted and hungry, as were their animals, as they plodded along a cart trail in a thick fog toward San Pascual.

Combined with Gillespie's small force, Kearny's Army of the West now numbered about 150 men. Twelve dragoons under Abraham Johnston led the army, with Kit Carson riding with them, followed by Kearny, Lieutenant Emory, and the engineers. Next in the column rode Captain Moore, Lieutenant Hammond, and fifty dragoons, most of them mounted on mules, followed by Gillespie with twenty men of the California Battalion, and Lieutenant John Davidson with two mountain howitzers and the crew to serve them. In the rear, the balance of the force, fifty or sixty men under the quartermaster, Major Thomas Swords, rode with the baggage train and Gillespie's brass four-pounder. The army was strung out, two columns wide, for nearly a mile along the brushy trail.

As the Indian huts of San Pascual came into view, lying at the east end of a flat valley, Kearny stopped his column in a narrow ravine that followed the valley floor into the village and there he gave some final orders to his officers. Precisely what these orders

were is unknown, but he appears to have given a version of Lord
Nelson's oft-used admonition that "every man is expected to do his
duty" and urged his officers not to depend upon musketry (much of
the army's powder had been dampened in the rain), but in true dragoon custom to rely upon the point of the saber. He had no real idea
of the enemy numbers or of their deployment, or of the terrain,
shrouded by the ground fog, and therefore he had no tactic. He
said something about surrounding the village and taking as many
prisoners as possible.

Ahead, gathered around the Indian huts, Andrés Pico and his
horsemen waited, wrapped in bright serapes and leather cuirasses,
their seven-foot-long, needle-pointed, fire-hardened, ashwood lances
couched. Pico, with poorer firearms and powder than the Americans, had but a single order for his men: "One shot and the lance!"

4

The battle began by mistake, its opening move like a miniature version of the charge of the Light Brigade at Balaclava. Kearny's order
to "Trot!" was apparently misheard by Abraham Johnston, who
suddenly yelled something, unsheathed his saber, and spurred his
horse down the valley, followed by Kit Carson and the twelve dragoons who led the American column. Captain Johnston's charge
toward the village, three-quarters of a mile away, was so startling
that gaps began opening in the line of march as Kearny, Benjamin
Moore, and others yelled orders to follow. Those in the front of the
column were able to spur their horses and mules, most of them weak
and blown already, but minutes passed before those in the rear even
realized that the army was on the move.

In the gray dawning, Johnston and the vanguard reached San
Pascual fatal minutes ahead of Moore and the fifty dragoons who
had followed closest behind, and Pico's horsemen were awaiting
them in a gully on the eastern edge of the village. The Californians
fired what few carbines they had, then wheeled to uncouch their
lances. Johnston was killed by one of the first shots fired—struck in

the forehead—and rolled off his horse; another bullet hit Carson's horse and the guide went down, his carbine flung from his grasp, and rolled off the path as the others thundered past. He retrieved his rifle but found it smashed, took a carbine and cartridge box from a wounded dragoon, and scrambled ahead on foot until finding a sniper's roost in the rocks bordering the gully.

Pico had by now realized the number of Americans opposing him, and after meeting the initial charge with a volley, the lancers fell back momentarily to a level stretch of ground a half-mile away on the west of the village. This maneuver was interpreted by Moore—commanding the main body of dragoons—as a retreat, and he led a charge against Pico's force with all the men who by now had reached the battle zone. The horses and mules picked their way forward through the brush and rocks until they came upon Pico and his men, who had in the meantime re-formed and now turned, leveling carbines and lances, and countercharged. Moore, some yards ahead of his men, rode directly at Pico. He fired his pistol, then slashed at the Mexican captain with his saber. The blow was parried as two of Pico's men rushed up, lances leveled, and speared Moore from his horse. The American was shot as he lay wounded on the ground, then killed by lance thrusts. Later, when his body was recovered, Moore was found still grasping his broken sword, his body torn by sixteen lance wounds.

As Moore fell from his horse, his brother-in-law, Lieutenant Thomas Hammond, rode up yelling to those behind him, "For God's sake, men, come up!" and was also lanced and unhorsed. He died in agony several hours later.

Within seconds, the fight devolved into a furious hand-to-hand combat, gun butts and sabers against gun butts and lances, engaging Pico's men both on the flat and in and around San Pascual village, where Kearny and the others were fighting. The Californians were not only skilled horsemen ("the very best riders in the world," Kearny later said), but adept with the *reata,* managing to drop their loops over several of the mule-mounted Americans and jerk them from their saddles.

Gillespie arrived in the midst of the fight, the artillery pieces in tow, but was thrown from his horse and gashed so deeply in the chest by a lance thrust that his lung was exposed. Afoot and yelling "Rally! Rally! Face them!" he fended off six other attackers, then was literally nailed to the ground by a lance. Incredibly, he managed to pull the spear free and struggle over to one of the howitzers. He fumbled with flint and steel and was able to light the *machero* (a wick in a box used to light the gun's fuse) before being knocked to the ground again, this time by a jabbing lance that split his lip and broke off a front tooth.

Kearny, too, was in the midst of the fight, slashing with his saber and trying to stay on his mount. At one point, he was surrounded by lancers, and before Lieutenant Emory and Captain Henry Turner could come to his aid, took two lance wounds, one in the upper arm, the other in the buttock. Emory, who dug in his spurs and forced his way forward, probably saving Kearny's life by slashing at the attackers with his saber, later said, "The old general [he was but fifty-two] defended himself valiantly and was as calm as a clock."

Gillespie, weak from loss of blood, now found the second of Kearny's howitzers and managed to light the *machero* with his flint and steel. After he handed it to one of the gunners and heard the flat bang of the gun, he fainted. Navy Lieutenant Edward Beale, Gillespie's second, then took over the gun and also managed to find the Sutter four-pounder and bring it into position. The gunners loaded both guns with grapeshot and fired each once toward the Californians. Pico was unwilling to put his lancers against the guns and wisely withdrew, leaving the field and dragging with *reatas* one of Kearny's howitzers—the one Gillespie had failed to fire—whose mule team had bolted into the enemy lines.

Beale's cannon shots ended the battle. It had lasted no more than thirty minutes, ten of them in the desperate hand-to-hand fighting that followed Johnston's first engagement with Pico's lancers and Moore's charge that followed.

San Pascual village was deserted, and as the Americans fell into it, exhausted, famished, and thirsty, their animals done in, the dragoon surgeon John Griffin used it as a dressing station. He had much bloody work to do. In all, three officers—captains Johnston and Moore, and Lieutenant Hammond—and nineteen men of the Army of the West had been killed in the battle and another eighteen wounded, among them Kearny, Gillespie, Lieutenant Warner of the Engineers, who suffered three wounds, and Robidoux, the guide. Only two men—Johnston and one dragoon—had been killed by musketry, the others by lance.

The casualties among the Californians was never dependably recorded. Pico claimed to have lost only eleven wounded. He also reported that he had defeated a force of two hundred Americans, killing over thirty, including the "despicable Gillespie." He made no mention of the one Californian taken prisoner by the Americans. Ironically, he said he suffered most of his casualties after retiring from the San Pascual field when he lost eleven men in an attack by a band of Luiseño Indians.

Kearny's report, written a week after the battle, was at least as exaggerated as Pico's. He wrote that he had defeated 160 Californians, that six dead were left on the field, the rest of the dead and wounded carried away by Pico's men.

During the battle, the general had brushed off Griffin's ministrations and ordered the doctor to attend to the more seriously wounded. Then, like Gillespie, he fainted from blood loss. The gashes in his forearm and buttock were deep and since he was not sure he could mount a horse, he turned over temporary command of the army to his adjutant, Captain Henry Turner, a Virginian and West Pointer who had served with Kearny since 1835.

With Kit Carson supervising the detail, the dead were buried on the night of the battle under a willow tree east of the San Pascual camp as wolves howled in the moonglow. Of the graves dug in the frost-covered ground, Emory wrote: "They were put to rest together forever, a band of brave and heroic men."

❀

CHAPTER SEVENTEEN

Mule Hill

1

For the moment, pursuit of Pico's horsemen was impossible and the Americans—"the most tattered and ill-fed detachment of men that ever the United States mustered under her colors," William Emory called them—spent the rest of the day of San Pascual in their sodden camp while Surgeon Griffin tended the casualties. There were no wagons for the wounded and some of the men fashioned travois by lashing buffalo robes between willow poles to be dragged behind mules. For the present, the men and animals were too fatigued to move on. The Indian village produced little food and the rations the dragoons had carried were but a memory.

As the day wore on, cold and gray-skied, fires were built and Captain Henry Turner, in temporary command of the army while the wounded Kearny was gathering his strength, wrote a letter to Stockton. He briefly described the fight, said that Pico's force was still hovering nearby, and asked for reinforcements, supplies, and carts for the wounded. Kearny approved the message, and Alexis Godey, a lieutenant with Frémont's California Battalion, was selected to make his way past Pico's outposts to deliver it to the commodore in San Diego, forty miles distant.

Before daybreak on December 7, accompanied by California

Battalion volunteer Thomas Burgess and an Indian sheepherder, Godey and the others mounted the choicest mules available and set out for San Diego through the low hills south of San Pascual.

At mid-morning, Kearny decided he could mount a horse despite his painful arm and buttock wounds and resumed command of the battered force, now consolidated into a single dragoon company under Captain Turner's command. The general announced to his officers that he needed to move on toward San Diego and join whatever relief force and provisions Stockton had sent out—assuming that Godey reached the commodore safely with Turner's letter.

By early afternoon, the Americans were on trail down the San Pascual Valley. They crossed a dry streambed and after several hours, the mule-drawn travois slowing the march to a crawl, reached a deserted rancho known locally as San Bernardo. Kearny's outriders had found a few head of stray cattle on the route and some chickens were captured on the property. After a brief respite at the rancho, during which the wounded were fed and their dressings changed, the column moved on to the San Bernardo riverbed, on the lookout for forage for the animals and for any enemy patrols in the vicinity.

When they reached the foot of a low hill that overlooked the streambed, a detachment of Pico's lancers burst from the brush and, at a distance too far for accuracy, opened fire on the dragoons. In the panicky seconds following the sudden gunfire, Emory and eight men scattered the Californians, then wheeled and scrambled through the tangle of cactus and thorny brush up the hill while Kearny and his officers led the balance of the army toward the summit on the other side. A number—Emory said forty—of Pico's horsemen rode up the hill to intercept the Americans but were chased off by Emory's men, and in minutes the Army of the West occupied the position with their two fieldpieces and the travois. The brief skirmish had cost no American casualties; Kearny reported five killed and wounded among the Californians.*

---

*Historian H. H. Bancroft treats this figure with an "(!)."

The hill, while an excellent defensive position, could not long sustain a large force, but the general determined to camp his army among a battlement of boulders and cactus for the night. Holes were dug by a patrol venturing down to the San Bernardo bed and this resulted in a small seepage of muddy water. During the brief fight, the few head of cattle that had been driven in front of the dragoons ran off, and several of the mules had to be slaughtered, the meat roasted over brushwood fires and the scraps boiled to a broth in pots of muddy water. The men quickly dubbed their high ground "Mule Hill."

On the morning of the eighth, the siege of Mule Hill was interrupted briefly by the arrival of a courier, riding under a truce flag, with a message from Pico. The courier carried a bag of sugar and tea and a request for an exchange of prisoners. Kearny's men had taken one Californian under guard from the San Pascual battlefield and the general was startled to learn that Pico had captured Alexis Godey, Thomas Burgess, and the Indian guide, the men who were to deliver Captain Turner's message to Stockton in San Diego. Lieutenant Emory escorted the Californian prisoner on the ride back with Pico's man and made the exchange, returning to the hill with Burgess. This man had disappointing news: he and his partners had delivered Turner's message to Stockton and had been captured near the San Bernardo while making their way back with packsaddles of food and clothing. Burgess said that Stockton's responding message had been cached in a tree to prevent it from falling into the hands of the enemy but that he knew its content: the commodore had said that he would be delayed in sending reinforcements until after sufficient horses were gathered, and that he had no carts or wagons for the wounded.

As the daylight dwindled, Pico, in a gentlemanly gesture, sent the captured packsaddles to Mule Hill but kept Godey and the Indian under guard and the hill patrolled by his lancers. Kearny held another war council with his officers and Gillespie's, the result of which was the writing of a second message to Stockton, to be carried to San Diego by Navy Lieutenant Edward Beale of the California

Battalion. Beale asked Kearny for Kit Carson to serve as guide and at first the general resisted this. He said he needed Carson's skills in the event the reinforcements did not arrive and the army had to fight its way off the hill and make its way west. Beale suggested that the scout's presence would greatly improve the chances for the success of the mission, and Carson opined that while he considered the plan a "forlorn hope" (the old British army term for a suicide mission), especially since they had to travel afoot through Pico's cordon of lancers, he hated to see the "boy"—meaning Beale—go alone. Kearny relented, and at dusk on December 8, Beale, Carson, and an Indian volunteer from among Gillespie's men crept down the hill on their bellies to an oak grove where they split up, intending to reunite after a safe distance from the Californians.

2

Kearny waited two days on Mule Hill, during which time one of his dragoon sergeants wounded at San Pascual died. In addition, Antoine Robidoux, who had taken a lance wound in the back during the battle, suffered greatly in the night freeze on the hill and was thought to be dying. He had served Kearny as interpreter among the Indians and, with Kit Carson, had led the Army of the West on its Gila River journey to California. The general thought highly of him, as did Lieutenant Emory, who tried to comfort him by bringing him a steaming cup of coffee to help ward off the cold. Emory later recalled that Robidoux seemed to rally and in gratitude gave him a sort of cake, an emergency ration that Emory described as "made of brown flour, almost black with dirt," that he said had "for greater security, been hidden in the clothes of his Mexican servant, a man who scorned ablutions." The lieutenant ate more than half of the cake "without inspection." Then, upon breaking off another piece, he said, "The bodies of the most loathsome insects were exposed to my view. My hunger, however, overcame my fastidiousness."

On December 10, as the Americans' horses and mules were allowed to nibble on the withered grass at the foot of Mule Hill, Pico's lancers drove a small band of horses into the grazing animals, intended to stampede them. Somehow, a number of dragoons scrambled down the hill in time to thwart this plan; a warning shot was fired from the Sutter canon, and the general's sharpshooters even managed to kill two of Pico's horses, adding the meat to their near-empty larder.

Kearny was determined that his force would fight its way off the hill the next morning and issued orders that everything that could not be carried be burned. He doubted that the three-man express party had reached San Diego and he could not continue to hold Mule Hill while awaiting reinforcements.

Beale, Carson, and the Indian apparently never regrouped after splitting up at the beginning of their mission, for the Indian—whose name, according to one of Stockton's men, was Che-muc-tah—arrived in San Diego first, at about six in the evening of December 9. Beale followed the next morning, so exhausted by the journey and affected by exposure that he collapsed and was said to be "mentally deranged" for several days thereafter. Carson, who had taken a more circuitous route to the town, arrived on the eleventh, limping on torn and bleeding feet. By then, a relief expedition had already reached Mule Hill.

An hour or two before dawn on December 11, as Kearny's men slept fitfully among the brush and rocks of their encampment, sentries spotted movement below and shouted "Who goes there?" "Americans!" came the reply as Stockton's aide-de-camp from the *Congress,* Lieutenant Andrew F. V. Gray, appeared in the moonlight at the San Bernardo riverbed leading a force of 215 sailors and marines.

The Army of the West and the relief force celebrated for hours among the hill's breastworks. Gray's men had brought coffee, tobacco, jerked beef, hardtack, and clothing; Kearny's men offered steaming mule soup and long accounts of what had happened at San Pascual and their survival in the five days since the battle. Everyone managed to sleep an hour or two before dawn, at which time Kearny intended to resume the march.

❁

The advent of Lieutenant Gray's tars and marines ended whatever plans Andrés Pico had to prevent Kearny from entering San Diego. The Californians had received their own reinforcements since San Pascual, over a hundred men sent from Los Angeles by General José Flores, but Pico, his strength presently at least 250 "effectives," made no use of them. By the time the Army of the West, now numbering about 350 with Gray's men, returned to the San Bernardo rancho at daybreak on December 11, Pico had abandoned the field, reporting to General Flores that the "want of horses" prevented him from pursuing the Americans any further. H. H. Bancroft provided another unsatisfactory explanation for Pico's action, or lack of it, writing that "the Californians had a pardonable aversion to charging on horseback up a hill to meet cannon-balls and rifle-bullets." In fact, it is impossible to believe that Pico ever contemplated an "attack" either before or after Gray's arrival, and least of all, up Mule Hill. He was too intelligent an officer to charge into the muzzles of the American howitzers. His "want of horses" explanation to his commander in chief was no more than a euphemism for his pardonable aversion to sacrificing his lancers to superior numbers and guns. With the addition of the hundred men from Los Angeles, he might have made it difficult for the Americans to continue to San Diego, but he could not have stopped them.

In their haste to quit the field, the Californians left their small cattle herd behind and it was captured by Kearny's men and driven ahead of the column. Camp was made at another abandoned rancho on the night of December 11, where the army was well fed for the first time in many days and fortified with confiscated wine by the time it resumed the march the next morning.

At four in the next afternoon, Kearny led the advance guard of dragoons into the nondescript adobe village of San Diego, ending a thousand-mile march that had begun at Fort Leavenworth six months less four days past.

Stockton and his officers from the *Congress* met the general on the eastern edge of the village and rode with him to the commodore's quarters, which were graciously offered to the haggard Kearny, still tortured by his wounds.

3

"It is difficult to regard the affair at San Pascual otherwise than as a stupid blunder on the part of Kearny, or to resist the conclusion that the official report of the so-called 'victory' was a deliberate misrepresentation of the facts." So wrote H. H. Bancroft forty years after the battle, when some of the participants (though not Kearny) were still living. The historian allowed that while the Americans had possession of the battlefield after Pico's lancers fled, "this fact by no means sufficed to make of defeat a victory. . . ." There was no reason for the attack on Pico at San Pascual, especially with a small force of exhausted men, Bancroft insisted, asserting that Kearny could have joined Stockton in San Diego "without risk or opposition" and proceeded as commander in chief to devise plans to recapture the lost towns and complete the conquest of California. Instead, as the historian wrote:

> Coming in sight of the enemy, he orders a charge and permits a use of his men, benumbed with cold, their fire-arms wet and useless, their sabres rusted fast in the scabbards, mounted on stupid, worn-out mules and half-broken horses, to rush in confusion upon the California lances, presenting a temptation to slaughter which the enemy—even if they are as cowardly as their assailants believe—cannot resist.

"Individually, the Americans fought most bravely; nothing more can be said in praise," Bancroft said, but "many lives are recklessly and uselessly sacrificed. An irresponsible guerrillero chief would be disgraced by such an attack on Indians armed with bows and arrows." But Kearny was no guerrillero chief, he was a brigadier general commanding regular troops of the United States and, said the historian, "Success would have brought him no glory; defeat would have brought him disgrace."

Apart from the lack of evidence that Kearny actually ordered a charge, the assertion that there would have been no glory had the attack been a success, and the ludicrous "rusted sabre" image (no dragoon would ever let his saber rust: it was his principal weapon and he oiled and sharpened it religiously), there is much that is undeniable in Bancroft's polemic, much that is inexplicable in Kearny's conduct.

Why did he move, with men and animals decrepit from their fatiguing march, against an enemy force about which he was utterly ignorant? He did not know the number in Pico's force, what arms they carried (he did not even know they were lancers), or what artillery might be supporting them. Of the deployment of the enemy and the ground over which it was deployed, he knew only what tidbits were told him by Lieutenant Hammond and the Indian spy when they returned from the disastrous reconnaissance patrol.

Bancroft and others made much of Kearny's dependence on the word of Kit Carson and Archibald Gillespie about the "cowardice" of the Californians, but no officer of Kearny's experience would have regarded such opinion as more than campfire badinage. He had heard of the "cowardice" of the British who had wounded him and taken him prisoner at Queenston Heights in 1812, and of the "cowardice" of the Poncas, Mandans, and Comanches he had fought as an officer of dragoons on the Western frontier.

Did Stockton's message urging him to attack Pico and "beat up the camp if the general thought it advisable" cause Kearny to act so precipitously? Did he hope to impress Stockton by some glorious result at San Pascual? This too seems unrealistic. Bancroft reluctantly states that "we may charitably suppose that he [Stockton] did not realize the condition of Kearny's force," but in truth, Kearny had no need to impress a naval officer who would become his subordinate, and in any event, he was not the kind of officer who fought to make an impression on anybody but the enemy.

His own biographer, Dwight Clarke, states that "General Kearny's tactics on the night of December 5—6 were at fault. 'Blunder' is one word applied to them with reason." But, Clarke argues, the chief blunder occurred when Hammond's troopers alarmed Pico's camp; the battle of San Pascual turned upon that happenstance and upon the overruling of Captain Benjamin Moore's argument to attack the Californians while they slept.

As would be expected, Kearny reported San Pascual as a "victory," as did Gillespie, whose lance wounds attested to his being in the forefront of the fight.

To Bancroft, San Pascual was a "criminally blundering" defeat for the Americans.

Kearny's biographer calls the fighting around San Pascual village a "check that came perilously close to defeat" and admits that the result was "a Pyrrhic victory" for the Americans.

Based on the "conduct" of the thirty-minute battle by the Americans, the negligible gains in ground and advantage, and the resulting casualties of the two sides—twenty-two dead (including three officers) and eighteen wounded among Kearny's force, perhaps a dozen wounded among Pico's—the word "victory" must have given Kearny pause in the writing. But he could say no less; nor could Andrés Pico say the truth about why he left the field to the Americans after the fight.

✳

CHAPTER EIGHTEEN

San Gabriel

1

For the first several days after reaching San Diego, Kearny was content to rest and let his wounds heal. He wrote his official account of San Pascual and sent soothing letters to his wife Mary in St. Louis, assuring her of his good health and of his fondest wish: that he could be home with her and their seven children with the Christmas holidays drawing close.

He had, pro forma, presented his War Department orders to Commodore Stockton but had not discussed the issue of command. In his thinking, there was little to discuss: when he could do so, he would assume both military and civil authority as his orders demanded. For the present, he would not interfere with the scheme of things.

Neither, at first, did Robert Field Stockton give attention to the command matter. The entry of the wounded, sick, starved, and weary dragoons into San Diego had delayed his plans to pursue and force the surrender of the rebels. He had five hundred sailors, marines, and a gang of volunteers drilling daily in the scrub near his presidio headquarters; he had search parties in the countryside, and in Baja California, gathering horses, mules, and cattle; he had Frémont, now somewhere in the Monterey vicinity, adding recruits to his California Battalion and also searching for horses in preparation to march south. He had a firm grip on the helm, knew the course his ship was headed, and would soon correct the unfortunate but "temporary interruption" caused by the seizure of Los Angeles by the California mob of malcontents.

Although Stockton's position had something in it of a patrician military officer's blind certitude of correctness, he had the history of the past five months of a sort of eminent domain at his advantage. His predecessor, Commodore Sloat, had raised the flag at Monterey on July 7—while Kearny was still en route from Fort Leavenworth to Bent's Fort. Stockton had taken command of the Pacific Squadron on July 22, a month before Kearny had reached Santa Fé. Moreover, he had five hundred men in his command; Kearny had only about sixty "effectives" who could join the march to Los Angeles.

The commodore did not question Kearny's orders, dated June 3, 1846, and did not see them as superseding his own orders from the navy secretary, dated eighteen days later. The War Department had directed the general of dragoons that "Should you conquer and take possession of N. Mex. and Cal., or considerable places in either, you will establish temporary civil governments therein. . . ." The general had fulfilled only the first part of these tentative "should you" orders. He had taken possession of New Mexico. But in the matter of California, the issue now at hand, Stockton had stolen the march five months earlier.

During the sixteen-day lull between the advent of the Army of the West in San Diego and the beginning of the 150-mile march to Los Angeles on December 28, both officers seemed certain in their knowledge of whose authority was paramount. Even so, as they prepared to march, each man made certain gentlemanly gestures. Stockton suggested that the general take command of the combined army and offered himself as aide-de-camp; Kearny declined, said the commodore should lead the force with himself, Kearny, as aide-de-camp. Stockton repeated his offer before the march began, and again Kearny declined.

H. H. Bancroft's explanation for Kearny's strange reluctance to take the command he assumed belonged to him by his seniority of rank and War Department order is that he felt he owed Stockton a favor. After the disaster of San Pascual, which Bancroft said "reflected no credit on his ability as an officer," he had entered San Diego under "peculiar circumstances, wounded, like so many of his men, deprived of his best officers who had been killed, his whole command perhaps saved from destruction by the commodore's aid." The delicacy of Kearny's position and the fact that Stockton was actively engaged in organizing an expedition against the enemy, the historian wrote, "prompted the general not only to abstain from demanding the chief command, but to decline it when proffered by Stockton."

The breech in the amenities opened on December 22 after Stockton described his plans to Kearny: he would advance to the coastal town of San Luís Rey, forty miles north of San Diego, and there determine the whereabouts of Colonel Frémont and the deployment of the enemy. Failing to join with Frémont, he said, might dictate a course of falling back to San Diego.

Kearny's soldierly brain could see no benefit in such a tentative movement, especially one that might leave Frémont and his California Battalion, the strength and location of which were unknown, in limbo. He said as much to Stockton in a letter counseling a quick march to Los Angeles via San Luís Rey and stating, "I shall be happy to . . . give you any aid either of head or hand of which I may be capable."

Stockton's reaction to this sensible suggestion was inexplicably harsh and filled with demonstrably false suggestions. The commodore asserted that the Californians might be fielding a more numerous army than his and Kearny's combined force of six hundred men, and that this phantom army "might get in my rear and cut off my communication with San Diego," and even put his ships off the California shore at hazard.

This exchange of ideas on the conduct of the Los Angeles campaign seems to have tipped the scale for Kearny. A few days before the march, he met with Stockton and said that in the national interest in completing the annexation of California, he needed to command the army.

In a later report to the War Department, he said that the command "was reluctantly granted to me by Commodore Stockton on my urgent advice that he should not leave Colonel Frémont unsupported to fight a battle on which the fate of California might for a long time depend."

Stockton's view differed. In his subsequent testimony in Washington, he said that Kearny "gave me to understand he would like to command and after a conversation I agreed to appoint him . . . but I retained my own position as commander in chief."

Kearny seemed to admit that while he had the immediate command, Stockton's authority was preeminent when he wrote that "during our march, his authority and command, though it did not extend over me, or over troops which he had himself given me, extended far beyond where we were moving. It extended to the volunteers stationed at Nueva Helvetia, Sonoma, Monterey and I think some few in San Francisco and over the California Battalion of mounted riflemen under Colonel Frémont's command which I had not then claimed."

The Stockton-Kearny army thus set out for Los Angeles on December 29, 1846, with the band from the *Congress* leading the force of forty-four officers, fifty-seven First Dragoons under Captain Henry Turner, and five hundred sailors, marines, and volunteer riflemen, the latter, the only men on horseback, commanded by Captain Archibald Gillespie. The column was armed with muskets, carbines, boarding axes, and six artillery pieces, followed by ten ox-carts of supplies, the bullocks so feeble that the men had to help drag the fieldpieces and stores wagons. They moved slowly, covering only thirty miles in the first three days on the route Kearny had taken into San Diego, and on New Year's Eve, they camped at the San Bernardo rancho.

"Our men were badly clothed, and their shoes generally made by themselves out of canvas," Stockton wrote; yet, as he perhaps thought befitted a commander in chief, he slept in a lavish tent suite complete with night tables and a bed with a mattress, while Kearny slept on the ground wrapped in a bearskin.

2

At about the time Kearny and his battered veterans of San Pascual first reached San Diego, Lieutenant Colonel Frémont had brought his California Battalion down the boggy trails from Monterey to San Luís Obispo. His call for volunteers had been answered and his battalion had grown to a demi-regiment made up of his old exploring company, immigrants newly arrived at New Helvetia, a company of Walla Wallas and a miscellany of California Indians, some sailors and marines detached from warship duty in San Francisco Bay, and the Bear Flaggers of the Sonoma garrison under Captain John Grigsby. He had 428 men in buckskins and moccasins and all manner of cobbled-together outfits, three fieldpieces, ammunition and stores wagons, and an enormous herd of nearly two thousand horses and mules, plus a small collection of cattle. All, men and animals, had been gathered and on the march in the space of two months.

It had taken nearly a month for his cumbersome party, moving in rain squalls along eroded mud paths, to reach San Luís Obispo, and when Frémont set up his camp in the mountain foothills above the mission village on the night of December 14, he had no idea what resistance the Californians might throw against him. He was operating in a vacuum three hundred miles from San Diego: he did not know of Kearny's fight at San Pascual, nor of the whereabouts of Stockton and his men, who were presumably coming north toward Los Angeles.

The San Luís Obispo Mission was surrounded and occupied quickly with no resistance. Frémont's men captured several local influentials, including José de Jesús Pico, a cousin of Andrés and Pío Pico, and thirty-five of his rebels who had fought Frémont's men at La Natividad in October. José Pico had surrendered to the Americans months before and had been granted "parole"—freedom under the promise that he would not bear arms or engage in any insurgent activities. However, a search of his quarters turned up letters and documents showing that he was in regular contact with General Flores, commander of the Californians. Amazingly, Frémont, supposed to be on the march toward the critical recapture of Los Angeles, decided to hold a court-martial to punish the captured officer for violating his parole. This was done on December 16 and Pico was sentenced to death by firing squad the next morning.

He was rescued minutes before he was to stand blindfolded before his executioners. After paying a visit to the condemned man, Frémont granted an audience to Pico's wife, a woman described by those who knew her as "striking." She was dressed in black and brought her children and knelt before the colonel to beg for her husband's life. Frémont raised her to her feet and promised he would consider her entreaties. He had the prisoner brought to him, later describing him as "calm and brave . . . a handsome man, within a few years of forty, with black eyes and black hair," and told him his life had been spared and for this, he should thank Señora Pico.

In his memoirs, Frémont said that Pico made the sign of the cross and said, "I was to die—I had lost the life God gave me—you have given me another life. I devote the new life to you."

In truth, Frémont may have intended sparing Pico's life all along; several of the California Battalion officers had come forward with the suggestion. It turned out to be a wise decision, as was the freeing of the other captives taken in the mission town. Pico volunteered to accompany the expedition to Los Angeles, and those freed from captivity—reluctant and unpaid volunteers to begin with—passed the word that the Americans had overwhelming numbers and it was futile to resist them.

The march was resumed on December 17 with Santa Barbara, a hundred miles south of San Luís Obispo, the next significant town en route to Los Angeles. Frémont led his battalion inland toward the western slopes of the Santa Ynez Mountains, traveling over country until recently stricken by drought. The new rains had produced only sparse grass, and the horses and pack train grew jaded and weak as the days wore on, each day ending with little more than fifteen miles of progress for the weary force.

On Christmas Eve, the Americans crossed San Marcos Pass, a few miles northwest of Santa Barbara, in a freezing mountain rainstorm. The trail, which virtually disappeared in the flash floods, caused a hundred pack animals to loose their footing and dump their packsaddles and baggage "like the trail of a defeated army," as Frémont put it. The battalion camped in the mud, ate cold rations since cook fires were impossible, crossed ravines choked with uprooted trees and dense brush, watched helplessly as mules and horses buried themselves in mud, and were hurtled into the rocks by winds so strong they could snatch a man off his feet. They struggled into the town in the afternoon of December 27 so trail-worn, hungry, and fatigued that it took a week for the men and animals to recover sufficiently to resume the march.

Fortunately for Frémont and his prostrate army, Santa Barbara, its shops closed and streets deserted, offered no resistance and no prisoners to worry about, and the flag was raised in the central plaza with no onlookers. The Americans themselves were too tired to cheer.

The six-hundred-man Stockton-Kearny force approached the vineyards of San Luís Rey Mission on January 4, 1847, and there the commodore exercised his authority as commander in chief. A party of three men arrived in the American camp under a truce flag, bringing a message dated January 1 from now-Governor José Flores, who proposed a suspension of hostilities. Rumors were abroad that Mexico and the United States were negotiating a peace settlement, Flores wrote, and further bloodshed should be avoided until these reports were verified.

Stockton, without consulting Kearny, angrily rejected the proposal, ridiculing Flores' claim to be governor of California and declaring to the couriers that the Mexican officer had broken parole and would be executed if captured.

As the combined army moved on from San Luís Rey to San Juan Capistrano, Stockton received a report that Frémont and his men had reached Santa Barbara. Upon reading this, the commodore sent Captain George Hamley, master of the whaler *Stonington,* to deliver a message to the colonel warning him of the near presence of the Californians, and of their belligerence after defeating Gillespie and Mervine—and Kearny at San Pascual. Hamley rode back to San Diego, then took passage upcoast on a trader to intercept Frémont.

By the time he reached the explorer, the last battle in the conquest of California had ended.

3

From his headquarters at San Fernando, north of Los Angeles, Governor-General José Flores had reached his wit's end. He had hoped to harass the Americans with hit-and-run guerrilla tactics, buying time until Mexico either sent him reinforcements—which he knew was little more than a dream—or signed a peace with the United States. He had close to five hundred men but they were unpaid, ill-equipped, and disgruntled. The American Frémont and his buckskinned battalion were heading south out of Santa Barbara, and the American Stockton, who had rejected the New Year's Day cease-fire proposal, was on the march north out of San Diego. The surrender of Gillespie and his garrison in Los Angeles three months past and the subsequent defeat of the Americans at San Pascual had inspired the Californians with renewed patriotic zeal. But the euphoria had been short-lived: the Americans were on the march from the north and south, with larger numbers than ever before, and they would converge on Los Angeles.

During the first days of the new year, Flores expected it would be Frémont he would first meet in battle. This expectation changed after his scouts brought news of Stockton's rapid advance, and on January 7, the Californian moved his force into camp on a steep bluff overlooking a ford of the San Gabriel River, twelve miles northeast of Los Angeles. It was an advantageous place amid willows and mustard brush on the American line of march, perhaps a perfect place for an ambush.

Stockton's scouts located Flores' potential ambuscade during the night and reported the enemy position. The commodore ordered a crossing of the river on a lower ford than originally planned and halted his force about a quarter-mile from the river at around two in the afternoon of the eighth, the anniversary of Andrew Jackson's 1815 victory at New Orleans.

The Californians watched the American advance and Flores stationed sharpshooters, Andrés Pico's lancers and two other squadrons of horsemen, all strung out along the fifty-foot-high-bluff four hundred yards west of the stream. He placed a large force of horsemen and his two nine-pounder cannons at the crossing ford.

Upon reaching the San Gabriel bank, Stockton's skirmishers exchanged rifle fire with the Californians, and by the time the crossing began in earnest, Flores' cannons were pelting the water with grape and round shot. The river, about a hundred yards wide and knee-deep, had a quicksand bed that slowed the crossing and gave the Californians fish-in-a-barrel targets from their positions on the bluff. But Flores' powder was of poor quality and there were few casualties.

As the main force of Americans reached the riverbank, Kearny ordered two nine-pounders brought forward to counter the Californian artillery, but Stockton, who had no experience in land fighting, countermanded the order and insisted that the guns not be unlimbered until after they had crossed the river. The cannons were pulled by flailing mule teams and manhandled with guy ropes across the spongy streambed under a hail of rifle and cannon fire. At one point, seeing one of the nine-pounders stalled and sinking, Stockton rode to it, grabbed a rope, and shouted at the desperate gunners, "Quicksand be damned, come on, boys!"

Incredibly, they managed to get the guns over and unlimbered as Stockton, who did have experience in laying guns at sea, took command of the pieces, yelling, "Steady, boys, don't waste a shot!" Meantime, his main force splashed across the San Gabriel, finding shelter under what Lieutenant William Emory called "a natural banquette, breast-high" while being deployed. Kearny directed the deployment, sending his dragoons, Gillespie's volunteers, and the tars from Stockton's ships up and downstream as the balance of the force continued the crossing under the galling musket fire from the bluff. The carts of the baggage train foundered in the sand and the terrified mules and horses were belabored to shore by the ropes and whips of the teamsters and the flat blades of dragoon sabers.

Stockton was too busy to notice the chaos in the stream. He took command of one of the nine-pounders, laid it so accurately toward Flores' guns on the bluff that the first shot smashed the carriage of one of the enemy cannons to splinters, rendering the piece useless.

Kearny now had most of his men deployed to his satisfaction and stood, big dragoon pistol in each hand, shouting to Stockton, "I am now ready for the charge!" The commodore nodded and yelled to the sailors and marines in front of him, "Forward, my Jacks! Charge!" They scrambled up the hill, bayonets fixed and shouting "New Orleans!" as Stockton's gun crews flogged their mule teams up at the same time.

Near the top of the bluff, Kearny's party swerved to the right, and the left wing of the Californians fell back after firing their weapons, abandoning their disabled cannon. But some of Flores' mounted troops circled the Kearny column as if to attack its flank and rear guard, and the general quickly ordered his men into a square formation. Faced with the hedgerow of bayonets, the Californians retreated out of range.

On Kearny's left, Stockton met a feeble charge by Flores' horsemen, but as the commodore later wrote, "finding so warm a reception . . . they changed their purpose and retired, when a discharge of artillery told upon their ranks."

By the time the Americans reached the top of the bluff, the enemy had disappeared, only the dust raised by their rear-guard horsemen marking their retreat.

The battle at the San Gabriel, from the first skirmisher's shots through the contested river crossing and the climbing of the heights, had lasted less then two hours. Two American sailors had been killed, eight men were wounded. The Californian casualties were never authenticated. H. H. Bancroft asserts that they were "probably the same in killed. . . . Each party as usual greatly overrated the enemy's loss."

With the animals too spent in the day's work to give chase, Stockton and Kearny made camp on the bluff. On the night of January 8, Flores' campfires could be seen flickering in the distant hills athwart the road to Los Angeles and a few desultory shots were exchanged in the darkness. In the morning, as Stockton ordered the march to continue, the Californians had again vanished.

Before leaving the bluffs on the morning of January 9, a courier rode into the American camp under a white truce flag, bringing news that Frémont and his men were now in San Fernando, about twenty-five miles north of Los Angeles. Stockton sent a message back urging the colonel to bring the force into the pueblo quickly and join his command. Presumably he told Frémont of the fight on the San Gabriel and that he and Kearny would enter Los Angeles later in the day.

The Americans detoured off the main road at noon after reports reached Stockton that Flores had regrouped what remained of his force—many of his men had deserted—and was drawn up in a horseshoe-shaped formation on an open plain on a mesa about six miles from the San Gabriel. Kearny again placed his men in a hollow square, the pack animals and provision and baggage carts in the center, and ordered that there would be no stragglers or breaking of ranks, that every man needed to keep his post and pace to thwart any cavalry charge by the enemy.

As Stockton's naval bandsmen played "Hail, Columbia" and the infantry square, dragoons, and skirmishers advanced toward the mouth of Flores' horseshoe, the Californian cannons opened fire and sent round shot bouncing harmlessly toward the American flanks. Stockton halted his army, brought his own fieldpieces forward and answered the fire. The exchange lasted for a quarter-hour before Flores ordered his lancers to charge the front of the enemy square—a foolhardy decision that, as contemporary militarists like to say, "defied all the rules of war."

The lancers, ten horsemen wide and three rows deep, thundered toward the square, their long, needle-tipped lances tucked under their armpits. Kearny held his two front ranks of dragoons and marines in check, shouting "Steady! Pick your men, boys!" Then, when the horsemen approached to within a hundred paces, he roared "Fire!" The rifles in the first rank cracked and produced a plume of smoke; instantly Kearny ordered "Front rank, kneel! Rear rank, fire!" The front rank fell to its knees, each man's bayonet at the ready to meet any horseman attempting to break the square, as the second rank rose, took aim, and fired. The volleys staggered the careening lancers; horses and men tumbled to the ground, upsetting others behind, and by the time the musket smoke cleared, the Californians and several riderless horses were fleeing back toward Flores' main force.

Kearny ordered the square forward, and as it lumbered across the mesa, the Californians again charged, this time on the left and right flanks simultaneously. Kearny ordered "Steady! Keep your ranks! Give 'em Hell!" and again the first two ranks on each of the square's sides volley-fired against the enemy horsemen, broke their order, and sent them reeling. A smaller attempt at the rear of the square was similarly repulsed while Stockton, expertly directing his cannoneers, sent such a shower of grapeshot after the retreating horsemen that Flores retired his entire force into the low hills surrounding the mesa.

For such a furious little engagement, the two-and-a-half-hour "Battle of the Mesa" produced few casualties. Among the Americans, there were only five wounded men (Gillespie was one of them, suffering a slight contusion from a spent bullet); Flores had at least one man killed and between twenty and forty wounded.

On the evening of January 9, Stockton and Kearny took their men across the Los Angeles River and set up camp three miles below the town.

❀

CHAPTER NINETEEN

Cahuenga

1

On the morning of January 10, three men approached the Stockton-Kearny camp on the Los Angeles River, the delegation sent as representatives of the town to say that no resistance would be made toward the Americans. Stockton promised that if this were true, there would be no reprisals and the peaceable citizenry would be protected.

At noon that day, the two officers led their men into the pueblo and dispersed them through all its principal streets and byways, converging on the central plaza to the drumbeat and martial airs of the navy band. Hundreds of Angelinos lined the streets and overlooking hills to watch the pageant, and there were some touchy moments along the route when, as Stockton wrote, his men were "slightly molested by a few drunken fellows who remained about the town." Several shots had to be fired to scatter the drunks, and two artillery pieces were hauled to the crest of a hill as a warning, but Gillespie was able to raise the flag over his old headquarters, abandoned four months earlier, without incident.

With sentries posted and horsemen patrolling the fringes of the village to watch for any sign of Flores' men, Stockton wrote his account of the San Gabriel "campaign" for the War Department. He extended a minimum of credit to Kearny and made no mention of the general's command of the square that had fended off the charges by the Californian lancers. The commodore said he had been "aided by General Stephen W. Kearny with a detachment of sixty men on foot from the First Regiment of U.S. Dragoons and by Captain A. H. Gillespie with sixty mounted riflemen." Subsequently, at a court-martial proceeding in Washington, he narrowed the credit even further, making certain that the government realized that he, Stockton, "was wholly and solely responsible for the success of the expedition" and that the campaign had merely been "sustained" by the "gallant and good conduct of General Kearny and all the officers and men under his command."

The commodore's pronouncements to his men for their "brilliant victories" and "steady courage," his proclamations to the Angelinos assuring them of peace and protection, and his reports to Washington, were the mortar holding together the shaky framework of his command. He needed to make sure there would be no question about who had conquered California and who, now that it had been accomplished, was in control.

✤

At first seemingly oblivious to Stockton's maneuvering, Kearny went about his business. He was comfortable with the knowledge that as the senior officer in the field, armed with what he fancied as explicit War Department orders, he was the military commander in chief in California and would soon assume control of its governance. More immediately, he needed to bring Frémont in. Just before the San Gabriel fight, Stockton had received a courier's message saying that the California Battalion had reached San Fernando, a short distance northwest of the pueblo. If Kearny was nettled by the lieutenant colonel's failure to join his and Stockton's force earlier, he made no hint of it in the message he dispatched to Frémont on the afternoon of January 10: "We are in possession of this place, with a force of marines and sailors, having marched into it this morning. Join us as soon as you can, or let me know if you want us to march to your assistance; avoid charging the enemy; their force does not exceed 400, perhaps not more than 300. Please acknowledge receipt of this, and dispatch the bearer at once."

These were orders from the superior officer. There could be no question of who was in command.

On January 12, with no response from San Fernando, Kearny wrote another note, and on January 13, two more, asking the battalion's whereabouts, and sent a note to Stockton expressing the fear that Frémont, if ignorant of the recapture of Los Angeles, might "capitulate and retire to the north." He offered to take a force out to find the missing battalion but this proved unnecessary when an express rider from Frémont arrived with startling news.

2

The fight at the Mesa had ended and the Americans were within a day of recapturing Los Angeles when George Hamley, master of the whaler *Stonington,* found Frémont a few miles east of San Fernando. He handed over Stockton's six-day-old message warning of the Californians' growing belligerence and urging caution in moving the battalion south.

The explorer had been cautious from the moment he had led his men out of Monterey in mid-December. He did not underestimate the threat posed by Flores' army after the fall of San Diego. He had the fight at La Natividad in mind and had learned of Kearny's battle at San Pascual. He had no idea of the Californian strength, armament, or whereabouts. His men were volunteers, untrained, undisciplined, and unpredictable. He was an officer of topographical engineers and had no experience in warfare, but he was no fool and saw his duty as bringing his men and animals safely to the conjoining with Stockton's army. The commodore's letter had confirmed the wisdom of his caution: "If there is one single chance for you," Stockton had written, "you had better not fight the rebels until I get up to aid you, or you can join me on the road to the pueblo [Los Angeles]."

More messages arrived. On January 11, as the battalion reached the summit of San Fernando Pass, two friendly Californios brought the news to Frémont of the fights at the San Gabriel and the Mesa and of the American reoccupation of Los Angeles. Another courier brought the "join us as soon as you can" note from General Kearny, dated January 10, urging the colonel to "avoid charging the enemy" and asking if he needed assistance in continuing on to the pueblo. A day later, more Kearny notes arrived, ordering Frémont to report to him at his headquarters and asking for an acknowledgment of the order and a time when he would reach Los Angeles. The notes made no mention of Stockton, a fact that might have given Frémont pause.

The explorer put the notes aside; he would answer soon, but for the present he was concentrating on a peace negotiation. José de Jesús Pico, who had been captured at San Luís Obispo, was a key figure in the effort. He had faced a firing squad for breaking his parole, his life had been spared by Frémont, and he now regarded the American officer not only as his savior, but as his friend. H. H. Bancroft said of Pico: "He was a man of some influence, came to men who had no fixed plans, dwelt with enthusiasm on the treatment he had received, and without much difficulty persuaded his countrymen that they had nothing to lose and perhaps much to gain by negotiating with Frémont instead of Stockton."

On January 11, Pico completed his talks with General Flores and Manuel Castro at their camps at San Pascual and a rancho nearby called Los Verdugos. By the end of the day, Flores turned over command of the Californians to Andrés Pico and, with his escort, rode toward Sonora. The next morning, as Frémont issued a proclamation at the San Fernando mission calling for a meeting to end all hostilities, Don José brought two of Andrés Pico's officers to Frémont's headquarters to "treat for peace."

The treaty and armistice were written and signed on January 12 at a deserted rancho on the north end of Cahuenga Pass,* between San Fernando and the northern outskirts of Pueblo de los Ángeles.

Antonio María Osio, the Monterey influential who apparently received a detailed description of the meeting at Cahuenga Pass, said of it: "When the two *jefes* encountered each other . . . Señor Frémont was recognized for his military expertise, and he correctly esteemed the courage of his opponents. Because he also was a shrewd man, he was convinced that these courageous Mexicans would be of use to the territory after it became a state. . . . With this in mind, Frémont proposed terms for a surrender to Señor Pico."

The document, its seven articles written by Theodore Talbot in both English and Spanish, was signed by Frémont and Andrés Pico. It forgave all past hostilities and allowed all Californian officers and volunteers to return home on parole after surrendering their arms and promising not to resume hostilities. It absolved them of taking an oath of allegiance until after a treaty between the United States and Mexico came into effect and guaranteed them the protection and equal rights of all American citizens. And it permitted any person who wished it the right to leave the territory.

The terms were exceedingly liberal and Frémont knew they might be questioned. But he did not seem to entertain the critical question: why make a treaty at all? He was being bombarded with increasingly petulant messages from Kearny and Stockton urging him to proceed to Los Angeles; he knew that both men were of superior rank, were a half-day distant, and either one more appropriate, even more "legal," for treaty-making than he.

H. H. Bancroft's answer to this question bore the pervasive cynicism that typified his treatment of the man he called a "filibustero chieftain": "Frémont's motive was simply a desire to make himself prominent and to acquire popularity among the Californians, over whom he expected to rule as governor. It was better to adopt conciliatory methods late than never."

The site is commemorated by a historical marker on Lankershim Boulevard in North Hollywood.

The generosity of the treaty's terms was to Frémont entirely defensible. Exacting punishment—perhaps even execution—for the Californian officers and draconian measures for the populace might have resulted in a rising similar to that which had ousted Gillespie's garrison from San Diego. Such an approach might have created guerrilla bands of angry citizens who would strike and run and prolong the fighting for months. The battles had been fought, Los Angeles was retaken, all the principal towns and ports were in American hands, the Californians had surrendered, their commanding general had escaped to Sonora, their best field commander was now cooperating in the armistice. Frémont expected the governorship of the new territory of California. What was to be gained by alienating the people he would govern?

In addition, he and his men had missed all the fighting. There was little glory left. Pico had turned over to him the howitzer captured from Kearny's dragoons at San Pascual and at least he could lead his battalion into Los Angeles with the cannon and with a paper that he later said "put an end to the war and to the feelings of war." The Cahuenga treaty, he said, "tranquilized the country, and gave safety to every American from the day of its conclusion."

In a dispatch to Stockton and Kearny, he wrote of the surrender of Pico and his men, of the recovered San Pascual gun, and of his imminent arrival in Los Angeles. He entrusted the letter and a copy of the treaty to Lieutenant William H. "Owl" Russell of the California Battalion to deliver to the American headquarters.

3

Since his arrival in Los Angeles, Stockton had received details on the suppression of a small rising in the north that bore some similarity to what had occurred to Captain Gillespie's garrison in San Diego. On December 8 past, at the time Stockton was learning of the San Pascual fight, a small band of Californians, reacting to what they considered unnecessarily harsh treatment by the Americans, had seized the acting *alcalde* of Yerba Buena, a Lieutenant Washington A. Bartlett. The rebels announced that they wished to trade this captive for another officer, Captain Charles Weber, whose behavior was said to be particularly oppressive and insulting. In late December, Marine Captain Ward Marston had set out with a party of marines and sailors for Santa Clara, where the rebels were camped. On January 2, Marston found a force of about 120 Californios under Francisco Sánchez, the former military commander at Yerba Buena. The skirmish that ensued cost the Californios four dead and five wounded, the Americans, two wounded. The next morning, Sánchez agreed to a cease-fire and on January 6, to an unconditional surrender.

Now, with the news of Pico's surrender at Cahuenga, the war was certainly over.

But the treaty pleased neither commander. Who was Frémont to write and sign such a document? Stockton was furious over the liberal terms of the surrender and shared Kearny's concern that a mere lieutenant colonel of volunteers would assume such a responsibility when his superior officers were within hailing distance.

Owl Russell was witness to the reactions of the commanders and, although leaving no precise record of it, must have been confused at what he heard, especially after Stockton, when finished ranting over the paper, told Russell he intended naming Frémont governor. The signals became further mixed in Kearny's headquarters, where Russell, who had known the general in Missouri, spent the night of January 13. Kearny seemed less concerned about the paper than Stockton did. True, the treaty had been written in haste by one not authorized to negotiate a peace, but the terms of it were in accord with what Washington wanted. Kearny agreed with Stockton that Frémont should be given the governorship.

The commodore, despite strong reservations over the treaty, gave it reluctant approval when he wrote to Navy Secretary Bancroft on January 15, "Not being able to negotiate with me, and having lost the battles of the 8th and 9th, the Californians met Colonel Frémont on the 12th instant on his way here, who, not knowing what had occurred, entered into the capitulation with them, which

I now send to you; and although I refused to do it myself, still I have thought it best to approve it."

The California Battalion entered Los Angeles in a rainstorm on the afternoon of January 14, 1847. Riding with his beloved, war-painted Delaware bodyguard in front of his four hundred men, pack animals, baggage train, and mule teams pulling six artillery pieces through the muddy streets, Frémont sat his horse straight as a lath. He was tanned and bearded, wore an open-collared, blue-flannel shirt, deerskin hunting jacket, blue-canvas trousers, moc-casins, a buccaneer's bandanna on his head, covered by a slouchy, wide-brimmed hat. The men who followed him looked more like a huge fur brigade riding to a mountain rendezvous than an authorized military force. They were a sunburned, trail-ragged, mud-caked, grizzle-bearded lot—farmers, frontiersmen, hunters, trappers, wanderers, sailors—in their favored buckskins and sun-faded shirts and big floppy hats, carrying huge knives, sidearms, and all manner of carbines, musketoons, and long rifles.

Owl Russell rode out five miles from the pueblo and gave his colonel the news of the reactions to the treaty. Russell reported that he thought Kearny more amenable to it than Stockton, and he prob-ably also gave Frémont his impressions of the rivalry between Kearny and Stockton and of the commodore's claiming credit for the battles of San Gabriel and the Mesa and for having rescued Kearny at San Pascual.

Frémont thus had a sense of the political problems rising in Los Angeles, but he had no idea of their gravity until he found himself enmeshed in them.

Since he had no doubt of which officer was the superior in Cali-fornia, he paid a visit first to Stockton. This was the man who had commissioned him in the navy (despite the fact that Frémont had no right to accept the commission since he was already an officer of the army's Topographical Corps and had not resigned), the man who had rescued Kearny at San Pascual, the man Russell said had offered to turn over to Kearny command of American military forces in California and had been refused.

The meeting was brief and polite. Stockton was not comfortable with the treaty and was prepared to write an additional article or two before sanctioning it, but he expressed no displeasure with his lieutenant colonel's actions.

The meeting with Kearny was similarly cordial. The two had not met since May, 1843, when, at Jefferson Barracks in St. Louis, Colonel Kearny, then in charge of the army's Third Military Department, had granted Frémont's request to be issued a brass field-piece, powder, and shot to take with him on his expedition to Oregon. That gun had been abandoned, but now the son-in-law of his friend Tom Benton of Missouri was "returning" another, the one lost at San Pascual. The general did not need to be reminded of this. He must also have disliked Frémont's unmilitary appearance and improper tendency to talk as if he alone had won the peace in California.

But Kearny allowed the man some latitude. He did not view Frémont as a military man—a topographical engineer was to a general of dragoons only nominally "army" to begin with, and the officer was young, ambitious, with a splendid wife and influential in-laws, and had accomplished much in his explorations. Soon after their initial meeting, Kearny wrote Senator Benton that Frémont had arrived in Los Angeles, fit and well. He asked, "Will you please in my name congratulate Mrs. Frémont upon the honor and credit gained by the Colonel and with my best wishes for her and all your family."

It was a kind thing to do and demonstrated Kearny's confidence that Frémont would serve well under his command.

✺

CHAPTER TWENTY

Last Battle

1

Owl Russell had warned Frémont that there were two camps in
Los Angeles and a wide gulf between them, that big trouble was
brewing between Commodore Stockton and the army's senior officer in California, Brigadier General Kearny. Owl had earned his
nickname—he saw things and heard things—and was an utterly dependable and loyal Frémonter. The explorer believed what Russell
said but when he marched into the village in mid-January, 1847, he
naively thought that he stood outside and aloof from the problems
of the two senior officers.

He had the Cahuenga treaty in his saddlebag, had confidence
that the commanders would work out their differences and that he,
a mere lieutenant colonel, had no role in their conflict. He had been
in California for thirteen months and under Stockton's command
for six of them. Kearny had a mere six weeks in the country and it
was common knowledge that he had bungled one battle, had to be
rescued by the commodore's men under Archibald Gillespie, and
had turned over land operations to Stockton at San Gabriel and the
Mesa.

To Frémont, the chain of command was not disputable: Stockton had led in the conquest of California, had recovered Los Angeles, and remained in command now.

But, trapped between the colliding forces, he learned that nothing was so simple: his arrival in Los Angeles with his four-hundred-man California Battalion served as a long-awaited signal to Kearny to assert his command over all American forces and all civil governance in California.

❈

The source of difficulty between the two senior officers was as old as war: ambiguous orders from a government far removed from the battlefield, orders written inexplicitly because of the time that would lapse between the issuance and receipt of them, orders rendered moot and unworkable by the time they reached their destination.

Kearny had marched to California with orders from President Polk dated June 3, 1846—six months before he arrived there—to subdue the country and take control of it, and these orders contained the ruinous ". . . should you conquer" equivocation.

Stockton's orders from the Navy Department were similar and dated nineteen days after Kearny's orders. But the commodore had been the senior officer *in situ* during most of the actual conquest and he maintained that he had already conquered California before Kearny arrived on the scene and that therefore the general's orders were nullified. Moreover, he said, Kearny did not have a sufficient force to win any battle and had had to be supplemented by the navy's sailors and marines and Frémont's volunteers. In Washington, he would later say, with a certain vagueness of his own, "My right to establish the civil government was incident to the conquest, and I formed the government under the law of nations."

Frémont saw all this as irrefutable, and of his partnership with the commodore, H. H. Bancroft said, "Notwithstanding the blunders and braggadocio and filibusterism of Frémont and Stockton, really the greatest obstacles to the conquest, these officers might plausibly claim to be conquerors. . . ."

The real obstacle, which Stockton did not mention but that did the greatest injury to his position in the argument, was the September 23 revolt in Los Angeles.

Had there been no revolt, President Polk and his entire government would have accepted Stockton's precedence without question. But the Los Angeles rising and Gillespie's surrender tainted and clouded the conquest thereafter. Stockton's attitude that California had been won by the time Kearny reached Warner's Ranch on December 3, 1846, overlooked the fact that with the exception of San Diego, all of southern California had to be re-won in three battles, in all of which Kearny played a role and Frémont none.

Bancroft said of Stockton-as-conqueror: "He had shown a creditable degree of energy and skill in overcoming obstacles for the most part of his own creation, in putting down a revolt that but for his own folly would have had no existence. No more can be honestly said in praise of the commodore's acts and policy in California." The historian gave Kearny credit for realizing he was in no position to supersede the commodore upon entering San Diego, and Kearny later said that he had acquiesced to Stockton's role as commander out of "respect for his [Stockton's] situation," but that he fully intended to supersede this junior officer "as soon as my command was increased."

Ironically, a month before Kearny entered California, clarifying orders had been dispatched west by the army's senior general, Winfield Scott, soon to command the Vera Cruz expedition against Mexico. Scott wrote to Kearny on November 3, 1846: "After occupying with our forces all necessary points in Upper California, and establishing a temporary civil government therein, as well as assuring yourself of its internal tranquillity . . . you may charge Col. Mason . . . or the land officer next in rank to your own, with your several duties, and return yourself to St. Louis."

He also ordered that Frémont's volunteers be mustered into the regular army service retrospective to May 13.

These orders were entrusted to Colonel Richard Mason of the First Dragoons, to be carried over the Isthmus of Panama and to California by warship.

Unfortunately, the orders did not arrive before the storm broke.

2

On January 14, Stockton, ready to sail south to Mazatlán and find some action along the Mexican coast, and still nettled over the unauthorized treaty his subordinate had written, fulfilled a promise by tendering to Frémont the appointment as governor of California. In his proclamation, the commodore took care to permit no question of his authority to make such an appointment; indeed, he seemed to have written it expressly for the eyes of his bête noire, Kearny.

> Having, by authority of the President and Congress of the United States of North America, and by right of conquest, taken possession of that portion of territory heretofore known as upper California; and having declared the same to be territory of the United States, under the name of the territory of California; and having established laws for the government of the said territory, I, Robert F. Stockton, governor and commander-in-chief of the same, do, in virtue of the authority in me vested, and in obedience to the aforementioned laws, appoint J. C. Frémont, esq., governor and commander-in-chief of the territory of California, until the President of the United States shall otherwise direct.

Kearny, as Stockton must have expected, reacted with barely contained fury and in a letter written on January 16, questioned Stockton's authority, asserting that such appointments were his, Kearny's, specific domain and that if the commodore had such authority from the President, or from "any other channel of the president's," he asked to see "certified copies" of the documents. "If you do not have such authority," the general wrote, "I then demand that you cease all further proceedings relating to the formation of a civil government for this territory, as I cannot recognize in you any right in assuming to perform the duties confided to me by the president."

The Frémont appointment, the ensuing Kearny letter, and Stockton's bitter response occurred with orchestrated timing. The commodore answered the general with alacrity and hid a round shot in his return note. He repeated his assertion that California had been conquered before Kearny entered it and that he had communicated to the President the details of the civil government he had formed before Kearny's arrival. Then he appended acidly: "I will only add that I cannot do anything, nor desist from doing anything, or alter anything on your demand; which I will submit to the president and ask for your recall. In the meantime you will consider yourself suspended from the command of the United States forces in this place."

Frémont was caught in the no-man's-land of this letter shrapnel from the outset. Stockton had appointed him governor on January 14; two days later, Kearny had written his objection to the commodore and the commodore had returned his blistering response; now, on January 17, Kearny summoned Frémont to his headquarters in an adobe building near the town plaza: "Dear Colonel, I wish to see you on business," the note said.

The explorer knew the subject of this meeting. Kearny, on the day he had voiced his objection to Stockton's appointment, had sent his adjutant, Lieutenant William Emory, with instructions for Frémont. Kearny said that the explorer was to maintain his command of the California Battalion, not to turn it over to Gillespie—which Stockton had ordered—and to remain in that position until notified otherwise. These orders, undermining Stockton's authority, were clearly the "business" at hand.

Before reporting to Kearny's headquarters, Frémont hastily wrote a letter to the general and left instructions that it be delivered by Kit Carson to Kearny's office as soon as it was copied.

The letter and its author arrived at the general's office almost simultaneously. Frémont reread it, signed it, and handed it over to Kearny. After a polite introductory, the letter got to the point:

> I found Commodore Stockton in possession of the country, exercising the functions of military commandant and civil governor, as early as July of last year; and shortly thereafter, I received from him the commission of military commandant, the duties of which I immediately entered upon, and have continued to exercise to the present moment. . . . I feel myself, therefore, with great deference to your professional and personal character, constrained to say that, until you and Commodore Stockton adjust between yourselves the question of rank, where I respectfully think the difficulty belongs, I shall have to report and receive orders, as heretofore, from the Commodore.

He signed the letter "Lieutenant Colonel, United States Army and Military Commandant of the Territory of California."

In all his career, since he was commissioned a first lieutenant in the 13th Infantry in 1813, Kearny had never heard, much less seen written down, such an astonishing case of disobedience of a lawful command of a superior officer, such an instance of prejudice of good order and military discipline—such a clearly defined example of *mutiny.*

Yet he made allowances that he would never have permitted any other officer in similar circumstances. Frémont was an explorer and topographer, scarcely "army," and doubtlessly unaware of the gravity of what he had written; he was the son-in-law of one of the most powerful of American political figures, Thomas Hart Benton, who was a Kearny friend, as was Benton's daughter Jessie, Frémont's wife, toward whom the general had a genuine affection.

The letter was a grievous mistake, Kearny counseled. He urged Frémont to destroy it and said that if he would do so, there would be no consequences, provided there would be no questioning the general's orders thereafter. On the matter of the governorship, Kearny said he intended to return to St. Louis within a month and implied a willingness to appoint Frémont to replace him as governor at that time. He called upon his long friendship with Senator Benton and Mrs. Frémont and urged that the colonel not destroy his career and embroil others in the consequences of his disobedience.

This momentous scene was unwitnessed and neither man left a satisfactory record of it. There were two extraordinary features of it: Kearny's uncharacteristic willingness to counsel his subordinate on the evils of his letter, and Frémont's failure to ask questions about the command controversy and seek Kearny's advice—even his assistance—on the matter of how he could serve two masters without alienating either. Kearny, probably because of his regard, if not his fear,* of Benton, seemed willing to help, but Frémont did not take advantage of the offer; instead, he seems to have said something about his decision having Commodore Stockton's support, then saluted and walked out of the room.

(A year later, in Washington, Frémont pointed out that Kearny, in suggesting he rescind the letter, was in effect willing to "break the rules of the service and of war." H. H. Bancroft's devastating rejoinder to this was that "dishonor in such cases pertains not to the officer who shows such leniency but to the recipient who uses it against him.")

Bancroft wrote further: "Against Kearny's position in the dispute, nothing can be urged, and against his conduct—his blunder at San Pascual affecting only himself and his men—nothing more than a savor of sharp practice in certain minor proceedings indicating a lack of confidence in the real strength of his position, or perhaps an excess of personal bitterness against his rival."

And of Frémont: "His action in disobeying Kearny's order, or

Brevet Major Henry S. Turner of the First Dragoons kept a journal of his experiences with Kearny on the march from Forth Leavenworth to California. He wrote that the reason Kearny failed to place Frémont in irons for mutiny was that the general "is afraid of giving offense to Benton." Turner was disgusted with his chief for his inaction in the matter and for not dealing decisively with Stockton, whom Turner characterized as "a low, trifling, truckling politician."

rather in leaving the two chiefs to settle their own quarrel, must I think be approved; that is, compared to the only alternative. Like Stockton, he merits no praise for earlier proceedings. He had perhaps done even more than the commodore to retard the conquest. His mishaps as a political adventurer call for no sympathy. . . . There is, or should be, honor even among filibusters."

3

Kearny had no choice but to bide his time. Addressing Stockton as "Acting Governor of California," he wrote, "I must for the purpose of preventing collision between us, and possibly a civil war in consequence of it, remain silent for the present, leaving with you the great responsibility of doing that for which you have no authority, and preventing me from complying with the president's orders."

To Secretary of War William Marcy he sent a dispatch stating that Stockton had prevented him from carrying out the President's orders "and as I have no troops in the country under my authority, excepting a few dragoons, I have no power of enforcing them." He included copies of his orders to Frémont on continuing in command of the California Battalion, Frémont's fatal letter, and his own exchange of letters with Stockton.

At about this time, he had made up his mind to arrest Frémont when they reached Fort Leavenworth, and see him court-martialed.

Stockton too wrote to Washington, addressing his remarks to the secretary of the navy on February 4, recounting his troubles with Kearny and demanding the recall of the general to "prevent the evil consequences that may grow out of such a temper and such a head!"

The Stockton-Kearny-Frémont imbroglio could not be kept secret. Even a newcomer such as twenty-seven-year-old artilleryman Lieutenant William Tecumseh Sherman, who arrived in California on the warship *Lexington* after a voyage around Cape Horn, saw the confusion, heard the arguments, and asked, "Who the devil *is* the governor of California?"

❈

As he promised, Kearny distanced himself from Stockton. On January 18, after sending Lieutenant William Emory east via Panama with dispatches on the command impasse, he gathered the remnant of the Army of the West—fifty reasonably able-bodied dragoons—and rode south to San Diego.

Within two weeks of his departure from Los Angeles, the descending star of his brigadiership began to rise; his enervating experiences with Stockton and Frémont were replaced by the exhilarating confirmation of his role as generalissimo of American military forces in California and head of its civil government.

The first of three arrivals in the abrupt turnabout of Kearny's fortunes was that at Warner's rancho of the Mormon Battalion of 350 volunteers led by Kearny favorite Lieutenant Colonel Philip St. George Cooke of Leesburg, Virginia, a West Pointer (class of '27), veteran of the War of 1812 battles and the Black Hawk War, and a fifteen-year veteran of the First Dragoons.

Kearny had explained to the War Department that he temporarily deferred to Stockton's leadership because, especially after San Pascual, he had too few fighting men under his immediate command to argue about it. He had depended upon adding Frémont's volunteers to his dwindled regulars to assert his right to the command in chief, but Frémont's disobedience had confounded that plan. Now the arrival of Cooke's battalion gave the general the manpower he needed to seize the military and civil supremacy the President had directed.

Cooke brought his haggard battalion into San Diego on January 29 and Kearny posted them at San Luís Rey to rest, recuperate, and await further orders while he and his staff sailed on the *Cyane* to Monterey. There, where Commodore John Sloat had first raised the American flag over California and launched the conquest six months earlier, Kearny intended to set up his headquarters. Consul

Thomas Larkin, now a Kearny ally, had generously offered his home for the purposes.

Monterey, the general had decided, would be the capital of American California during his governorship.

With an uncanny interdicting precision, while the general and his officers were making a leisurely eight-day voyage upcoast from San Diego, there arrived in Monterey Bay the naval officer sent to take over command from Robert F. Stockton of the Pacific Squadron.

Commodore William Branford Shubrick was a solid, stolid, fifty-seven-year-old salt from Bull's Island, South Carolina, and from a family of navy men. His older brother, John Templar Shubrick, had been a hero of the War of 1812 and was lost at sea in 1815. William Branford Shubrick, commissioned a midshipman in 1806, had, like Stockton, served in 1812, in the Mediterranean, West Africa, and the West Indies. There the similarities ended. He had none of Stockton's flamboyance and vainglory, no wealth, no political connections, and, as it quickly became evident, no use for Robert Field Stockton.

Shubrick arrived in Monterey on the razee—a refitted frigate—*Independence* in late January, and when the *Cyane* sailed into the harbor, the new commodore ordered a thirteen-gun salute in Kearny's honor. At dinner aboard his flagship, Shubrick got a lengthy briefing on the command question, took one look at the general's orders from President Polk and instantly concurred with them. He notified Kearny that new and clarifying orders would soon be arriving from Washington and wrote the Navy Department that "I have recognized in General Kearny the senior officer of the army in California; have consulted and shall cooperate with him as such. . . ." Stockton's civil government measures, Shubrick said, "have been, in my opinion, prematurely taken . . . and an appointment of governor made of a gentleman who I am led to believe is not acceptable to the people of California."

Frémont, on February 7, wrote to Shubrick to explain the difficulty of his position. "The conquest of California was undertaken and completed by the joint effort of Commodore Stockton and myself," he said, "in obedience to what we regarded paramount duties from us to our government." Once the surrender of the province had been accomplished, a civil government was organized, "designed to maintain the conquest by the exercise of mild and wholesome civil restraints over the people, rather than by the iron rule of military force." The results of his and Stockton's labors "were precisely what was contemplated by the instructions of General Kearny," and the record of the Stockton-Frémont conquest had been communicated to the President by express but no response had yet been received. "General Kearny's instructions being, therefore, to the letter fully anticipated by others, I did not feel myself at liberty to yield a position so important to the interests of my country until, after a full understanding of all the grounds, it should be the pleasure of my government that I should do so."

This sensible explanation, which might have illuminated the controversy for Shubrick, seems to have made no impression on the commodore but would resurface a year later in a courtroom in Washington.

❈

The next arrival in California proved the most significant of all in Kearny's—and Frémont's—future.

The warship *Erie* came through the Golden Gate on February 12 and Kearny traveled north to confer with its highest-ranking army passenger, Colonel Richard Barnes Mason of the First Dragoons, lately Kearny's second and successor as colonel of the regiment. He was pale and sick from the rough sea voyage from Panama when he stepped ashore at Yerba Buena.

The scion of distinguished Fairfax, Virginia, forebears, Mason had spent thirty of his fifty years in the army and had compiled an excellent record of service. In 1824, he had commanded a keelboat on a Kearny-led expedition to the mouth of the Yellowstone River; in 1832, he took part in the Battle of Bad Axe, which terminated the

Black Hawk War, and a year later, at Fort Gibson, Indian Territory, he was promoted major of the newly created First Dragoons.

He was a primary Kearny crony and a Kearny-like, no-nonsense professional soldier with a reputation as a duelist.

At Yerba Buena, Mason handed over to his chief orders from General of the Army Winfield Scott dated November 3, 1846, giving Kearny command of all land operations in California and the office as governor of California until such time as a civil government could be appointed. Scott also ordered Kearny to muster Frémont's California Battalion into the army and instructed that when the general could be confident of the safety and tranquillity of the country, he was to turn over all duties to Colonel Mason and return with a troop escort to St. Louis.

By the time Kearny and Mason returned to Monterey on February 23, the question of authority in California seemed to be settled. In his diary, Colonel Philip St. George Cooke gave a biting view of the matter: "Gen. Kearny is supreme—somewhere up the coast; Col. Frémont supreme at Pueblo de los Angles; Com. Stockton is 'commander-in-chief' at San Diego; Com. Shubrick, the same at Monterey; and I, at San Luís Rey; and we are all supremely poor, the government having no money and no credit, and we hold the territory because Mexico is poorest of all."

And in Washington, President Polk took note in his diary of the "unfortunate collision" in California between General Kearny and Commodore Stockton "in regard to precedence in rank" and said, "I think General Kearny was right. It appears that Lieut. Colonel Frémont refused to obey General Kearney and obeyed Commodore Stockton and in this he was wrong. . . ."

4

In Los Angeles, unaware of the fateful comings and goings at Monterey and Yerba Buena that February, Frémont was trying to run a government with no money. With Stockton at sea off Baja California, he was reduced to writing desperate letters to Kearny and

Shubrick begging for financial aid to keep the primitive military administration running. He needed money to pay the volunteers, to purchase equipment, supplies, horses, saddles, arms, and livestock, and to pay for the appropriated goods and resultant bills incurred during the conquest of California. He proposed that six hundred thousand dollars would settle the accounts—a sum that benumbed Shubrick, who refused to authorize any funds and notified Frémont in a curious non sequitur that until he, Commodore Shubrick, heard from Commodore Stockton, Kearny was the senior commanding army officer in California.

Frémont borrowed money over his personal signature, including one personal debt of five thousand dollars to purchase Bird Island (later named Alcatraz) to prevent its sale by its owner to a foreign power that could have used it to control the entrance to San Francisco Bay. On February 25, he sent Kit Carson, Lieutenant Edward Beale, Ted Talbot, Stepp the gunsmith, and others as a delegation to Washington with urgent dispatchs to Senator Benton and President Polk on the desperately impecunious and debt-burdened state of affairs in California.

By the time the California party departed overland, Kearny had returned to Monterey, where he and Shubrick began issuing a series of orders and proclamations defining the roles of the two services, placing the army in control ashore and limiting naval duties to customs and port regulations. Other public declarations assured Californians that their religious rights would be held sacrosanct, that they would be protected from enemies, foreign and domestic, that present laws would continue in force, that local magistrates and similar officials would retain their posts after taking oaths of allegiance to the United States, and that any losses realized in the American annexation would be reimbursed.

These preludes to Kearny's ascendancy ended on March 1 with a notice to the people of California that Brigadier General Stephen W. Kearny had assumed the governorship and had selected Monterey as the seat of his government.

Frémont's fifty days as governor ended with this announcement and with orders from Kearny dated March 1. Lieutenant Colonel Cooke would relieve Archibald Gillespie as military commander in Los Angeles, and Frémont would report to military headquarters in Monterey and bring with him all the California Battalion records and property, this preparatory to mustering out the volunteers and reenlisting those who wished to serve in the regular army. The orders were signed "S. W. Kearny, Brig. Gen., and Governor of California."

✤

CHAPTER TWENTY-ONE

Return

1

No Kearny man had any use for John Charles Frémont. Among the dragoon officers, he was regarded as an arrogant parvenu, jumped up by his political connections, an amateur "soldier" who should have been clapped in irons for his mutinous defiance of the general's orders. Now, with the Kearny star risen at last, it was time for the new governor to take the usurper to task.

The first of the several agents to essay this work was Philip St. George Cooke, the smart, capable, former commander of the Mormon Battalion. In mid-March, he took over as military chief of the "Southern District"—principally Los Angeles—sent his predecessor, Archibald Gillespie, packing, and called upon Frémont.

There is no detailed record of their meeting, only its aftermath, but it was an unpleasant one for both men. Frémont told Cooke that once mustered out, the men of the California Battalion would not enlist in the army, and because of alarming rumors of a possible rising against American authority, he could not turn over any military property—not even the howitzer that had been captured by the Californians at San Pascual. Men, arms, and materiél, he said, might be needed to defend Los Angeles.

Frémont also made known his intention to journey to Monterey to report on the unrest and other critical matters directly to General Kearny.

Cooke's immediate reaction to these announcements is unknown, but his wrath spilled over in his later report on the confrontation: "I denounce this treason, or this mutiny, which jeopardizes the safety of the country and defies me in my legal command and duties. . . ."

A hundred years after the Cooke-Frémont encounter, Bernard DeVoto wrote that the rumor of a native revolt in Los Angeles was the product of a Frémont "whoop up," mere bluster and oration, one ploy among many in the explorer's continuing "acts of treason" designed, the historian said, for the purpose of making a record for use later, when "he could play his ace, the support of his father-in-law." But there is no evidence of such a sinister and cynical design. The rumors were real: reports claiming that Californians were massing and arming in Baja California, their strength increased by the arrival of Mexican army regulars, and were intent on retaking their lost territory. Other reports reached Frémont stating that he would be "deposed by violence" because of the nonpayment of debts that Americans had incurred during their presence in California and because of proclamations issued in Stockton's absence that were, as Frémont put it, "incompatible with the capitulation of Cowenga."

This "commotion," as he called it, genuinely alarmed him. Gillespie's lamentable experience in Los Angeles proved what an ardent and armed mob of nationalists and a handful of trained officers could do against a small military garrison. The California Battalion was tenfold larger than Gillespie's pitiful force, but Frémont had no information on the extent of the army rumored to be massing against him. For all he knew, José Castro, José María Flores, Andrés Pico, and all the other Mexican commanders who had decamped to Sonora were putting together a huge army in Baja California and preparing to march on San Diego and points north.

He determined to ride to Monterey and report to Kearny in person, and on March 22, 1847, he set out with Jacob Dodson, his black manservant and an expert wrangler who minded six extra unsaddled horses, and José de Jesús Pico, who had been instrumental in the surrender at Cahuenga Pass. Pico's role in the ride north is unclear but Frémont may have intended that he would confirm the reports and rumors of a brewing counterrevolt.

Principally due to Senator Benton's extolling of it in Congress, the 420-mile ride from Los Angeles to Monterey was later described as "epic." One of Frémont's most protective biographers called it "theatrical" and "unnecessary." At the least, the ride was remarkable: after brief rests at Santa Barbara and San Luís Obispo and a near-miss bear attack in their night camp, the three men reached the outskirts of Monterey at dusk on March 25, covering the 420 miles in three days and ten hours.

Frémont left Dodson and Pico to set up camp about a mile outside the town and rode his lathered horse to Kearny's headquarters at Thomas Larkin's home. The consul escorted him to the general's office, but the explorer's epic ride clearly did not impress the busy new proconsul, who announced that he would meet with Frémont the next morning.

That night, Lieutenant William T. Sherman, now a Kearny aide, paid the explorer a "courtesy call." He wrote later that, "feeling a natural curiosity to see Frémont . . . I rode out to his camp and found him in a conical tent with one Capt. [Dick] Owens . . . I spent an hour or so with F. in his tent, took some tea with him, and left without being impressed with him." It seems likely that Sherman, at this time as much a Kearny toady as Cooke or Mason, paid the visit to test the explorer's temperament and to obtain as much information as he could to report to the general in preparation for the next day's interview.

From the outset, the March 26 meeting was ruinous for Frémont. He was angry. He had worn out three horses getting to Monterey to deliver crucial information, only to be told he must wait the night to see the general. He had been rudely informed that he was relieved as governor and as commander of the California Battalion. His confrontation with Lieutenant Colonel Cooke still rankled. He had been rubbed raw between two senior officers in a command dispute that any ensign and second lieutenant could have settled amicably. He needed to present his case to Kearny in a frank, open dialogue. But when he was ushered into the general's office, he found that the meeting would not be private. Soon after their disastrous January 17 confrontation in Los Angeles, Kearny had determined that once they returned to Fort Leavenworth, he would place Frémont under arrest on charges of mutiny and disobedience of lawful orders and request that a court-martial be convened. Five months would pass before the explorer learned of this plan and realized why, on the morning of March 26, he was not meeting with Kearny alone.

Seated with the general in his headquarters office was Colonel Richard B. Mason. Frémont did not know the man or his mission but objected to his presence and suggested to the general that it was perhaps to witness some "unguarded remark." Kearny regarded this as an insult and the meeting, which dragged on over two days, corroborated for him the justice of his plans for the explorer and confirmed for Frémont that the general and his gang of lickspittles were more his enemy than the Californians had ever been.

Kearny did not appear concerned over the rumors and reports of a potential revolt among the Californians in the southern province, nor did he rise to Frémont's pointed question about whether the new civil government would assume the debts of the conquest. (In Washington subsequently, Kearny could remember neither the question nor his reply, although he said he "should have answered in the negative.")

Frémont said that he would resign his army commission, but Kearny refused to accept the proposition.

The meeting culminated with Kearny asking Frémont if he intended obeying his order to hand over the California Battalion and its records. The general, with Mason hanging on to every word, cautioned the explorer to take care in responding to the question and gave him a day to think it over.

In the end, Frémont agreed to obey and was ordered to return to

Los Angeles to gather the battalion and accompany it back to Monterey, together with its supplies and papers.

After the explorer departed with Dodson and Pico, Kearny dispatched Colonel Mason to Los Angeles with a letter giving him full authority to oversee the battalion's debarkation at San Pedro and to order Frémont to report to Monterey no more than twelve days after the battalion sailed.

2

Mason arrived in Los Angeles on April 5 and set up his office in the home of Nathaniel M. Pryor, a Kentucky-born silversmith and clockmaker who had lived in the pueblo since 1830. Once established there, the colonel sent for Frémont.

Neither man was apt to be holding an olive branch, but any chance of a reasonably friendly encounter disappeared when Frémont saw that Mason, following the lead of his general, had a witness present. Lieutenant Colonel St. George Cooke may have smiled when the explorer entered the room; he was as eager as any Kearny man to witness the fall of this mutinous subordinate.

Mason repeated Kearny's orders and asked Frémont to join him the next day at Mission San Gabriel to visit the battalion and ascertain which of the volunteers wished to stay in the service.

The muster followed its commander's prediction. Mason announced to the gathered men that they were to be disbanded but that all who wished to continue to serve would be sworn into the regular army. When none stepped forward, Mason directed his anger at Frémont, ordered the battalion to be discharged immediately, the naval personnel among them to be sent north on the sloop-of-war *Warren*. He instructed the explorer to gather his original Topographical Corps party and march it to Monterey, there to report to Governor-General Kearny, and to turn over to the appropriate officer of the First Dragoons all horses, mules, arms, ammunition, and supplies.

Frémont, unhumbled in the stripping of his command, had, or contrived to have, a final encounter with the man he considered a Kearny chauvinist. The issue centered on a sizable horse herd that Frémont had gathered for "service in Mexico." He informed Mason by letter that he intended leading a regiment into Mexico for service with Zachary Taylor, an option given him in correspondence to Kearny from War Secretary William Marcy.

Mason curtly dismissed this idea as contrary to new orders from the general and sent an orderly to Frémont's quarters demanding that the horses be surrendered to the government forthwith.

The clash between the contemptuous colonel and the refractory lieutenant colonel switched from a paper duel to the threat of the real field of honor when, on April 14, Frémont was summoned to Mason's office. There would be no further dispute or discussion of the horse issue, or of any other issue, Mason said heatedly, and when the explorer objected to the tone of the admonition, Mason exploded, "None of your insolence, or I will put you in irons!" In his version of the event, Frémont took the threat calmly, saying to the choleric Kearny agent, "You cannot make an official matter of a personal one, sir; as a man, do you hold yourself personally responsible for what you have just said?"

Whether Frémont walked out of the meeting or Mason terminated it is not clear, but within an hour of its end, the explorer sent a note to Mason demanding a written apology for his "insult" and making a threat of his own: failure to offer the apology would be translated as an "official challenge." Then, when Mason, perhaps calculatedly, did not respond, Frémont threw down the last gauntlet, making the challenge official by letter and inviting his opponent to choose his weapon.

His folly in defying Kearny had cost him his career; his recklessness in challenging Mason came close to costing him his life: the colonel of dragoons, who was believed to be familiar with dueling and was certainly familiar with bird-hunting, chose shotguns—double-barreled and buckshot-loaded. Frémont had never fired such an arm in his life and had to send an aide to locate one.

He was saved from certain death by the blind good fortune that often follows the foolhardy: the day after the challenge, the dragoon colonel sent his second to Frémont's quarters to say that the duel would have to be delayed until after they reached Monterey. A few days later, upon hearing of the pending confrontation, Kearny intervened, writing to his lieutenant colonel: "It becomes my duty to inform you that the good of the Public Service, the necessity of preserving tranquillity in California . . . require that the meeting above referred to should not take place at this time, and in this country, and you are hereby officially directed by me to proceed no further in this matter. A similar communication has been addressed to Colonel Mason."*

In the end, Frémont grudgingly obeyed orders: the horse herd was surrendered, the California Battalion was mustered out on April 19, Mason sailed to Monterey to assume command of the Tenth Military District—now the official army name for California—and soon afterward, the explorer followed with what remained of his original topographical party.

On May 13, Kearny notified the adjutant general of the army in Washington that he would soon be returning to the East with Lieutenant Colonel Frémont, whose conduct in California, he said, "has been such that I shall be compelled on arriving in Missouri to arrest him and send him under charges to report to you." He did not say that Frémont had yet to be informed of the impending action against him.

Toward the end of May, at about the time he learned from Washington dispatches that General Scott had captured Vera Cruz and

---

In 1850, Mason, having returned from his service as governor of California, wrote to his old adversary in Washington offering to fight the duel if Frémont would come to St. Louis. Frémont wisely chose not to answer the letter. The quarrel ended with Mason's death that year at the age of fifty-three.

was marching on Mexico City, Kearny met with Frémont and the Topographical Corps men and had orders read that they were to proceed east under his command on May 31 and that any who sought to be discharged from the service would be permitted to remain in California.

Frémont had several requests to make of the general. He asked for time to locate two of his original expedition men, Ned Kern, the artist and one-time officer in charge at Sutter's Fort, and Henry King, a veteran of the explorer's western treks. This was refused. He asked if Kearny would authorize payment of financial obligations that Frémont had incurred as governor and was told no. He asked that members of the California Battalion who did not join the army receive back pay due them and this was denied. He asked permission to return to St. Louis, even if at his own expense, by either the Gila River in the south or the Salt Lake in the north and the answer was no. He asked for time to gather up his geological and botanical specimens and scientific instruments left in Yerba Buena, and this too was denied.

He was required to turn over what surveying equipment he had to Kearny aide Lieutenant Henry W. Halleck, and in a particularly galling order, was instructed to camp outside Monterey with his men while awaiting the return home.

3

On May 31, 1847, General Kearny, with Colonel Cooke and sixty-two men plus a mule pack train and small horse herd, marched out of Monterey, capital of the new United States Territory of California, on the trail north to New Helvetia. Six months had passed since he and Kit Carson had led his small, trail-weary dragoon force into Warner's Ranch.

Among those in the Kearny column were Lieutenant Colonel Frémont and nineteen of his original topographical force, including his Delaware escort. Eighteen months had passed since he had led his small and exhausted exploring party into Sutter's Fort.

Frémont and his men were posted a mile or two in the rear, as if in quarantine, "compelled to trail eastward at the chariot wheels of the General," as the explorer's biographer, Allan Nevins, put it.

The collection of indignities devised by Kearny for the pariah in his assemblage were numerous and uniformly petty. When the group arrived at Sutter's outpost on June 13, the hospitable Swiss greeted the general with a salute from the fort's cannon and invited him and his officers to a dinner he had prepared in their honor. Frémont was not invited, a circumstance entirely agreeable to Sutter, who still smarted over the explorer's commandeering of his fort during the Bear Flag revolt and over the jailing of General Vallejo and the other prisoners there.

Another calculated insult arose when the company departed New Helvetia for the long journey east and it was learned that Kearny had hired Le Gros Fallon as his guide through country well known to Frémont and any number of his veteran explorers.

As the final irony in the journey home, Commodore Stockton and his party of fifty officers (including Archibald Gillespie), sailors, and marines departed from Sonoma about a month behind the Kearny column. Thus, with Kearny in the lead and Stockton in the rear, Frémont was once again sandwiched between the rival conquerors of California.

The single memorable event on the return journey was the arrival at Truckee Lake on June 22, where Kearny and his company saw the pitiful remains of the Donner party, a rubble of bones, remnants of wagons, scattered goods and clothing and shattered crockery, rickety, fire-blackened cabins and lean-tos. The essentials of what had happened to the emigrants during the past winter were known, and Sutter, among others, told the story often about how the Missouri farmers George and Jacob Donner and their emigrant train had reached this place at the end of October, 1846, four months out of Independence.

They had abandoned the proven California Trail after being told of a shortcut to the Sierra foothills, and by the time they reached the Humboldt River in September and Truckee Lake a month later, the Sierra winter had locked them in. They had rested for five fatal days before attempting to cross the mountains, allowing their surviving livestock to wander and become buried in snow. They had not gathered sufficient firewood; there was no game. They camped in cabins on the lake and in tents and brushwood arbors and huts at Alder Creek. There were eighty-seven of them, nearly half small children, and they were reduced to eating brush mice, powdered bone, bark and twigs, and boiled rawhide. A group of fifteen of them started on December 16 from the lake camp to cross the Sierras on makeshift snowshoes with six days' rations. Their travail lasted thirty-two days. Eight of them died in the snow and two Indian guides were shot. The corpses were eaten by the survivors. The dead were also cannibalized at Truckee Lake. Once word finally reached Sutter's Fort and ranches around New Helvetia, relief parties were sent out through the snowbound passes to rescue the survivors. Of the eighty-seven Donner party emigrants, forty-eight reached California.

Kearny's and Frémont's men buried what bones they found and burned the remains of the cabins, then moved on to the Truckee River, the Humboldt Sink, the Humboldt River, across the Snake and on to the Oregon Trail. South Pass was reached on July 24 and Fort Leavenworth on August 22, ending a sixty-six-day march of nearly two thousand miles.

Frémont had no time to enjoy the journey's end; indeed, he barely had time to find billets for his men and smack the trail dust from his hat before being summoned to the office of Lieutenant Colonel Clifton Wharton, the post commander. There he found Kearny waiting in the ominously familiar arrangement of having a witness on hand. In Wharton's presence, the general read a document instructing the explorer to turn over all horses, mules, and other public property to the Leavenworth quartermaster, to arrange for the accounts of his nineteen men to be paid, and "having performed the above duty," Kearny intoned, Lieutenant Colonel Frémont "will consider himself under arrest, and will then repair to Washington City, and report himself to the adjutant general of the army."

Although he certainly suspected that he faced some kind of official reprimand—his exile at the rear of Kearny's party and similar affronts signaled that—the pronouncement of August 22 was the first that Frémont knew of Kearny's plan, formulated six months before, to place him under arrest. And he had enough familiarity with the procedures of military justice to know that "arrest" was but a step removed from court-martial.*

Frémont claimed that after news of his arrest spread, none of the officers at the post would speak to him or extend to him or his men any of the courtesies that were normally commonplace. He said that when he brought the horses and mules up for delivery to the post quartermaster, he, his men, and the animals were forced to wait in the sun five hours before they were officially received.

Stockton, Gillespie, and the commodore's party arrived at Fort Leavenworth a few days after Kearny, and in the last week of August, Frémont boarded the steamer *Martha* for the short voyage south on the Missouri to Westport Landing, where Jessie waited.

Twenty-seven months had passed since they were last together; Lily was just a baby when he had left. Jessie noted the graying of her husband's beard and was delighted at his garish Californio outfit of broad hat, fancy trousers, and red sash.

---

*Dwight L. Clarke, Kearny's biographer, in attempting to mitigate the six-month delay in informing Frémont of his fate, provides an inadvertent indictment of the dragoon officers the explorer regarded as lackeys. "The Lieutenant Colonel should have been very grateful that his arrest had been so long delayed," Clarke says, adding the telling comment that had the explorer been arrested when Kearny first decided on it and a court-martial convened then, "What chance would John C. Frémont have stood with a court composed in part of Mason, Cooke, Swords, Turner and Sherman?"

The Frémonts took the *Martha* downriver for a reunion with Senator Benton before moving on to Washington.

Kearny preceded them and by the time they reached St. Louis, the general was en route to Washington for a meeting with President Polk.

CHAPTER TWENTY-TWO

Court-martial

1

Frémont returned to St. Louis a conquering hero. A mob of well-wishers hoping to catch a glimpse of him and the always-luminous Jessie greeted the *Martha* at the pier-head and clamored for a speech; invitations poured in from the city's social and political elite. But the explorer made only a few innocuous remarks referring to his California adventures and attended no parties. He could not linger in St. Louis; he needed to move on to Washington to clear his name of the grave charges Kearny had leveled against him. What time he had he spent with his family, giving Jessie, and especially her father, the history that had led to his arrest, from the fatal January 17 meeting with the general in Los Angeles to the August 22 arrival at Fort Leavenworth, where he had been placed under arrest.

Benton and Jessie had learned some of the story before the *Martha* docked and their hero stepped ashore. Frémont himself, in the infrequent letters he wrote home, had told of the Stockton-Kearny feud and his ordeal between the two men, and there had been other sources of information out of California as well.

In June, Major William "Owl" Russell, the explorer's close friend and, during his brief governorship, his secretary of state, came through St. Louis. He brought the unsettling news of Kearny's assumption of power in California and was carrying to Washington petitions signed by many influentials in the southern part of the Territory beseeching federal authorities to reinstall Frémont as governor.

(Neither Russell nor the explorer knew it at the time, but anti-Frémont petitions and letters were also arriving in the capital, said to have been gathered by disgruntled former California Battalion volunteers "clamorous for their pay." Other letters opposing Frémont were written by his mortal enemy, Richard Mason, by Thomas Larkin, and by certain *arribeños* who had not forgotten the murders of José Berreyesa and the De Haro brothers at San Rafael in June 1846.)

Newspapers were another source of information, mostly dubious, on the controversy. The New Orleans *Picayune,* Louisville *Journal,* and St. Louis *Republican,* among others, carried peculiarly skewed reports and first-person "columns" giving readers the scenario that Kearny was the honorable professional soldier trying to do his duty, thwarted at every step by the power-hungry amateurs, Stockton and Frémont. Since some of the unsigned newspaper work contained details known only among Kearny's intimate circle of officers, the authors were suspected to be Colonel Richard Mason, Lieutenant Colonel Philip St. George Cooke, and Lieutenant William Emory.

Kit Carson, Edward Beale, and Alexis Godey had also preceded the explorer to St. Louis and brought news to Senator Benton of the dire events in California—Kearny's seizing of the command primacy in Stockton's absence, his usurpation of the governorship, his humiliating initiatives against Frémont.

Carson had arrived in St. Louis in May and told what he knew. Benton, his always volatile temperament by now roiling over his son-in-law's predicament, took Kit and Jessie with him to Washington to make a personal visit to the President.

On June 7, 1847, at the time Frémont and his nineteen men were camped in exile at Sutter's Fort awaiting the departure east, Jessie escorted the celebrated frontiersman to the President's office. Polk was charmed by Carson and they chatted at length, the President acknowledging the scout's services in the war by awarding him a commission as a second lieutenant "of Mounted Rifles" at a monthly pay of $33.33 plus $24 for rations, $16 for forage for two horses, and a servant at $16.50—a total of $89.83 a month. Kit thus happily left the capital to return home to Taos and his wife Josefa.

Jessie held Polk in much less thrall. He listened with as much patience as he could summon, giving her the same courtesy he extended to her powerful father, whose several visits on behalf of the California intrigues had taxed the presidential patience. The man who, with his cabinet secretaries, had created the command commotion in California, noted in his diary, "Mrs Frémont seemed anxious to elicit from me some expression of approbation for her husband's conduct, but I evaded. In truth, I consider Colonel Frémont was greatly in the wrong when he refused to obey the orders issued to him by General Kearny. I think General Kearny was right also in his controversy with Commodore Stockton."

On September 16, three days after General Winfield Scott's victory at Chapúltepec, the final battle of the war in Mexico, Frémont arrived in Washington and reported to Adjutant General of the Army Roger Jones. He asked for a thirty-day delay in his trial in order to amass his papers, make a study of newspaper reports, and await Commodore Stockton's arrival in the capital.

"I wish a full trial, and a speedy one," he wrote in a letter for the record to General Jones. "The charges against me by Brigadier General Kearny, and subsidiary accusations made against me in all the departments of my conduct (military, civil, political, and moral) while in California, if true, would subject me to be cashiered and shot, under the rules and articles of war, and to infamy in the public opinion." He said it was his intention to "meet these charges in all their extent and for that purpose to ask a trial upon every point of allegation or insinuation against me, waiving all objections to forms and technicalities, and allow the widest range to all possible testimony."

Frémont, aware that Kearny had preceded him to Washington and had been closeted with high-ranking army officers, the War Department, and the President, made certain that the adjutant general understood the indignities he had suffered before charges were made against him, as well as the circumstances of his arrest. He said bitterly, "Brought home by General Kearny, and marched in his rear, I did not know of his design to arrest me until the moment of its execution at Fort Leavenworth. He then informed me that among the charges which he had referred were mutiny, disobedience of orders, assumption of powers, etc. . . ."

In late October, a few days before the court-martial was to open, Benton paid a final visit to the President and, in a fireplace lecture, made a virulent argument against his one-time friend, Stephen Watts Kearny. Polk, true to his custom, was exasperatingly noncommittal. The President considered Kearny "a good officer and an intelligent gentleman" and, after a visit with the general on September 11, recorded in his journal that neither man had talked about the "difficulties" in California. "I did not introduce the subject and I was glad that he did not," Polk noted.

As to Benton's importunities, the President wrote, "I have always been on good terms with Senator Benton but he is a man of violent passions and I should not be surprised if he became my enemy because all his wishes are not gratified. . . ."

2

After a day of preliminaries, the trial opened on the overcast Indian-summer Wednesday of November 3, 1847, at the Washington Arsenal, a shabby wooden building dimly lit by sunlight filtering through windows up near the high-domed roof. The court consisted of fourteen officers—three colonels, five lieutenant colonels, and four majors—led by Brevet Brigadier General G. M. Brooke of the Fifth Infantry and Major John Fitzgerald Lee, judge advocate. Eleven of the fourteen officers had thirty or more years of army service; four were graduates of the military academy at West Point.

In the audience there were newspapermen, congressmen, a miscellany of Washington bureaucrats and hangers-on, and Frémont faithfuls such as Alexis Godey and Dick Owens (Kit Carson had returned to California). Jessie was there, dressed in a lovely wine-colored dress, her striking oval face shaded by a burgundy-velvet bonnet, and her sister Eliza, in a gay blue ensemble. Eliza had suggested they dress in black for the occasion, but Jessie rejected the idea as too funereal.

Frémont sat with his advisors. At the prosecutor's table were General Kearny; his Army of the West second in command, Captain Henry S. Turner; and Major Lee, the judge advocate.

After the administering of oaths, the explorer requested of the court permission to have his brother-in-law, William Carey Jones, an attorney married to Jessie's older sister Eliza, and Senator Thomas Hart Benton as counsel at his defense table. This was granted under military rules, which permitted civilian attorneys to serve in advisory roles but did not allow them to cross-examine witnesses. In this, Frémont would have to serve as his own defense lawyer.

Following various courtesies and questions, the hushed audience heard the judge advocate read the charges against John Charles Frémont.

The first and weightiest of these was the charge of mutiny, the allegation that Frémont had refused to obey orders of his superior, Brigadier General Stephen Watts Kearny, beginning on January 17, 1847, when he declared that he would continue to "report and receive orders, as heretofore, from the Commodore [Stockton]" and that he would continue, against contrary orders, as "Military Commandant of the Territory of California," which title he had employed in signing his letter to Kearny.

There were eleven specifications under the mutiny charge, with documents supporting them dating between January 17 and May 9, 1847, the latter date approximating the dispute with Colonel Mason in Los Angeles.

The second charge, "Disobedience of the Lawful Command of his Superior Officer," contained seven specifications between the same dates, and the third, "Conduct to the Prejudice of Good Order and Military Discipline," carried five specific charges.

In the course of the trial, Frémont characterized the charges as a "comedy of three errors," the first being "the faulty order sent out from this place [Washington]; next, in the unjustifiable pretensions of General Kearny; thirdly, in the conduct of the government in sustaining these pretensions." The last of these, he said, was the greatest of the three.

He pleaded not guilty to each of the twenty-three specifications.

His defense strategy centered on the struggle for command between Kearny and Stockton, this having at its source the circumstances he had explained in his February 7, 1847, letter to Commodore Branford Shubrick, who had been sent out to Monterey to relieve Stockton of command of the Pacific Squadron. Frémont had written Shubrick that "The conquest of California was undertaken and completed by the joint effort of Commodore Stockton and myself in obedience to what we regarded paramount duties from us to our government" and that this conquest was complete and a civil government had been established before Kearny's arrival in California.

The explorer was also able to demonstrate that the charges against him derived from this rivalry and from Kearny's vindictiveness and temper, attributes shared by a circle of sycophants such as Commodore Shubrick, colonels Richard Mason and Henry Turner, Lieutenant Colonel Philip St. George Cooke, and Lieutenant William H. Emory. And he was permitted to place into the record all the affronts he had suffered during the contretemps between his superior officers, especially those inflicted by Kearny during the march home, the keeping of the charges against him secret for six months, the outrageous manner of his arrest, and the subsequent demeaning treatment at Leavenworth.

Of the great latitude the court extended the defense, Bernard DeVoto said that the court, in permitting extraneous testimony and records, allowed the explorer and his counsel "to turn a military trial into a political circus," and characterized it as a "creature of oratory and newsprint."

But Frémont proved to be a formidable advocate, especially relentless when, referring to himself in third person, he questioned his accuser. Their first exchange did not reflect well on the general.

"At what time did you form the design to arrest Lieutenant Colonel Frémont?" Frémont asked.

"I formed the design shortly after receiving his letter of January 17. That word 'shortly' would not imply immediately. It may have been a week."

The explorer then bored in on another critical matter. Kearny, in mid-February, 1847, had received orders from General Winfield Scott, carried to California by Colonel Richard Mason. These orders gave Kearny command of all land operations in the province and the office of military governor and authorized him to muster the California Battalion into the army.

Why, Frémont asked, had Kearny not informed Lieutenant Colonel Frémont of these orders—which would have ended all debate on the command issue?

Kearny answered haughtily, "I am not in the habit of communicating to my juniors the instructions I receive from my seniors, unless required to do so in those instructions."

(Frémont biographer Allan Nevins calls this response "a very lame excuse for a base act.")

Kearny made a poor start and was a poor witness overall. His chief weakness lay in his inexplicable memory lapses—or, as the defense had it, his highly "selective" memory. He claimed he could not remember that Frémont had made his ride from Los Angeles to Monterey for the purpose of warning about the rumors of an armed Californian force planning to recapture the southern province; he could not remember that it was Kit Carson who had delivered Frémont's letter to his office on January 17; he claimed never to have heard of the conquest debts Frémont had begged his assistance in paying; nor did he remember Frémont's attempt to resign from the army. He could not remember who had recovered the cannon he had lost in the San Pascual battle, could not remember Lieutenant Archibald Gillespie or Lieutenant Edward Beale, two of the officers who had led the Stockton relief force of sailors, marines, and California Battalion volunteers who had joined him on the eve of the battle.

One thing the general did remember clearly was that Lieutenant Colonel Frémont had attempted "bargaining" for the governorship of California.

"He asked me if I would appoint him governor," Kearny said from the witness stand. "I told him I expected shortly to leave California for Missouri . . . that as soon as the country was quieted I should, most probably, organize a civil government in California; and that I, at that time, knew of no objections to my appointing him as the governor."

He then accused Frémont of stating that he intended to see Stockton to demand the governorship, and failing to get it, he would no longer obey the commodore's orders.

Few with any knowledge of the events in California believed Kearny's account of the January 17 conversation. Frémont himself vehemently denied it in court, saying that he had received appointments from three Presidents, Jackson, Tyler, and Polk, but that he had never begged or bargained for one in his life. Furthermore, there was ample record that both Stockton and Kearny had offered him the governorship and that Stockton actually gave him the appointment on January 14, the day he rode into Los Angeles and delivered the Cahuenga treaty to the commodore.

Through his direct questions and lengthy diversions disguised as questions, Frémont was able to dwell on Secretary of War Marcy's June 3, 1846, orders to Kearny, the "Should you conquer and take possession of New Mexico and California" orders. He declared that Kearny and his Army of the West had not taken possession of anything in California, that the conquering and possessing had been done by Stockton and Frémont and that Kearny had been in no shape to possess or conquer anything; indeed, he had had to be rescued from Mule Hill after the San Pascual fight by 215 of Stockton's sailors and marines.

Kearny was forced to make damaging admissions. He had addressed official correspondence to Stockton as "His Excellency, R. F. Stockton, Governor of California," which gave a tacit concession that Stockton had superseded him in setting up a civil government. And on the charge of mutiny, he admitted that he had not imprisoned or placed Frémont in irons despite the fact that mutiny was a capital offense in wartime.

The defense was getting high scores in newspaper reports, and it was pointed out that Robert F. Stockton, a key figure in the entire controversy, had yet to take the stand.

3

Philip St. George Cooke testified for a week with no great consequence for Frémont. The judge advocate chose not to call William H. Emory as witness, but Frémont managed to reveal his role as probable author of a letter in the New Orleans *Picayune* that extolled Kearny as the hero of the conquest of California, told of the rivalry between Kearny and Stockton, and said that the commodore had drawn Frémont "on his side."

At last, on December 6, the first anniversary of the Battle of San Pascual, Stockton was sworn in as a witness. From the start, he proved a great disappointment for the defense and a source of frustration for the court, which grew far more impatient at his extemporizations than at Kearny's memory lapses. Self-confident and abnormally self-possessed, accustomed to talking more than listening, the commodore gave a windy, rambling history of the war in California but seemed uncertain about specifics and vague in answering the questions both Frémont and Major Lee posed.

He tried to be helpful to the defense, and his meandering testimony contained some coherent statements that to some extent mitigated Frémont's actions. He said that the conquest of California had been "interrupted" by the events in Los Angeles in September, 1846, when the pueblo had temporarily surrendered to the insurgents. Peace was soon restored, he said, "and therefore there was nothing for me to do in relation to the establishment of a civil government, except to hand to Lieutenant Colonel Frémont the commission as governor, which I had pledged my word to do; which I had informed the government I would do, and which I probably would have done, on the 25th day of October [1846], if the insurrection had not broken out."

As to what he called "the position of the parties"—meaning himself, Kearny, and Frémont—he said, "in my judgment and opinion . . . General Kearny had laid aside, for the time being, his commission as brigadier general, and was serving as a volunteer under my command." He asserted that after the San Gabriel battle, as their combined forces marched to Los Angeles, the troops placed by his orders under the command of General Kearny were the dragoons, sailors, and marines and Captain Gillespie's two companies of the California Battalion, "and no other." As to the disposition of the battalion after reaching Los Angeles, Stockton said, "On the arrival of Lieutenant Colonel Frémont, he reported to me; and I did not give, nor did I intend to give, General Kearny any control or command over that part of the California Battalion. It was under my own immediate command." He testified that he had appointed Captain Gillespie to take command of the battalion after he appointed Frémont governor, and said, "If I understand the matter before this court, the disobedience of orders charged against the accused, whilst I was commander-in-chief, is, that he would not obey an order which required him not to recognize my appointment of Captain Gillespie as a major of the battalion."

At one point in the questioning by Major Lee, a significant point was made for Kearny when Stockton admitted that he had no specific orders to form a civil government in California. "I formed the government under the law of nations," he said, without defining a law that apparently existed only in his mind.

Archibald Gillespie testified on Frémont's behalf, as did Lieutenant Andrew F. V. Gray and Owl Russell. Gray, the naval officer who had led the force Stockton sent to relieve Kearny and his dragoons on Mule Hill, said he witnessed Kearny's offer to serve as Stockton's second in command in the march to Los Angeles. Owl Russell supported this testimony and added, "I remember distinctly that he [Kearny] spoke of his intention of appointing Colonel Frémont governor."

At the beginning of the trial, newspaper coverage of it was extensive, with editors such as James Gordon Bennett of the influential New York *Herald* regarding it as the *cause célèbre* of the era. But as the proceedings rolled on six days a week through December and January, the tedium of dull and repetitious testimony had a palling effect. There were signs of ebbing editorial support for the defense and a growing sympathy for the old soldier Kearny, belabored at such length by defense witnesses and the relentless interrogations by the accused.

Kearny returned to the stand on January 5, 1848, the first session of the new year, and three days later provided a startling moment in his testimony when he asked the court permission to read a statement he had prepared. The courtroom was silent as the general read in an obviously troubled voice:

> "I consider it due to the dignity of the court, and the high respect I entertain for it, that I should here state that, on my last appearance before this court, the senior counsel for the accused, Thomas H. Benton, of Missouri, sat in his place making mouths and grimaces at me, which I considered were intended to offend, to insult, and to overawe me. I ask of this court no action on it, so far as I am concerned. I am fully capable of taking care of my own honor."

This astonishing statement shocked the court and audience momentarily; General G. M. Brooke, president of the court, nervously said that he had not observed any offensive facial expressions of the senator's and proceeded to read from the Articles of War the caution against "menacing" words or gestures in a court-martial proceeding.

Then Benton, towering, smoldering, stood and ignoring admonitions that he had no right to speak at the trial, launched into a booming response, saying that in earlier testimony, Kearny had made certain insinuations and "fixed his eyes upon Colonel Frémont . . . insultingly and fiendishly." He went on:

"When General Kearny fixed his eyes upon Colonel Frémont, I determined if he should attempt again to look down a prisoner, I would look at him. I did this day; and the look of today was the consequence of the looks in this court before. I did today look at General Kearny when he looked at Colonel Frémont, and I looked at him till his eyes fell—'til they fell upon the floor."

The president of the court cooled the senator's ardor by asserting that he had observed Kearny looking with "kindness" toward Colonel Frémont, and General Brooke permitted Kearny the last word on the subject: "I have never offered the slightest insult to Colonel Frémont, either here as a prisoner . . . or anywhere, or under any circumstances whatsoever."

4

"My acts in California have all been with high motives, and a desire for public service," Frémont said on January 27, 1848, standing before his accusers and judges to end the summary of his defense. "My scientific labors did something to open California to the knowledge of my countrymen; its geography had been a sealed book."

In the grim, gray Washington armory courtroom, he appeared anything but the vainglorious filibustero chieftain, the self-promoting frontier Napoleon—and the mutineer—his opponents styled him. Nor, for that matter, did his appearance give a hint of the truer man.

It was difficult to credit that this man, described in newspaper columns as "slight," "trim," "erect," "olive-skinned," "dark-eyed," "sad of countenance," "handsome," and—often—"Gallic," was the celebrated explorer whose name was as synonymous with the great unknown West as Lewis and Clark's. He did not appear to be the same Frémont whose books revealed a man who found his greatest comfort among the Kit Carsons of the mountains. Was this slight, well-spoken, neatly dressed, lawyer-like figure the same man who killed Indians who opposed him, smoked pipes of willow-bark shavings, and thumbed "trapper's butter" from the cracked bones of a fresh-killed brute buffalo among Indians who befriended him?

His self-defense, if overlong and tedious in its drumming counter-accusations against General Kearny and his minions, had been brilliant for a man so out of his element. But as the trial lumbered to its close, Frémont, as if perceiving the inevitable outcome of it, grew more defensive, betraying, some said, the narcissism that was his fatal flaw.

"My military operations were conquests without bloodshed," he said untruthfully. "My civil administration was for the public good. I offer California, during my administration, for comparison with the most tranquil portions of the United States. I offer it in contrast to the condition of New Mexico during the same time."*

---

*The reference was directed at the aftermath of Kearny's conquest of New Mexico. In Taos in January, 1847, at the time of the Kearny-Frémont-Stockton dispute in California, Governor Charles Bent, whom Kearny had selected to serve as the first civilian governor of the territory, was killed with six others by Pueblo Indians believed under orders from Mexican conspirators. Kit Carson's wife Josefa and her sister, Bent's wife, were unharmed but had to remain over a day in the house with the governor's scalped corpse. Colonel Sterling Price of Missouri led 353 men and four howitzers through deep snowdrifts to Taos, reaching the town on February 3. Fifty-one insurgents were killed; Price lost seven killed and forty-five wounded in ending the revolt. Much of Carson's later enmity toward Kearny was traceable to the fact

He ended his final statement with strength: "I prevented civil war against Governor Stockton, by refusing to join General Kearny against him; I arrested civil war against myself, by consenting to be deposed—offering at the same time to resign my place of lieutenant colonel in the army."

Then, as he placed his papers on the defense table, he said, "I have been brought as a prisoner and a criminal from that country . . . I am now ready to receive the sentence of the court."

✻

The court deliberated three days and delivered its verdict on Monday, January 31, 1848.

Frémont was found guilty on all charges and every specification under each charge, and the court sentenced him to be dismissed from the service.

Six of the twelve sitting members of the court recommended that President Polk grant clemency, issuing a statement laden with irony:

> Under the circumstances in which Lieutenant Colonel Frémont was placed between two officers of superior rank, each claiming to command-in-chief in California—circumstances in their nature calculated to embarrass the mind and excite the doubts of officers of greater experience than the accused—and in consideration of the important professional services rendered by him previous to the occurrence of those acts for which he has been tried, the undersigned members of the court, respectfully commend Lieutenant Colonel Frémont to the lenient consideration of the President of the United States.

The six signatories, in admitting that the explorer had been caught between feuding commanders and in circumstances that

---

that if he had not been ordered to guide the general and his dragoons back to California, he might have foreseen the dangers of the unrest and been able to protect his family.

would have daunted a veteran officer, had borrowed the main leaf from the Frémont defense book.

James Gordon Bennett's *New York Herald* expressed no surprise at the verdict, seeing "during the progress of the assizes . . . evidences of hostility on the part of members of the court against Lieutenant-Colonel Frémont . . . a greater, though a younger man, than a majority of his triers."

On February 16, the President responded to the recommendation of clemency and surprised the court by dismissing the more serious charge against Frémont by writing, "Upon an inspection of the record, I am not satisfied that the facts proved in this case constitute the military crime of 'mutiny.'" He sustained the other charges and convictions but wrote:

> . . . in consideration of the peculiar circumstances of the case, of the previous meritorious and valuable services of Lieutenant Colonel Frémont, and of the foregoing recommendations of a majority of the members of the court, the penalty of dismissal from the service is remitted. Lieutenant Colonel Frémont will accordingly be released from arrest, will resume his sword, and report for duty.

Despite the urgings of Senator Benton that he accept the President's offer to reinstate him, Frémont resigned the army on February 19, 1848. He was not guilty of any of the charges against him, he said, and to accept Polk's remission of his sentence was tantamount to admitting guilt.

As he saw it, it was a matter of honor: he had been in California before the conquest began, had had a role in starting it, had seen it unfold, had seen it botched to near ruination by two warring officers, had won the surrender treaty at Cahuenga Pass, and suffered the consequences of being forced to choose between the two lesser men who were his superior officers.

Ten days before the court's verdict, Frémont had passed his thirty-fifth birthday.

He had time for other conquests.

Epilogue

✸

1

On January 24, 1848, a week before the court-martial verdict, gold was discovered at a sawmill owned by John A. Sutter on the South Fork of the American River. The man who first saw the gleam in the millrace was James Marshall, the eccentric New Jersey wheelwright who had ridden with Frémont, Segundai, Gillespie, and Kit Carson into Sonoma after the skirmish at Olómpali.

✸

On February 2, 1848, two days after the verdict, the war officially ended with the signing of the Treaty of Guadalupe Hidalgo. The pen strokes made just outside its capital city divested Mexico of forty percent of its territory. Five hundred and thirty thousand square miles, including all of present-day New Mexico, Nevada, Utah, Arizona, and California, plus parts of Colorado, Idaho, and Wyoming, were ceded to the United States, with the Rio Grande established as the boundary between the two nations.

In return, President Polk agreed to pay $3.25 million in indemnities owed by Mexico, plus $12 million for its annexed lands north of the river.

Epilogue

The 1846 settlement with England had already added lands that became known as Washington and Oregon, and most of Idaho, to the Union.

Between the Mexican War and the Oregon settlement, the United States nearly doubled in size, adding 1,200,000 square miles of territory, with the country now stretching "from sea to shining sea."

2

Following the Frémont trial, Stephen Watts Kearny joined Winfield Scott's army of occupation in Mexico and served briefly as military commander at Vera Cruz. He contracted yellow fever and came home an invalid in July, 1848. That month he was nominated by the army for promotion to major general for "gallant conduct at San Pascual and for meritorious conduct in California and New Mexico." Senator Thomas Hart Benton filibustered in the Senate for thirteen days against the promotion, repeating most of the testimony against Kearny that had emerged in the court-martial. "After the conspiracy of Catiline, Cicero had a theme for his life; since this conspiracy against Frémont, and these rewards and honors lavished upon all that plotted against his life and character, I have also a theme for my life." This "ludicrous overshooting of the mark," as H. H. Bancroft said of the tirade, had no effect. Kearny won the major generalcy but did not live to enjoy its benefits. He died in St. Louis on October 31, 1848, of the effects of the fever he had contracted in Mexico.

James Knox Polk accomplished all he had set out to do in his presidency, from the annexation of Texas to the settlement of the "Oregon question" to the extension of the Union to the Pacific. He had announced early his intention to retire at the end of a single term and happily turned the presidency over to Zachary Taylor on March 5, 1849. In his diary, Polk wrote, "I am sure I shall be a happier man in my retirement than I have been during the four years I have filled the highest office in the gift of my countrymen." He enjoyed his retirement for only three months. After the inauguration of his successor, he took a month-long summer tour along the Atlantic seaboard and the gulf states and spent his final weeks working on his papers at his home in Nashville. He had fallen ill during his tour, possibly from a cholera outbreak in New Orleans. On June 15, 1849, he died at age fifty-three.

Both Senator Benton and Thomas O. Larkin, the latter the consul at Monterey and "confidential agent" during the conquest of California, died in 1858.

General José Castro returned to California in 1848 and lived as a private citizen in Monterey until 1853, when he was appointed military chief and *jefe político* along the border of Baja California and American California. In 1860, he was killed, Bancroft says, "in a drunken brawl—or, as some say, assassinated."

Robert Field Stockton resigned from the navy in 1850 and served in the United States Senate, representing his home state of New Jersey from 1851 to 1853, during which time he introduced a successful bill to abolish flogging as a punishment in the navy. In 1861, he served in a peace commission promoted by former President John Tyler in an effort to avert the impending Civil War, then became president of the Delaware and Raritan Canal Company. He devoted his retirement years to importing race horses from England. He died at Princeton on October 7, 1866.

José María Flores, who directed the last Californio resistance against the Americans, remained in Mexico after the war and rose to a generalcy in the Mexican army. He died in 1866.

John Drake Sloat died in New York in 1867. He was the original "conqueror" of California who raised the American flag at Monterey on July 7, 1846, and served as Stockton's predecessor as commander of the Pacific Squadron.

Christopher Houston "Kit" Carson returned to New Mexico in 1849, often leaving his beloved Josefa to serve as a military scout and guide in Apache country. In 1861, he reentered the army as a colonel of the First New Mexico Volunteer Regiment and saw action on February 21, 1862, at the Battle of Valverde on the Rio Grande, after which he received the brevet rank of brigadier general. He was then ordered to western New Mexico and Arizona to war against the Navajo, one of the tribes terrorizing New Mexican settlers. With a force of four hundred men, he led a scorched-earth campaign, burning villages and crops, killing cattle, driving the Indians to starvation, and in the summer of 1864, he invaded their stronghold in the Canyon de Chelly in northeastern Arizona. There he forced the surrender of some eight thousand Navajos who were subsequently marched to Fort Sumner, New Mexico, for internment.

Carson's last Indian campaign took place in November, 1864, when he led an expedition of 335 men and seventy-five Ute and Apache scouts against marauding Kiowas and Comanches on the Canadian River in the Texas Panhandle.

A colonel in the regular army after the Indian wars, Carson took command at Fort Garland, Colorado Territory, in July, 1866, and was released from military service the next year.

Now, at age fifty-eight and after forty-two years of strenuous living, his health began to fail. He suffered from chronic bronchitis, noticed a weakening of his legs, and had persistent neck and chest pains that seemed to signal a faltering heart. With Josefa and their six children, he settled at Boggsville, near present-day Las Animas, Colorado. There a physician visited him and diagnosed an aneurysm of the aorta so large it was destined to be fatal.

Despite his weakened state and Josefa's nearing delivery of their seventh child, he made a last journey in February, 1868. As superintendent of Indian Affairs for Colorado Territory, he led a delegation of Utes to Washington to press for a treaty guaranteeing the tribe exclusive hunting rights to lands on the Western Slope. In the capital, he met his old comrade, John C. Frémont, who was so distressed at his friend's haggard appearance and obvious suffering that he called upon some eminent doctors to examine the frail scout. The aneurysm diagnosis was confirmed.

Carson returned home in April to the great tragedy of his life. On April 13, his wife gave birth to their seventh child, a daughter, and ten days later, Josefa Jaramillo Carson died.

He lasted a month after that. He was moved to Fort Lyon, Colorado, where, at his insistence, he slept on the floor of the post surgeon's quarters under a big buffalo robe. He made his will, leaving his estate to the care and benefit of his children, and on the afternoon of May 23, 1868, he called out, "Doctor, *compadre*—adios." Blood gushed from his mouth as the aneurysm burst and he died.

Archibald Gillespie, the courier who found Frémont at Klamath Lake on May 9, 1846, and who surrendered Los Angeles to Californian insurgents the following September, died at age sixty in San Francisco in 1873.

Andrés Pico, who commanded the Californians in the battle at San Pascual on December 6, 1846, and later negotiated the treaty of Cahuenga with Frémont, served in the California assembly and state senate after the war. He died in 1876.

John Augustus Sutter, the lord of New Helvetia, became a delegate to the convention that in 1849 drafted California's state constitution. The discovery of gold on his lands, rather than making him rich, ruined him, and by 1852 he was bankrupt. He was granted a pension by the California legislature, moved to Lancaster County, Pennsylvania, and died there on June 18, 1880.

Richard Henry Dana, Jr., whose 1840 book, *Two Years Before the Mast,* gave Americans their first real glimpse into life in California before the conquest, died in Rome in 1882. His best-selling memoir had made the Boston patrician famous, so much so that Charles Dickens, upon first visiting the United States in 1842, asked to meet the young author. In his law practice, Dana specialized in maritime matters, especially the plight of the common sailor. "The truth is," he said, "I was made for the sea. My life on shore is a mistake." In 1859, he returned to California—by sea—and paid a visit to the Frémonts and Colonel Vallejo. He spent the last decade of his life traveling in Europe and studying international law.

Don Mariano Vallejo, arrested by the Bear Flaggers in June,

1846, like Sutter, served in the constitutional convention in 1849. He became a state senator and a leading proponent of cooperation with American authorities in his homeland. He died at his Lachryma Montis estate in Sonoma on January 18, 1890.

Pío Pico was the longest-lived of all the principal Californios. Born at the San Gabriel Mission in 1801, he saw his home country ruled by Spaniards, Mexicans, and Americans. His career as political partisan, most often in opposition to the governors Mexico sent to their far-western province, had begun in 1831, his opposition to American incursions in the early 1840s, and he served as the last Mexican governor before the American takeover. He returned to California in 1848 and took up residence near San Luís Obispo. He lost his extensive land holdings—sixty thousand acres—to an American swindler and was left a pauper. He died at his daughter's home on September 11, 1894. Bancroft judged Pico to have been a man "abused far beyond his just deserts; a man of ordinary intelligence and limited education; of generous, jovial disposition, reckless and indolent; with a weakness for cards and women; disposed to be fair and honorable in his transactions, but [unable to] avoid being made the tool of knaves; patriotic without being able to do much for his country."

3

In a wise assessment of John Charles Frémont, Irving Stone said, "In his every success there was contained the germ of his next defeat; in every defeat, the seed of his next victory."

He lived forty-three years after the conquest of California, remaining a Child of Fortune—"He was essentially a lucky fellow," Bancroft said—to the end of his days.

But his fortune was not always good and his luck did not always hold out.

In the winter of 1848, he led his fourth expedition west, into the San Juan Mountains of southern Colorado, exploring a railroad route to California. The venture ended in disaster: ten of his thirty-three men were trapped in the mountains by heavy snows and perished.

In 1853, on his fifth and last exploration, he successfully crossed the San Juans—in the winter.

He became a millionaire when gold was found on the Las Mariposas lands he had purchased for three thousand dollars in the Sierra foothills, near Yosemite Valley. He acquired real estate in San Francisco, for several years lived in affluence with Jessie and their children in Monterey, and in 1850 was elected one of California's first senators, serving through a single year of Congress, giving up his seat to return to his Las Mariposas mines.

In 1856, he was nominated the first presidential candidate of the new Republican Party ("Free Speech, Free Press, Free Soil, Free Men, Frémont and Victory!") but lost to James Buchanan in the era's most disgraceful political campaign. Frémont, accused of being anti-Catholic, a mountebank, a drunkard, a bastard, a foreigner, and a convicted mutineer, managed to carry eleven states to Buchanan's seventeen and received 1,341,264 popular votes to Buchanan's 1,838,169.

During the Civil War he resumed his army commission and was sent to St. Louis as a major general and commander of the army's Western Department. He was obliged to work without funds, arms, or supplies, and had to organize an army in a slave state that had a strong and vocal core of secessionists. He imposed martial law and worked indefatigably to make the city safe for the Union—even issuing his own emancipation proclamation—but was removed by President Lincoln after a controversial one-hundred-day command.

In 1864, he was endorsed as candidate for president by the radical wing of the Republican Party but withdrew for the sake of party unity.

He lost his Maricopa lands and fortune in unprofitable railroad ventures.

He served as territorial governor of Arizona from 1878–1881, after which undistinguished and absentee tenure, he was granted a pension by Congress.

Epilogue

In 1890, while visiting Washington, Congress restored him to a major generalcy and awarded him a six-thousand-dollar annual pension, but on July 13 that year, he died at age seventy-seven of peritonitis from a burst appendix in a New York City hotel at 49 West Twenty-fifth Street. His only son, John Charles, Jr., was at his bedside and placed in his hand a locket containing a miniature portrait of Jessie. She had remained in their modest Los Angeles home, unable to afford the trip east with her husband.

Kit Carson told his biographer in 1856, "I was with Frémont from 1842 to 1847. The hardships through which we passed I find it impossible to describe and the credit to which he deserves I am incapable to do him justice in writing. But his services to his country have been left to the judgment of impartial freemen and all agree in saying that his services were great and have redounded to his honor and that of his country."

Carson paid special tribute to how Frémont "cheerfully suffered with his men when undergoing the severest of hardships" and said, "His perseverance and willingness to participate in all that was undertaken, no matter whether the duty was rough or easy, is the main cause of his success."

Jessie's epitaph for her husband: "From the ashes of his campfires have sprung cities."

The second of Senator Benton's six children, Jessie had married Frémont on October 18, 1841, when she was eighteen, a bright, pretty, boisterous tomboy, and he twenty-eight, a solemn, ardently ambitious, handsome, and gallant suitor. She was pregnant with their first child when he departed in May, 1842, to explore the Oregon Trail to the South Pass in the Wyoming Rockies, and thereafter she transformed the raw data of his oral narrative and notes into memorable books.

She was also pregnant during her husband's trial, and the couple lost the baby three months after its birth.

She argued with Lincoln on her husband's conduct in Missouri in 1861—so forcefully that the exasperated President called her, after she left his office, "a female politician."

When their fortune disappeared in bad speculative investments, Jessie, now fifty, had to take up her pen and write reminiscences and children's stories to earn a subsistence wage.

But even in Frémont's brooding and bitter last years, when he went east without her, she wrote, "Love me in memory of the old times, when I was so dear to you," and assured him that their advancing age and uncertain future changed nothing. "I love you now much more than I did then," she said.

After her husband's death, Jessie and her daughter Lily lived in an eight-room cottage in Los Angeles given them by the Women of California Club. In her parlor, sitting near the Gutzon Borglum portrait of her hero, she received occasional visitors and eked out an income by writing magazine articles. She eventually received a two-thousand-dollar annual widow's pension, and to the end of her twelve-year widowhood, sheltered the flame of her "Jason of California."

She died in her sleep at age seventy-eight on December 27, 1902, and was buried beside her husband at Piermont, New York, overlooking the Hudson River.

✤

Hubert Howe Bancroft came to California in 1853, following his father, a forty-niner with a claim on the Sacramento River. He opened his book-selling and publishing company in San Francisco in 1856, amassed a sixteen-thousand-volume library (sixty thousand by 1905), and launched publication of his histories in 1874. In all, there are thirty-nine volumes in his series, *The Native Races of the Pacific States* and *The History of the Pacific States*. Of the twenty-eight volumes in the latter, the seven volumes devoted to California appeared between 1886 and 1890.

No one is certain of how much of Bancroft's work was written by Bancroft himself. He certainly could not have written the histories alone, although he is listed as sole author, and the personal pronoun can be found frequently in the voluminous footnotes in the books.

It is known that he employed many capable "assistants," as he called them, and the names of several of these researchers, editors, and writers are known.

Whatever the weight of his contribution as author, it is to H. H. Bancroft and his band of unsung heroes that I owe my greatest debt. By preserving most of the significant documents of the era, and in citing them, often fully quoting them, his California volumes have become quite priceless, providing a narrative of inestimable value to any writer interested in the conquest, or in any other episode in Pacific Coast history.

And, for so massive and scholarly an undertaking, they are a delight to read, as I hope the material I have quoted directly demonstrates.

❋

Of the three principals in the story of the Bear Flaggers and the conquest of California, Frémont, as one might expect, has been the biographers' favorite. The best among these books, in my belief, is Ferol Egan's thorough, eminently fair, and spiritedly written *Frémont: Explorer for a Restless Nation*. The explorer's own *Memoirs* is invaluable if used carefully.

Dwight Clarke's *Stephen Watts Kearny: Soldier of the West* is a keen defense of the dragoon general, meticulously researched and an apt example of the author's assertion that "It is essential to a good biography that its author show some partiality for his subject." I agree, and this is the principal reason I like Egan's *Frémont*.

There is no modern biography of Stockton, a curious omission for a figure of such magnitude in the era of Manifest Destiny. Bancroft provides a wonderfully irascible portrait of this irascible figure, and fortunately there are good, dispassionate essays on him in Spiller and similar military references, and in the histories of the U.S.—Mexican War.

Bernard DeVoto's *The Year of Decision, 1846* is indispensable as an endlessly entertaining, personal, polemical *view* of the era. As a source on the conquest of California, it is quotable but erratic, and the author's anti-Frémont bias makes even Bancroft's attacks on the explorer pale by comparison.

As always, I am indebted to my late friend, Dan L. Thrapp, for his *Encyclopedia of Frontier Biography*, a monument to the history of the American West.

BIBLIOGRAPHY

American Guide Series. *California: A Guide to the Golden State.* New York: Hastings House, 1939.

Bancroft, Hubert Howe. *History of Arizona and New Mexico, 1530–1888.* San Francisco: The History Company, 1883–1888; three vols.

——. *History of the Pacific States of North America: California.* San Francisco: The History Company, 1886–1890; seven vols.

Bashford, Herbert and Harr Wagner. *A Man Unafraid: The Story of John Charles Frémont.* San Francisco: Wagner Publishing Co., 1927.

Bauer, K. Jack. *The Mexican War, 1846–1848.* Lincoln: University of Nebraska Press, 1992. (Originally published 1974.)

Bean, Walton and James J. Rawls. *California: An Interpretive History.* New York: McGraw-Hill, 1983.

Beck, Warren A. and Ynez D. Haase. *Historical Atlas of California.* Norman: University of Oklahoma Press, 1974.

Bergeron, Paul H. *The Presidency of James K. Polk.* Lawrence: University Press of Kansas, 1987.

Bidwell, Gen. John. *Echoes of the Past.* New York: Citadel Press, 1962. (Originally published 1900.)

Blackwelder, Bernice. *Great Westerner: The Story of Kit Carson.* Caldwell, Idaho: Caxton Printers, 1962.

Blevins, Winfred. *Give Your Heart to the Hawks.* Plainview, New York: Nash Publishing Co., 1973.

Burdett, Charles. *Life of Kit Carson.* New York: A. L. Burt, 1902.

Caughey, John W. *California: A Remarkable State's Life History.* Englewood Cliffs, N.J.: Prentice-Hall, Inc., 1970.

Clarke, Dwight L. *Stephen Watts Kearny: Soldier of the West.* Norman: University of Oklahoma Press, 1961.

Cleland, Robert Glass. *California Pageant: The Story of Four Centuries.* New York: Alfred A. Knopf, 1946.

Connor, Seymour V. and Odie B. Faulk. *North America Divided: The Mexican War, 1846–1848.* New York: Oxford University Press, 1971.

Dana, Richard Henry, Jr. *Two Years Before the Mast.* Pleasantville, N.Y.: Reader's Digest Association, 1995. (Originally published in 1840, this edition contains Dana's full narrative plus his "Twenty-Four Years Later" memoir and the essay, "Richard Henry Dana, Jr.'s Endless Voyage" by Thomas Fleming.)

DeVoto, Bernard. *The Year of Decision, 1846.* New York: Houghton Mifflin, 1989. (Originally published 1941.)

Dillon, Richard. *Humbugs and Heroes: A Gallery of California Pioneers.* Garden City, N.Y.: Doubleday, 1970.

Egan, Ferol. *Frémont: Explorer for a Restless Nation.* New York: Doubleday, 1977.

Eisenhower, John S. D. *So Far From God: The U.S. War With Mexico, 1846–1848.* New York: Random House, 1989.

Frémont, John C. "Conquest of California," *The Century Magazine,* April, 1891.

———. *Memoirs of My Life.* New York: Belford, Clarke & Co., 1887; two vols.

Gilbert, Bil. *The Trailblazers.* New York: Time-Life Books, 1973.

Grant, Blanche C., ed. *Kit Carson's Own Story of His Life.* Taos, N. M.: Kit Carson Memorial Foundation, Inc., 1955.

Hafen, LeRoy R. and Carl Coke Rister. *Western America.* Englewood Cliffs, N.J.: Prentice-Hall, 1950.

—— and W. J. Ghent. *Broken Hand: Life of Thomas Fitzpatrick, Chief of the Mountain Men.* Denver: Old West Publishing, 1931.

Hansen, Harvey J. and Jeanne Thurlow Miller. *Wild Oats in Eden: Sonoma County in the 19th Century.* Santa Rosa, Calif., n.p., 1962.

Hawgood, John A. *America's Western Frontiers: The Exploration and Settlement of the Trans-Mississippi West.* New York: Alfred A. Knopf, 1967.

Henry, Robert S. *The Story of the Mexican War.* Indianapolis: Bobbs Merrill, 1950.

Herr, Pamela and Mary Lee Spence, eds. *The Letters of Jessie Benton Frémont.* Urbana: University of Illinois Press, 1993.

Jackson, Donald and Mary L. Spence, eds. *The Expeditions of John Charles Frémont.* Urbana: University of Illinois Press, 1970; two vols.

Johannsen, Robert W. *To the Halls of the Montezumas: The Mexican War in the American Imagination.* New York: Oxford University Press, 1985.

Lavender, David. *Bent's Fort.* Garden City, N.Y.: Doubleday, 1954.

Lynch, Robert M. *The Sonoma Valley Story.* Sonoma, Calif.: The Sonoma Index-Tribune, 1997.

Marks, Paula Mitchell. *Precious Dust: The American Gold Rush Era, 1848–1900.* New York: William Morrow, 1994.

Marti, Werner H. *Messenger of Destiny: The California Adventures of Archibald Gillespie, 1846–1847.* San Francisco: John Howell, 1961.

McCaffrey, James M. *Army of Manifest Destiny: The American Soldier in the Mexican War, 1846–1848.* New York: New York University Press, 1992.

Morison, Samuel Eliot. *The European Discovery of America: The Southern Voyages, 1492–1616.* New York: Oxford University Press, 1974.

—— *The Oxford History of the American People.* New York: Oxford University Press, 1965.

Nevin, David. *The Mexican War.* Alexandria, Va.: Time-Life Books, 1978.

Nevins, Allan. *Frémont: Pathmarker of the West.* New York: Longmans, Green, 1939.

Osio, Antonio María. *The History of Alta California: A Memoir of Mexican California.* Madison: University of Wisconsin Press, 1996.

Papp, Richard Paul. *Bear Flag Country.* San Francisco:, n.p., 1996.

Parkman, Francis. *The Oregon Trail,* ed. by E. N. Feltskog. Lincoln, Neb.: University of Nebraska Press, 1994. (Annotated new edition of the 1849 original.)

Paul, Rodman. *California Gold.* Lincoln: University of Nebraska Press, 1969.

Pittman, Ruth. *The Roadside History of California.* Missoula, Mont.: Mountain Press, 1995.

Proceedings of the Court-Martial of Lieutenant Colonel John C. Frémont. Washington: 30th Congress, Executive Document 33, n.d. [1848].

Richman, Irving B. *California Under Spain and Mexico.* Boston: n.p., 1911.

Rogers, Fred B. *William Brown Ide: Bear Flagger.* San Francisco: John Howell, 1962.

Rolle, Andrew. *John Charles Frémont: Character as Destiny.* Norman: University of Oklahoma Press, 1993.

Rosenus, Alan. *General M. G. Vallejo and the Advent of the Americans.* Albuquerque: University of New Mexico Press, 1995.

Royce, Josiah, "Montgomery and Frémont," *The Century Magazine,* March, 1891.

Sabin, Edwin L. *Kit Carson Days, 1809–1868.* Lincoln: University of Nebraska Press, 1995 (originally published 1935); three vols.

Singletary, Otis A. *The Mexican War.* Chicago: University of Chicago Press, 1960.

Sources

Smith, Justin H. *The War With Mexico*. New York: Macmillan, 1919; two vols.

Spiller, Roger J., ed. *Dictionary of American Military Biography*. Westport, Conn.: Greenwood Press, 1984; three vols.

Stone, Irving. *They Also Ran*. New York: Doubleday & Co., 1943.

Thrapp, Dan L. *Encyclopedia of Frontier Biography*. Glendale, Calif.: The Arthur H. Clark Co., 1988, 1994; four vols.

Vestal, Stanley [Walter Stanley Campbell]. *Kit Carson: The Happy Warrior of the Old West*. Boston: Houghton Mifflin, 1928.

Weems, John Edward. *To Conquer a Peace: The War Between the United States and Mexico*. Garden City, N.Y.: Doubleday, 1974.

Woodward, Arthur. *Lances at San Pascual*. San Francisco: California Historical Society, 1948.

INDEX

Index

Index

Index

Index

Index